The Land of the Lune

A guide to the region within the Lune Watershed

The Land of the Lune
– and its tributaries

A guide to the region within the
Lune Watershed

John Self

Drakkar Press

First published in 2008 by
Drakkar Press Limited
20 Moorside Road, Brookhouse, Lancaster LA2 9PJ
info@drakkar.co.uk

Printed 2008 by Stramongate Press
Aynam Mills, Little Aynam, Kendal LA9 7AH

ISBN: 0-9548605-1-9
          978-0-9548605-1-6

Additional photographs:
Front cover: the Lune at the Crook o'Lune
Back cover: Carlin Gill from Grayrigg
(The identity of the twenty-five bridges shown in these front pages is left as a challenge! They are presented in the order met in the journey described in the text, and none of the bridges are illustrated in the main text. If you would like to know the names and locations of the bridges please contact the publisher, address details given above.)

Contents

Two views from the Crook o'Lune

The Land of the Lune - and its tributaries

Introduction

The view from the Crook o'Lune at Caton is tranquil. The River Lune, nestled deep within its banks, meanders toward us from the hazy hills in the distance. But on a few days each year the scene is very different. The Lune then is a muddy torrent, raging halfway up Penny Bridge and stretching wide across the floodplain. An obvious question on such a day is: where does all this water come from?

This book answers this question as a pretext for providing a guide to a part of northwest England that is generally overlooked. As we will see, the region within the Lune watershed includes parts of the Lake District, the Yorkshire Dales, the Forest of Bowland and the Howgills, and all of what lies between them. Our region, however, gets little attention. For example, the National Trust, whose mission is to preserve "places of historic interest or natural beauty", owns about 350 sq km in the Lake District and 60 sq km in the Yorkshire Dales but within the Lune watershed only one public house, and that it did not actively acquire but gained through a bequest.

Perhaps this is understandable because the region within the Lune watershed has none of England's greatest buildings, no major historic events happened here, none of England's greatest men or women were born or lived here, and there are no sites of international ecological importance. Even so, if we approach the region without great expectations, we will find a great deal of interest and appeal – not on the majestic scale of the best of the Lake District but certainly not deserving of complete neglect. There have been thousands of books written on the Lakes but hardly a handful on the Lune region.

The reputation of the region suffers from it being hurried through by people on their way to the Lakes and the Dales. It has long been regarded as a kind of consolation for those unable to reach their intended destination. For example, *The Pictorial History of the County of Lancaster*, published in 1854, said "The vale of the Lune may now be visited from London in a day, thanks to railroads; and if the stranger go not as far as Furness or Westmoreland, he may still say he has entered the portal of the northern scenery of England, and found that alone has repaid his visit, especially if he prefer the tranquil in nature to the severe and grand – to pore over the bubbling brook, rather than listen to the thunders of the cataract".

We will follow the waters of the Lune and all its tributaries as they make their way from the fells to the estuary. This will take us through a variety of landscapes – fells, moors, crags, valleys, pastures, floodplains and estuary – but all the while, in our mind's ear, we will be accompanied by the comforting sounds of the beck and river. The Lune itself is not a long river, a mere 105km, but it drains 1285 sq km of varied terrain that fortunately remains in a condition relatively unaffected by so-called development. The Lune valley is a fine one but much more of interest is added if we widen our scope to include its tributaries.

A Word on Terminology

The phrase "the region within the Lune watershed" is cumbersome. I will co-opt the old, now largely disused, word 'Loyne' as shorthand for this phrase. 'Lunesdale' or 'Lonsdale' will not serve my purpose because they are usually taken to refer narrowly to the valley of the Lune itself. The few authors who have written on Lunesdale have some difficulty in deciding how far to creep up the tributaries – Sedbergh?, Bentham?, Ingleton? … My rule is simple: if rain falling on an area makes its way to the Lune estuary then the area is within my scope.

Loyne may seem an artificial construct compared with the familiar counties and National Parks. In fact, it is the administrative boundaries that are arbitrary – witness the 1974 creation of the boundaries of Cumbria, Lancashire and North Yorkshire, with the loss of Cumberland and Westmorland, and the on-going debate about changing the National Park boundaries. The Lake District includes the Shap Fells but not the similar Birkbeck Fells across the A6, although many regard both as not really part of the Lakes. The Yorkshire Dales National Park includes the southern half of the Howgills but not the similar northern half. Many consider that the Howgills should not be part of the Dales and would rather include, say, Wild Boar Fell.

To anyone looking from the Crook o'Lune, Loyne seems perfectly coherent. Everything we see is within Loyne, and a great deal of Loyne can be seen. Ingleborough and Whernside, for example, seem clearly to belong to Loyne.

Lancaster's "Luck to Loyne" crest

The Aim of this Book

The implicit aim of most guides is to encourage readers to visit that which is described. My aim is the opposite. I intend to describe a virtual, vicarious journey that may be enjoyed in an armchair by the fireside, thereby saving you time, energy and expense and protecting the serenity and loneliness of Loyne for those who enjoy that sort of thing, like me. (Reviewers of a draft manuscript have warned me that readers cannot see the tongue in my cheek, so I will henceforth remove it.)

A Note about the Walks

There are outlines of 24 walks in this book. It is strongly advised that the suggested route be traced on the appropriate 1:25000 Ordnance Survey (OS) map before you embark on any of the walks. The descriptions given here are not adequate unless used in conjunction with the OS map. The region is covered by maps OL19 (Howgill Fells and Upper Eden Valley), OL7 (The English Lakes, south-eastern area), OL2 (Yorkshire Dales, southern and western areas), OL41 (Forest of Bowland and Ribblesdale) and Explorer 296 (Lancaster, Morecambe and Fleetwood).

The outlines do not give step-by-step instructions as in specialist walking books. The idea is that, once you have traced the proposed route, you should adapt it as necessary to suit your own needs. Each route passes points of interest mentioned in the pages preceding the walk description. Always bear in mind that the walk details, such as they are, are provided in good faith but their continued correctness cannot be guaranteed.

All the suggested walks are full-day (five or six hour) loops from a car-parking spot. If you can reach the starting point by bicycle or public transport please do so. Unfortunately, the details of public transport are too changeable to be given here.

The walks require a good standard of fitness but there is no need for the heroic scrambling of some Lakeland walks. However, some walks do venture into wild, remote areas and accidents can happen anywhere. To be on the safe side, here is a list of items that you should take (created by merging the lists in half a dozen serious walking books on my shelf): map, compass, food, drink, waterproofs, hat, gloves, survival bag, whistle, torch with spare batteries, mobile phone, a GPS (global positioning system) and three people. The last are to help carry all the clobber, or you, if you should have that accident. Always leave information or tell someone about your intended route and estimated time of return, check weather conditions and forecasts before setting out, and wear appropriate clothes and footwear. (To avoid being hypocritical, I admit that some of my reconnoitring involved running around with only a map stuffed in my shorts. Very foolish.)

Walking on the fells had been accepted (except in the Bowland Fells) even where there was no right of way. The Countryside and Rights of Way Act 2000 has provided official access to what I will refer to as 'CRoW land'. Always enter CRoW land by public footpaths or official entry points, where there is generally a 'welcome' sign or a brown 'walking man' sign.

The 24 walks are listed in the Index (page 229).

Acknowledgements

Writing a general guide such as this is a humbling experience. I found that every topic, however obscure – be it within history, botany, geology, or whatever – on which I needed to venture a sentence or two has been the subject of a lifetime's devoted study by somebody. In a non-academic book, extensive references and footnotes are not appropriate but I am nonetheless very grateful for their unacknowledged work and hope that they will not pounce upon me for my superficial misrepresentation of it.

I will, however, name with gratitude those brave friends who commented upon a draft manuscript: Jim Foster, Lesley Jordan, Bob Lauder, Michael Mumford and Clare Napier. I have done my best to respond to their views – even though it wasn't always easy to reconcile them! Overall, I much appreciated that they found time for this. As is traditional, I claim full responsibility for all the errors and faults that remain.

I am particularly grateful for the comments and encouragement of my son Martin and daughter Pamela, and for their advice on matters of technology and design. Without their enthusiasm the project might never have gotten underway.

Most of all, I'm grateful to my wife Ruth for being much more of a partner in producing this book than it appears from the text. Apart from giving opinions and encouragement and overseeing overall 'quality control', she accompanied me on many of the exploratory expeditions. I have mainly used the first person singular in the text because the reviewers found it disconcerting to keep switching between "we" and "I", depending on whether Ruth happened to be there or not, and it seemed odd for me to write "we" for those occasions when Ruth was not present. On all occasions, Ruth was there in spirit if not in reality.

Feedback

All feedback – comments, suggestions, questions and (especially) corrections and updates – will be gratefully received. I have tried to ensure that the content is factually reliable and up-to-date, but Loyne covers a large area and although it may not seem to change much it does change a little. Therefore, all help in keeping later editions up-to-date will be very welcome. Please send all comments to the publisher, Drakkar Press, at the address given in the front pages.

The Flow of the Book

The flow of the book is determined by the flow of the becks and rivers that eventually reach the Lune estuary. We will take an imaginary journey in which we follow the Lune from its source, surveying points of interest nearby, and whenever we meet a significant tributary we will be magically transported to the source of that tributary and will begin a journey from there, eventually to continue the journey down the Lune. If we meet a significant sub-tributary, we will similarly be transported to its source. So, for example, when, travelling down the Lune, we meet the River Rawthey, we will be transported to its source on West Baugh Fell – and in due course when we meet Clough River, a tributary of the Rawthey, we will be transported to its source on East Baugh Fell – before eventually resuming our journey on the Rawthey and later the Lune.

In this way, we will systematically cover every part of Loyne. The emphasis on the watercourses is partly a structural device but serves also to highlight their importance in shaping the character of the region and to bring to the fore some of its more attractive features. The imagined flight to the source of the tributaries will take us from the valleys, where habitation and its consequent changes are concentrated, to the fells, which change little from one generation to the next. Throughout Loyne, the fells provide a reassuring background, supporting a quiet reflection on the heritage and attractiveness of the region.

For those who wish to follow the narrative closely, the next three pages give a more detailed list of the book's contents, followed by a map of Loyne. Twenty-two tributaries of the Lune (from Bowderdale Beck to Broad Fleet) are given section headings. These have single indents in the list below. Some of the tributaries have sub-tributaries that have been given section headings. For example, the River Rawthey has sub-tributaries of Sally Beck, Clough River and the River Dee. Sub-tributaries have double indents. A "…" in a section heading means that the description of that river is continued in a later section. For example, the Rawthey is described in four sections, separated by the three sub-tributaries.

Detailed Contents

Scale: 10 cm to 35 km

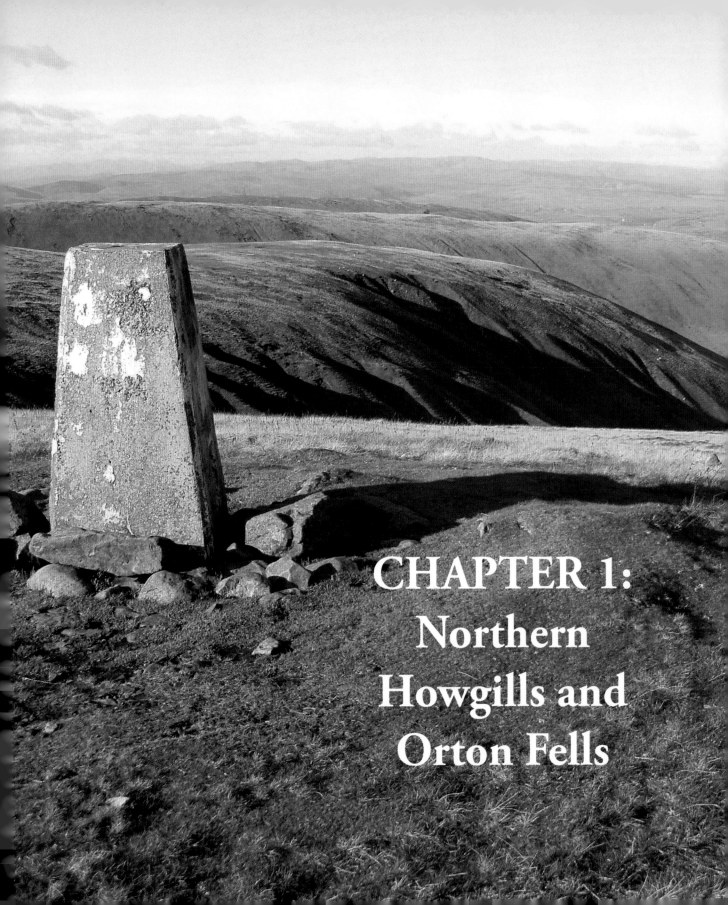

CHAPTER 1:
Northern Howgills and Orton Fells

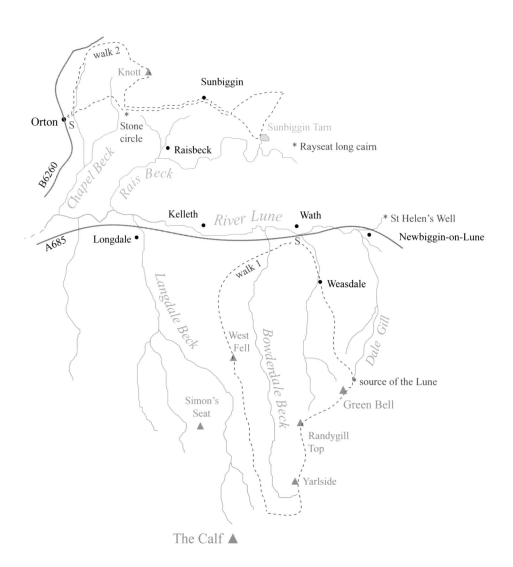

Scale: 1 cm to 1 km

0   5 kilometres

The River Lune ...

A great oak may grow from a single acorn but great rivers need very many sources. For some reason, we like to distinguish one of these as *the* source of the river, although there are no agreed rules for doing so. The determination of the source of the Lune has been made easy for us by the fact that its name continues far upstream along one particular branch among its many headwaters, to the helpfully named village of Newbiggin-on-Lune, 9km east of Tebay.

Above Newbiggin-on-Lune, various becks run north off Green Bell to form the infant Lune. Of these the longest and highest is Dale Gill, arising from a spring 200m northeast of the Green Bell summit (605m). Since any rain falling just north of Green Bell will drain into the Lune we may regard Green Bell itself as our sought-for source. Green Bell is an appropriate name for the rounded, grassy hill but then so it would be for most of the fifty or so other named summits in the **Howgills**. Green Bell, however, is rightly honoured with a trig point, one of only four in the Howgills (the others being at Winder, Middleton and The Calf).

Dale Gill runs 4km north from Green Bell, changing name twice (to Greenside Beck and Dry Beck), to become the Lune at Newbiggin-on-Lune. Here, Bessy Beck joins the Lune after refreshing the three lakes of a trout fishery. Bessy Beck may be named after Elizabeth

The **Howgills** is the name given to the homogeneous group of hills in the triangle of about 100 sq km between Ravenstonedale, Sedbergh and Tebay (or between the A685, the A683 and the Lune valley).

The hills are well drained, rounded and grassy, with no bogs and little heather. There are no walls above the pastures and only one fence. There are significant rocks in only two places, Cautley Crag and Carlin Gill. So, the Howgills is a place for striding out along the ridges – but not across them for then you would have steep eroded slopes to contend with.

The highest point is The Calf (676m), from which the ridges radiate to over twenty further tops above 500m. Walking is easy and airy but, according to *Walking Britain* (2005), edited by Lou Johnson, "the Howgills have little interest underfoot ... The reward for scaling the heights comes from the superb views of the Northern Pennines, the eastern fells of the Lake District, and the higher peaks of the Yorkshire Dales".

This, however, is the wrong frame of mind for tackling the Howgills. The Howgills must be appreciated on their own merits. There is no need to be envious of the other peaks (yes, the views are good but a little distant to be "superb"). As often the case, Harry Griffin captured the required spirit best in one of the last of the Country Diary vignettes, usually about the Lake District, that he contributed for over fifty years to the Guardian: "the Howgill Fells have always entranced me. Compared with Lakeland, overrun by the hordes and vastly over-publicized, they have retained their quiet, unspoiled beauty."

Previous page: Green Bell trig point, looking over Weasdale.

Left: The view north standing at the source of the Lune on Green Bell.

Left: Bowderdale, from the slopes of Randygill Top.

Gaunt of Tower House, near Brownber Hall, who in 1685 gained the dubious distinction of being the last woman to be burned at the stake in England. Although she may now be regarded as a virtuous, charitable lady only too willing to help those in need, the fact seems to be that she knowingly helped someone involved in a plot to assassinate Charles II. The penalty for high treason duly followed.

Newbiggin-on-Lune is spread out along what is now a large lay-by, bypassed by the A685 but not by far enough, as it is quite noisy. At the eastern end of Newbiggin-on-Lune is the old St Helen's Well, which some people insist is the source of the Lune, because it is never dry, unlike the Green Bell springs. As this would add dignity to the Lune's birth, it deserves investigation. I was informed at the Lune Spring Garden Centre that the well lies just across the A685 behind the chapel. The chapel, it transpires, is a small mound and the well just a seepage in the field, which is most uninspiring compared to the slopes of Green Bell.

The fledgling Lune turns west and after 2km reaches Wath, which most on-line encyclopedias assert is the start of the Lune, at the confluence of Sandwath Beck and Weasdale Beck. This seems absurd, as we have already passed Newbiggin, which insists it is on-Lune. The appendage, however, is a new one: the 1861 OS map has a simple Newbiggin. But the map considers the stream, which the encyclopedias regard as Sandwath Beck, resulting from the merger of becks east of Wath to be the River Lune, as I have done.

Weasdale Beck, equal in size to the Lune at this point, runs north from near Randygill Top (624m) through the fine, deep valleys of Weasdale and Great Swindale. These valleys, however, are not as fine as the adjacent, parallel Bowderdale, through which flows Bowderdale Beck to join the now undisputed Lune 1km below Wath.

Bowderdale Beck

There is nobility in the simplicity of Bowderdale. What you see is definitely what you get: there are no hidden secrets. And yet it is a marvellous valley, running due north for 6km or so and forming the prototypical U-shape that illustrates the **effects of glaciation**. There are also fine examples of Holocene (that is, post-glacial) fluvial erosion, with alluvial fans, terraces, meanders and braided channels.

Bowderdale Beck runs uneventfully from the head of Bowderdale, 2km from The Calf, to the small community of Bowderdale and then to join the Lune. The region provides a typical Howgills walking area, with its long, open ridges and steep, grassy slopes, striped with sheep tracks, falling to an enclosed valley, empty of manmade objects apart from a few old sheepfolds. There is little excitement to be found on the ridge tops: Yarlside has a distinctive dome; Kensgriff a few crags; Randygill Top a small cairn; otherwise, there are just gentle rises that provide extensive views.

> The **effects of glaciation** are widespread in Loyne. It has been covered with ice several times and in the last glacial period, ending about 10,000 years ago, all but the highest tops were under ice.
>
> Glaciation has two general effects: erosion and deposition. The most apparent erosive effect is the scouring of valleys (such as Bowderdale and Kingsdale), deepening and straightening them to form the characteristic U or parabolic shape. When ice accumulates in the lee of valleys, it may form bowl-shaped cirques with deep sides (such as Cautley Crag and Combe Scar in Dentdale). Generally, though, Loyne rocks are too soft to provide the more spectacular glacial forms seen, for example, in the Scottish Highlands. In addition to these large-scale effects, there are many, largely unnoticed, striations caused by the ice scratching the rocks.
>
> Deposits are in the form of till or boulder clay, that is, largish pebbles in clay dropped by the ice, and sands and gravel left by the actions of glacial meltwater. Drumlins – the rolling, hummocky hills formed from boulder clay and then shaped by the ice into distinctive alignments – are common in Loyne. Sometimes, the deposits at the ends or sides of glaciers (terminal or lateral moraines) form barriers sufficient to change watersheds (as in Quernmore). The most intriguing deposits are the erratics (such as at Norber), which are rocks carried on glaciers and left in an alien landscape.
>
> The detailed effects of glaciation are difficult to unravel, especially when they involve major changes such as the breaking through of watersheds and the formation of new flow directions as glaciers block one another. Also, it is not possible to separate glacial erosion from water erosion, since glaciers tend to have vast streams flowing under them and huge volumes of meltwater are created, which if blocked and released can cause immense damage as floods.

Walk 1: A Circuit of Bowderdale, including Green Bell

Map: OL19 (please read the general note about the walks in the Introduction).
Starting point: Near Wath on the road south of the A685 (685050).

There are three obvious routes between Bowderdale Foot and the head of Bowderdale – the west ridge, the east ridge, and the valley bottom. Higher mathematics shows that there are six loops possible.

The walk along the valley bottom should be experienced, but not on a first visit. Impressive though the symmetrical valley is, it becomes claustrophobic after a while. There is only one view and only the odd sheepfold to break the monotony. The west ridge, beginning with West Fell, is the better one, providing good views into Bowderdale and Langdale and, in the distance, an evolving panorama of the hills of the Lakes and Dales.

So begin by setting off southwest, past Brow Foot, to Bowderdale Foot and then onto the footpath that leads to West Fell and Hazelgill Knott. You will meet many sheep, a few ponies perhaps, and, only if you are really lucky (or unlucky, as the case may be), one or two other walkers.

Continue 2km south of Hazelgill Knott and, as the path begins to swing right (heading for The Calf), leave it to turn east to Hare Shaw and Bowderdale Head to the unnamed hill south of Yarlside, from where there is a good view of Cautley Spout. Head north over Yarlside, Kensgriff and Randygill Top, with distant views of Cross Fell, Wild Boar Fell, Ingleborough and the Lakes skyline.

Continue to Green Bell, where you may locate the spring that is the source of the Lune, just below some ruins off the Green Bell to Knoutberry path. As you wish, follow the fledgling Lune down or, better, the path over Stwarth, in both cases cutting across to Weasdale and thence to Wath.

The distances are long but walking is easy apart from on the slopes of Yarlside. Route finding may be a challenge on the eastern ridge but the trig point on Green Bell is a reassuring presence.

The Lune from Bowderdale Beck ...

The Lune runs due west, more due than it used to as it has been straightened to run alongside the A685. The A685 was rebuilt on the line of the old Newbiggin-on-Lune to Tebay railway after it closed in 1962. Becks, such as Flakebridge Beck and Cotegill Beck, continue to enter the Lune from the south but very little comes from the north. The old limestone quarries and limekilns that are seen on the slopes between Potlands and Kelleth hint at the reason for the dryness of the northern slopes.

Limekilns, which usually date from the 18th or 19th century, were used to burn limestone to make quicklime. This was then slaked with water and used to reduce the acidity of pastures and also to lime-wash buildings. The limestone was tipped into the kiln from the top onto a fire of coal or wood, and then more coal and limestone layered on top. The open arch provided air to keep the fire going.

The members of Kelleth Rigg's herd of pedigree Blonde d'Aquitaine cattle look lime-washed too. Kelleth itself is a small village, recently enlarged by new building, aligned along the now quiet road by-passed by the A685. The Lune reaches the rather ornate Rayne Bridge, built of red sandstone. Well, the parapet and wall are of red sandstone – the bridge itself isn't, as a side view from the east reveals. The bridge was built in 1903 to replace one that required an abrupt turn on the road. Soon after Rayne Bridge, Langdale Beck joins the Lune.

Langdale Beck

Langdale Beck runs north from The Calf for 12km through the deserted valley of Langdale to emerge at the small village of Longdale, close by the Lune. There is sometimes debate about which of Langdale or Longdale has been misspelled but they are surely different renditions of the northern vowel sound that we have in auld lang syne. Anyway, the dale is undoubtedly the largest in the Howgills.

The Calf is the focal point of the Howgills and from it there are extensive views in all directions. To the south, the Lune looks like a snail's trail entering Morecambe Bay, and circling around we see the Bowland Fells, Ingleborough, Whernside, Pen-y-Ghent, Baugh Fell, Wild Boar Fell, and Cross Fell. Most eyes, however, will be drawn westwards in the attempt to identify the classic Lakeland peaks, such as Crinkle Crags, Great Gable and Blencathra. The Calf itself is hardly a peak, being merely slightly higher than several nearby mounds. There is no bird's eye view into nearby valleys that the best peaks provide.

A walker near the head of Langdale (to the left), heading for The Calf

The Calf has many ridges leading towards it but it is closer to the southern point of the Howgills triangle than it is to the northern base. To the south there is one main ridge (from Winder by Arant Haw) but to the north there are many long, complicated, interlocking ridges, all very similar in appearance. Langdale Beck itself drains a vast area, with several significant tributaries creating deep gullies with ridges between them.

Walking around Langdale is deceptively easy. Physically, there is little problem because the grass is easy to walk on and the slopes are gentle. There are more tracks than are marked on the map, thanks to the farmers' quads rather than walkers or sheep. Most people will opt to walk on the ridges but if you wish to sample a Howgills valley then Langdale is the best, because the middle section has a flat valley bottom that provides an openness lacking in other valleys, such as Bowderdale, and there is an interesting series of incoming gullies.

The main problem is one of navigation. This is an area where you should heed the advice to know where you are on the map at all times. Don't walk for two hours and then try to work it out because there are few distinctive features to help you. Keep careful track of the few features there are (sheepfolds, gullies, scree) and if on the ridges identify the few distinguishable tops (Green

Bell and Middleton with trig points, Randygill Top) and keep them in perspective as you move along. Above the pastures, there is no sign of past human habitation or exploitation, such as quarries, to serve as a guide.

It is my duty not to exaggerate the attractions of walking in the Howgills. Given a choice between walking in the Lakes or the Howgills, I would choose the former nine times out of ten. But on that tenth occasion, I'd look forward to wandering lonely less the crowd. The ordinary walker will relish the scenery and solitude but specialists such as geologists and botanists will find more of interest, especially within the eroded gullies and scree slopes that are rarely visited by human or sheep.

Langdale Beck is formed by the merger of West, Middle and East Grain below The Calf, with the relatively distinctive top of Simon's Seat (587m) to the west. Near a picturesque packhorse bridge, Nevy Gill and the combined waters of Churngill Beck and Uldale Beck join Langdale Beck, which then continues through wooded pastures that are not part of CRoW land.

Langdale Beck is a fair size by the time it reaches Longdale, a village of one farm, one row of cottages, a couple more buildings, and the old school house. Within the last began the education of Thomas Barlow (1607-1691), who became Bishop of Lincoln. He is a

Langdale, near Langdale Knott, with fell ponies

candidate model for the traditional folk song character, the Vicar of Bray, who blithely adapted his religious beliefs to meet the changing political needs of the day. This is surely a calumny, for northerners are known for the stalwart independence of their views.

To the west of Longdale is the growing village of Gaisgill, on the Ellergill Beck tributary of the Lune. New 'luxury homes' are being built on the site of an old garage. Nearby are a number of slightly less new residences, and beyond them New House, dated 1848, and beyond that Barbara's Cottage, with a defiant date of 1648.

Langdale Beck almost doubles the size of the infant Lune, which is next joined by the first significant tributary from the north, Rais Beck.

Rais Beck

Rais Beck drains the broad, tranquil pastures that lie between Sunbiggin and the ridge of 300m hills to the north of the Lune between Newbiggin-on-Lune and Raisgill Hall. It is formed by becks that run west from Sunbiggin Tarn and south from the small village of Sunbiggin.

The area around Sunbiggin Tarn is much appreciated by ornithologists, botanists and malacologists (that is,

experts on molluscs) – and also by leisurely picnickers watching the shadows lengthen on the Howgills. Although Sunbiggin Tarn is only 0.06 sq km of open water, it is the largest for some distance around and is therefore an oasis for many birds. Breeding species include wigeon, teal, tufted duck, gadwall, mallard, little grebe, sedge warbler, water rail, lapwing, curlew, redshank and snipe. The large colony of black-headed gulls for which the tarn was known has recently moved away.

The tarn lies within a limestone upland and is surrounded by heath, acid grassland, swamps, and areas of chalky mire. These soils support a rich variety of plant life, including various sedges, rushes and mosses as well as the marsh orchid and rare bird's eye primrose.

And for those malacologists, there are two rare snails: *Vertigo geyeri* is known at no other British site and *Catinella arenaria* at only three others. So, there's something of interest underfoot here at least.

The outflow from Sunbiggin Tarn joins Rayseat Sike to form Tarn Sike. Rayseat Sike runs by a Neolithic barrow that was excavated in 1875 by William Greenwell, who was, amongst many other things, a canon at Durham Cathedral. In his remarkable 98-year life he investigated 400 burial sites and provided thousands of artefacts for the British Museum. He served as a magistrate until the age of 85 when he gained notoriety for suggesting that speeding motorcyclists should be shot.

I would expect Rayseat Long Cairn to rank highly among Canon Greenwell's 400. The barrow is 70m long and has a number of chambers in which burnt human remains were found. Archaeologists speculate that it could be one of the oldest such relics in the region. It is an evocative site, now isolated on a rather bleak moor.

Tarn Sike runs into a large pond at Holme House, where it seeps away – except after heavy rain, when it continues to form Rais Beck proper at Slapestone Bridge, joining with becks running from the quietly rural hamlets of Sunbiggin and Raisbeck. The latter has a notice board with a helpful OS map so old that all colour has long disappeared. The roads have wide

Sunbiggin Tarn, with the northern Howgills beyond

grass verges, indicating their origin as drove roads, with limestone walls and scattered Scots pine and ash.

Rais Beck now gathers pace as it passes Fawcett Mill, built in 1794 and now a holiday home. Five fields north of the mill may seem unexceptional but they have been designated a Site of Special Scientific Interest (SSSI) for their very naturalness. The site is one of the few remaining traditionally managed plant-rich hay meadows, relatively unspoilt by modern agricultural practices. The flora includes betony, orchid, burnet, primrose, cowslip and fescue.

Below Fawcett Mill is Raisgill Hall, a place with a long history. There is an ancient tumulus nearby but it is not worth a visit unless you are a trained archaeologist. Manorial courts, to regulate the use of the commons, were held at Raisgill Hall until the 18th century. They were then taken over by the court at Orton, not without considerable animosity and legal wrangling about the boundaries and use of Orton and Raisbeck Commons. However, the present owners of the Hall do not wallow in the past: they are leaders of an active local farming cooperative, which has received support from Prince Charles, no less.

On a bench overlooking the Lune at Raisgill Hall Bridge is carved "Go softly by this riverside for when you would depart you'll find it's ever winding tied and knotted round your heart", which, if there weren't five differences, I'd assume to be an unacknowledged quotation from *The Prairie* by Rudyard Kipling. We bear the sentiments in mind as we follow the Lune for 1.5km with Tebaygill Beck joining from the south and then Chapel Beck from the north.

The view across Sunbiggin Moor to the Howgills

Raisbeck pinfold, near Pinfold Bridge

Chapel Beck

The Lune watershed north of the A685 is formed by the Orton Fells, comprising Orton Scar, Great Asby Scar and Little Asby Scar. These are examples of **karst**, a kind of landscape that we will meet elsewhere in Loyne. The Orton Fells provide the largest area of limestone pavement in England outside the Yorkshire Dales. It is unfortunately not as large as it was because of earlier quarrying but the area is now protected by law.

The best undamaged pavements are found on Great Asby Scar, to the north of Raisbeck and Sunbiggin, and are now protected as a reserve by English Nature. The folding and jointing of the pavements is particularly notable. The exposure of the site and the effects of over-grazing have left only a few stunted trees, such as hawthorn and holly. Within the grikes further woody and non-woody species flourish, especially various ferns and herbs.

The dry surface of these limestone plateaus was no doubt partly why it was a favoured area for human habitation long ago, as shown by the many remains of ancient earthworks on the Orton Fells. Castle Folds, near the trig point on Knott, is an Iron Age site, with the ruins of hut circles on a natural limestone platform. Below Knott there's an ancient 40m-diameter circle of about thirty stones, of variable size, all but one of pink granite.

The pink granite may be a surprise, below the limestone scars, but the occasional pink boulder can be seen perched on the limestone pavements and scattered in fields. They are erratics, brought here from the Shap Fells by glaciers. Prehistoric man is not alone in finding a use for these intriguing boulders: some amusement can be obtained in spotting them in barn walls, protecting beck banks, ornamenting houses, and marking boundaries (for example, Mitchell's Stone, 1km north of Sunbiggin Tarn).

The headwaters of Chapel Beck run from Orton Scar by and through Orton, the largest settlement so far, as shown by the fact that we find our first public house. Orton was made a market town in the 13th century and the numerous converging roads, tracks and paths indicate Orton's importance in the old droving days. This rural heritage is echoed in the Orton Market that today wins prizes, such as National Farmers Market of the Year 2005, for its emphasis on local produce.

In 2006 Orton hosted the first "Festival of the Rough Fell" to celebrate the ancient breed of Rough Fell sheep, its history and the crafts associated with Rough Fell farming. The majority of Rough Fell sheep are found on the Howgills and surrounding fells. As the name indicates, the Rough Fell is hardy enough to live on the poor upland grasses of exposed fells. It is a large sheep, with a black and white face and curved horns, renowned

---

Karst refers to any terrain with soluble bedrock where, as a result, there is little or no surface drainage. It is named after an area of Slovenia but there are many kinds of karst in the world, depending on climate, location, type of bedrock, and so on. In our case, the bedrock is limestone, which is dissolved by the mildly acidic rainfall formed by the absorption of carbon dioxide.

The rainwater dissolves fractures in the bedrock, gradually enlarging them into deep fissures called grikes. The limestone blocks between grikes are called clints. On the surface, these limestone pavements look barren, as little soil forms on the clints, but within the deep, sheltered grikes specialised plant communities flourish.

Underground, the rainwater continues to erode the limestone, until meeting an impermeable lower layer, giving rise to several characteristic features, such as: caves with stalactites and stalagmites; sinkholes, shakeholes, swallowholes and potholes, through the collapse of bedrock above a void; springs, as water emerges at an impermeable layer; disappearing streams, through water flowing into a pothole. Over time, as underground passages are adopted and abandoned, complex and extensive cave systems may develop, to be explored by potholers.

Limestone pavement at Great Kinmond on Orton Fells

for its thick wool, which is used to make carpets and mattresses, and high quality meat.

The festival marked a recovery from the foot and mouth epidemic of 2001, which caused great problems throughout Loyne and, in particular, reduced the number of Rough Fell sheep from 18,000 to 10,000. As the fells were closed, the epidemic threatened the traditional methods of fell management, whereby every flock knows its own territory or 'heaf', with each lamb learning it from its mother.

The mingling of old and new typifies modern Orton: from the stocks near the church to the chocolates from the recently established industry. Likewise, among the few modern dwellings are some fine old buildings. Petty Hall has a door lintel dated 1604. Orton Hall, to the south, was built in 1662 and was once the home of Richard Burn (1709-1785), vicar of Orton and author of texts on the law and local history.

The All Saints Church was built in the 13th century, replacing earlier temporary structures, and has been rebuilt several times since. Inside the church there is a display of three old bells, the oldest of 1530, and a list of vicars back to 1293. The early 16th century west tower is the oldest remaining part and today is an eye-catching off-white. After modern methods to seal the leaking tower failed, it was decided to resort to the traditional treatment of lime washing. So far, it has worked.

Chapel Beck gains its name as it runs south past Chapel House, where there is a spring, Lady Well, which was known for its health-giving properties. As Chapel Beck approaches the Lune we may glance east up the Lune valley towards Newbiggin-on-Lune and reflect on the contrast between the hills to the north (Orton Fells) and to the south (the Howgills).

The geology of Loyne has a major impact on the appearance and activities of the region but it is not as complicated as, for example, the Lake District's geology. In general, rocks are of three types: sedimentary (formed by the settlement of debris), igneous (derived from magma or lava that has solidified on the earth's surface) and metamorphic (rocks that have been altered by heat and pressure). The bedrocks of Loyne are almost entirely

Walk 2: Orton, Orton Fells and Sunbiggin Tarn

Map: OL19 (please read the general note about the walks in the Introduction).
Starting point: The centre of Orton (622082).

Head for the unmistakable All Saints Church and walk east past the vicarage to locate the path north to Broadfell (on the left bank of the beck). Take this path and after 100m follow the sign left through the houses. Thereafter, the path is clear, beside the beck and beyond its spring, and emerges at a disused quarry on the B6260.

Cross the cattle grid and walk east on the north side of the wall to the monument on Beacon Hill. Within the extensive panorama of the northern Pennines and the Howgills, locate on the skyline, 1km southeast, the trig point on Knott to the left of a tree. That is your next objective.

Follow the wall east to a gate near the corner and through the gate turn half-left to another gate, picking up the bridleway. Keep the tree in view and when the bridleway turns south leave it to head between limestone crags towards the tree. From the trig point, there's an excellent view, with Castle Folds prominent nearby.

(Unfortunately, Castle Folds cannot be visited without climbing a wall: the stile that can be seen is over an adjacent wall. In any case, I would not recommend walking east over the limestone, as the clints are fragile and the grikes are deep. If you prefer to do so, a gate in the wall east at 658094 might be welcome.)

From the trig point, walk west on grass between the limestone to regain the bridleway and enter Knots Lane. Turn left on a clear path (part of the Coast-to-Coast route) just north of the stone circle. Continue east to Acres and then along the quiet lane to Sunbiggin and Stony Head, after which the road becomes a track.

Shortly after entering the CRoW moorland, the bridleway forks. Take the left branch heading northeast, to reach the road north of Spear Pots (a small tarn now almost overgrown). Walk south on the grassy roadside verge to Sunbiggin Tarn, with good views of the Howgills beyond.

Past the cattle grid, take the bridleway right to reach the branch you met earlier. Now return to Knots Lane. This is the only significant retracing of steps in our 24 walks but the path is excellent, with good views in both directions, and much better than walking on the limestone scars or on the nearby roads. Cross Knots Lane and continue west past Scarside, across fields to Street Lane and on to Orton.

Rough Fell sheep

sedimentary, with the sediments having been laid down in the following order (youngest on top, naturally):

- about 300m years ago: Carboniferous (Silesian) – mainly millstone grit
- about 350m years ago: Carboniferous (Dinantian) – mainly limestone
- about 400m years ago: Devonian – mainly sandstone
- about 450m years ago: Silurian and Ordovician – mainly slates and shales

The Howgills (apart from the northeast corner) have had all layers eroded away to the Silurian and Ordovician. Orton Fells have been eroded to the Carboniferous limestone. Clearly, if the Howgills still had a limestone layer it would be much higher than Orton Fells. This implies a tilt or slip (a fault) to raise the Howgills side, which would have made it more exposed and vulnerable to erosion. The word 'fault' suggests a minor matter but the slippage, spread over millennia,

All Saints Church, Orton

would have been of a kilometre or more (the 2005 Asian tsunami is thought to have been caused by a slippage of a few metres). There are literally all sorts of twists and turns – some sudden, some slow (but over unimaginable timescales) – to complicate this brief outline but it may serve as a starting point for understanding Loyne geology.

The Lune from Chapel Beck ...

Immediately after Chapel Beck joins, the Lune passes under Tebay Bridge, a sign that we are approaching Tebay. The village is split in two by the A685: the original part now called Old Tebay and the newer part Tebay. In the early 19th century Old Tebay was a community of about ten houses, with Tebay consisting of little more than the 17th century Cross Keys Inn.

In one of those houses lived Mary Baines (1721-1811), who was alleged to be a witch and is said to still haunt the Cross Keys Inn. She was feared for various diabolical deeds, such as foretelling "fiery

horseless carriages" (that is, trains), but why she should be feared for a forecast that did not come true before her death is hard to see.

When the railways did arrive, they transformed Tebay. With a station on the west coast main line, which opened in 1846, and a junction to the line that ran through Newbiggin-on-Lune to the east coast, Tebay was a key part of the **Loyne railway network**. In addition, there were many sidings for the engines that were used to boost trains over the Shap summit. The village migrated south to be closer to the rail-yards, with terraces for rail-workers and a Junction Hotel being built a kilometre south. St James Church, with its distinctive round tower and conical top, was built in 1880, paid for by the rail company and workers.

Tebay's image has not recovered from the reputation it gained in those times, which is hard to do when guide-writers persist in repeating old opinions, such as this one, from Clement Jones's *A Tour in Westmorland* (1948): "The traveller … is apt to think - and how rightly - of Tebay as a grim and grimy railway junction blackened

At its peak, the **Loyne railway network** consisted of eight lines, plus lines out of Loyne to places such as Carlisle, Kirkby Stephen, Skipton, Preston, Morecambe and Windermere:

> Tebay – Lancaster (1846-)
> Wennington – Lancaster (1849-1966)
> Clapham – Wennington (1850-)
> Newbiggin-on-Lune – Tebay (1861-1962)
> Lowgill – Clapham (1861-1964)
> Wennington – Carnforth (1867-)
> Settle – Carlisle (1876-)
> Lancaster – Glasson (1883-1930).

We will encounter these lines, derelict or alive, many times on our journey and some general comments are in order, not on the details that railway enthusiasts are fond of but on the railways' impact on Loyne.

The building of the railways brought welcome employment but they generally harmed local industry. This was almost entirely small-scale activity to meet local needs, such as basket-making, pottery, quarrying and coal mining. It became easier and cheaper to import coal from where it was plentiful, and while new markets were opened up for local products they could not compete in terms of price or quality with the outputs from the rapidly-growing industrial towns. Consequently there was an exodus from the villages to those towns.

The railways affected local transport. It was much cheaper to send beef by train than by hoof. Therefore, the drove roads fell into disuse, along with the associated activities en route. Otherwise, most country tracks, used on foot or on horse, were not much affected until the advent of the car.

Scenically, the railways have now merged into the countryside and are fondly regarded. Derelict lines are often unnoticeable, except for structures such as the Lowgill Viaduct and Waterside Viaduct, which still impress us. They must have been awesome in the 19th century.

with the smoke of many locomotives and consisting mainly of the ugly dwellings of workmen employed on the railway."

Today things are different. The Newbiggin branch line closed in 1962, Tebay station was demolished in 1970, and the Junction Hotel is no longer a hotel. The terraces are painted in multi-coloured pastel shades and, below the green hills on a sunny day, present a handsome, if not pretty, sight. But Tebay cannot fully escape the impact of its location in a traffic corridor. There is an ever-present hum or roar, depending which way the wind is blowing, from the motorway, broken frequently by the rattle of the London-Glasgow expresses.

Beyond the motorway the Lune passes a mound that when glimpsed by motorway drivers might be assumed to be the remains of a slagheap. It is in reality what's left of the motte of a Norman motte and bailey castle, now called Castle Howe. Such castles consisted of an artificial mound (the motte), with a wooden or stone building on top, and a larger enclosed yard (the bailey) containing stables, workshops, kitchens and perhaps a chapel. The earth from ditches around the motte and bailey was used to create the motte.

Castle Howe is the first of ten such remains that we will meet on our journey. The castles were built soon after the Norman Conquest to provide security against rebellious northerners. It seems that Loyne's locals were not as obstreperous as elsewhere because its castles were at the smaller end of the scale of over five hundred such castles built in England. Mottes are typically from 3m to 30m high, with Loyne's being nearer the lower end of the range. Also, there are no remains of stone buildings on any of Loyne's mottes, indicating that the more vulnerable wood was considered adequate.

The Loyne castles were probably for the strategic and administrative use of landlords rather than for military garrisons. They were built overlooking river valleys and close to fertile meadows. Castle Howe is the closest to the river itself and has lost half its motte to flood erosion. The motorway at least has swerved to avoid it, if only just. By Castle Howe the Lune, flowing east, meets Birk Beck, flowing west.

Left: A Tebay terrace.

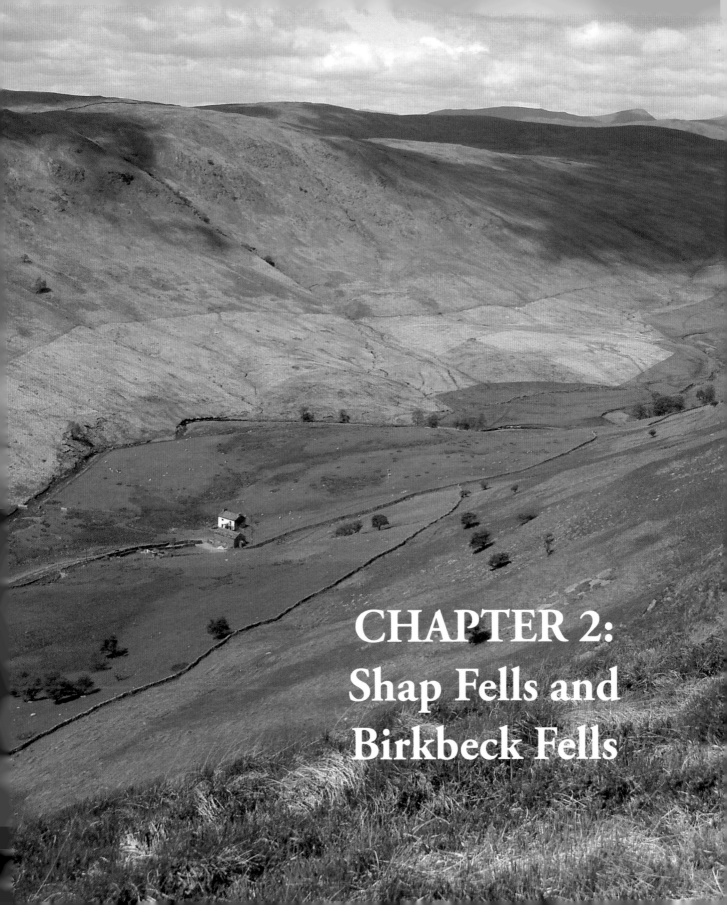

CHAPTER 2:
Shap Fells and
Birkbeck Fells

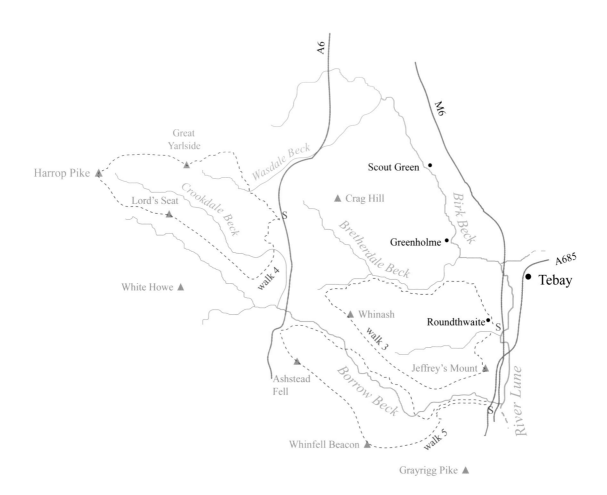

Scale: 1 cm to 1 km

0   5 kilometres

Birk Beck

Birk Beck arises in Wasdale, as Wasdale Beck, below Great Yarlside, which at 598m and 14km from the junction with the Lune is only a little lower and nearer than Green Bell. The most prominent feature of this region is the cliff face of Shap Pink Quarry, the existence of which tells us that there are locally rare and valued rocks. There is an exposure of 'Shap granite', an igneous rock with, amongst many other minerals, crystals of orthoclase feldspar (potassium aluminium silicate) so large that they may be studied with the naked eye. Large pink boulders can be seen in the surrounding fields and, as we saw, some made their way to the stone circle near Orton.

The Shap granite is an uprising of the granite that underlies the Lake District. It is seen in the western Lakes around, for example, the more famous Wasdale. This prompts consideration of how our Wasdale relates to the Lake District. The Shap Fells are officially part of the Lake District National Park, the eastern border of which is the A6, but lovers of Lakeland tend to ignore them. For example, Wainwright's classic seven volumes on Lakeland include a volume on the Eastern Fells and another on the Far Eastern Fells but still do not go far enough east to include the Shap Fells.

He argued that the Lakeland fells are "romantic in atmosphere, dramatic in appearance, colourful, craggy, with swift-running sparkling streams" but that the Shap Fells have a "quieter and more sombre attractiveness". But then Wainwright loved a scramble: anywhere where it was possible to settle into a brisk walking rhythm was usually described as dull or tedious. Rather ironically, the fact that the Shap Fells *are* in the National Park is now being used to try to extend the boundary yet further eastwards to include similar terrain.

South of the granite intrusion, the Shap Fells bedrock is of the Silurian slates and grits that underlie the Howgills. Here, however, deep peat gives blanket bog, with some heather moorland. The variety of upland vegetation supports breeding waders (curlew, lapwing, redshank, snipe) and raptors (peregrine falcon, merlin), although not very many, as far as I have seen. There's also a herd of red deer.

The headwaters of Wasdale Beck run off the slopes of Great Yarlside and Wasdale Pike, heading northeast to meet Longfell Gill, which passes the brother quarry, Shap Blue Quarry, which mines darker shades of granite.

At the junction is Shap Wells Hotel, built in 1833 for visitors, including royalty, to the nearby Shap Spa.

The beck, now called Birk Beck, passes Salterwath, a farmstead that lends its name to Salterwath Limestone. This first came from quarries 1km to the east, now beyond the railway and motorway, and more recently from Pickering Quarry 4km north. The limestone, which is blue-grey when quarried and polishes to a brownish shade, is a fine building and paving stone.

Below the 5m waterfall of Docker Force, Stakeley Beck and Eskew Beck join Birk Beck off Birkbeck Fells, a dull triangle of common land between the A6, M6 and Bretherdale, heathery to the north and grassy to the south. There's a good path from Ewelock Bank to the highest point, Crag Hill (400m), but the top is disappointing as it is little higher than nearby hillocks, lower than the A6 and surrounded in all directions by higher fells. Still, it provides reasonable views of those fells, especially the Cross Fell range and the Howgills.

Birk Beck runs past the small, secluded communities of Scout Green and Greenholme. It is hard to imagine now that they once lay on the route of an important drove road. Then, when there was no M6 or railway, it would have been quiet enough to hear the approaching clamour of a thousand cattle and accompanying throng; at the villages, excitement would grow – perhaps the visit coincided with a local market, with a lively exchange of beasts; the drovers would eat and drink (it was thirsty work); maybe the cattle would be penned overnight; and then the whole procession would move on to the next stop a few miles along.

The drove roads were, of course, not roads as we know them. They were wide tracks, often on high ground, partly for the free grazing there and partly to avoid the risk of ambush. A drover was a person of prestige and responsibility. The annual pilgrimage of cattle from Galloway to the south for sale or for fattening in the milder climate occurred for centuries before the railways made the practice obsolete. The drove roads were not restricted to cattle: they became the standard route of passage for people transporting other essentials of life, such as wool, coal and salt.

Surviving drove roads are characterised by their wide margins. The routes of the Galloway Gate (the

Previous page: upper Borrowdale from High House Bank.

name of the drove roads between Scotland and northwest England) through Loyne can be traced by place names (e.g. Three Mile House, reflecting the typical distance between stops) and inn names (e.g. Black Bull, Drover's Arms). The Galloway Stone, a large Shap granite boulder north of Salterwath, probably had significance for drovers.

More recently, Scout Green and Greenholme became known to railway enthusiasts as locations to view trains struggling up from Tebay to Shap. South of Greenholme, at Dorothy Bridge, Birk Beck is joined by Bretherdale Beck.

Docker Force
(Birk Beck may be only a tributary of the Lune but up to this point the Lune has been tame in comparison)

Bretherdale Beck

Bretherdale Beck runs between the A6 and M6 in the valley of Bretherdale, which was quiet and ignored until it came into the public limelight after a proposal to erect 27 wind turbines, 115m high, in a 6km by 2km area on its southern ridge. The proposal for what came to be called the Whinash Wind Farm was eventually rejected by the Secretary of State in 2006 because "the Whinash site is an important and integral part of a far-reaching landscape which is highly sensitive to change".

The proposal for what would have become England's largest land-based set of wind turbines became a test case for the conflict between protecting the landscape and securing renewable energy. Many factors provoked heated debates – too many to summarise here – but one that, judging from the 127-page inspector's report, seems to have been decisive is that the wind turbines would have impacted on views from the Lakes and Dales National Parks, from Orton Fells, and from locations further north. So, the views of Whinash were apparently more important than the merits of Whinash itself.

It is difficult to argue for those merits: "People love Bretherdale for its wild, open solitude" … "But nobody ever goes there" … "But if they did they'd love the solitude." How bleak and empty does a region have to be to be appreciated for that very bleakness and emptiness? How much intrusion can an empty region absorb before losing its emptiness? This is an argument not just for Bretherdale: many parts of Loyne appeal because so few people go there.

The debate about Whinash was obfuscated by opinions that the National Park boundaries might or would soon change. In particular, some professed to believe that the Birkbeck Fells, Bretherdale and Borrowdale were about to become part of the Lake District National Park – and of course it is unthinkable to have wind turbines in the Lake District. At the moment, the Lake District is ringed with wind turbines but there are none within its boundaries. On the other hand, the proposal, if approved, might have prevented the Birkbeck Fells joining the Lake District or might have set a precedent for further wind turbines in the Lake District.

Right top: derelict Parrocks in upper Bretherdale.
Right below: lower Bretherdale, looking west.

Among those who contributed to the debate were long-established groups such as Friends of the Earth and English Nature and newly created ones such as Friends of Bretherdale. Bretherdale never knew it had so many friends. The valley today has many abandoned farmsteads, which visitors, if there are any, might find charmingly derelict. But each of them was the home, perhaps for centuries, of families that were forced, in despair, to abandon their houses and their livelihoods. Where were the friends when these families needed them? Are a few wind turbines so much more important than the ruination of people's lives? Again, these are questions not just for Bretherdale. Loyne is and always has been predominantly rural and many communities continue to struggle to find a role in the 21st century.

As far as Bretherdale is concerned, all is far from lost. Although it may be too late for higher Bretherdale, except perhaps some buildings of Bretherdale Head, from Midwath Stead downstream there has been some reinvigoration. For example, Bretherdale Hall has been renovated despite uncertainty about the wind turbines. Midwath Stead itself seems a lively group of homesteads, with, according to its sign, "free range children".

Overall, it is a pleasant, sheltered valley, with rocky outcrops on the surrounding hills and an unobtrusive conifer plantation with other natural woodlands. Below Midwath Stead some of the fields are, like those near Raisbeck, traditional unploughed meadows and consequently rich in grasses, herbs and flowers.

After the Bretherdale Beck junction, Birk Beck proceeds uneventfully for 2km past Low Scales farm and under the three-arched Birkbeck Viaduct to join the Lune.

The Lune from Birk Beck ...

At their junction Birk Beck and the Lune are much the same size and if the matter hadn't been pre-empted by the naming it might have been unclear which was the tributary. They meet head on and as a significant, placid river run south, heading for a narrow gap, extravagantly called the Lune Gorge, between steep hills. This gap is an obvious transport corridor, as the Romans recognised with their road from Carlisle and as the drovers appreciated in the Middle Ages. More recently, the A685, the railway and the **M6** have squeezed themselves into the gap but only after it had been widened by blasting away the side of Jeffrey's Mount.

The **M6** in the Lune Gorge cannot be ignored so let us try to make a virtue of necessity: it is, after all, the recipient of a Civic Trust award, the plaque (which is in the A685 lay-by below Grayrigg Pike) saying "This award for an outstanding contribution to the appearance of the Westmorland landscape relates to the 36 miles of M6 Motorway between the Lancaster and Penrith bypasses". This contribution will not be appreciated at the level of the Lune. Distance lends enchantment and you really need to view the M6 from Grayrigg Pike, Blease Fell, Linghaw or even further away.

The A6 route via Shap, reaching 424m, was notorious for its bad visibility and winter conditions. The 1962 report on the proposed Lancaster-Penrith M6 route whittled the possibilities down to three: the A6, the Lune Valley, and the Killington routes. Of the two Lune Gorge routes, the Killington route was preferred to the Lune Valley (phew!), although a cost-benefit analysis found the A6 route better than both. The Killington route was selected because of the A6 weather problems and because the necessary tunnels would have "placed restrictions on the movement of dangerous goods" (?).

So Killington it was. The design and engineering problems were immense. The A685 was re-aligned; long constant gradients were designed, reaching a maximum height of 315m; 77 bridges were needed (plus three for the A685) – and all intended to blend into the landscape. Construction began in 1967 and the motorway opened in October 1970. By now millions of travellers on the M6 have admired the Howgills, but how many of the few of us on the Howgills have admired the M6?

The lines of transport jostle the Lune for space. Within 3km, the Lune is crossed nine times: four times by the M6, twice by the railway, once by the A685 and twice by footbridges. This is not the most soothing section of the Lune. Visually, the Lune is pleasant, running over a wide stony bed, bleached white in summer. Aurally, the M6 dominates.

The Lune is joined from the west by Roundthwaite Beck, which runs from Roundthwaite Common. The beck passes Roundthwaite Farm, which is the home of the Lunesdale fell ponies, about forty of which browse the fells between Bretherdale and Borrowdale. Fell ponies are hardy, strong, active, versatile, stubby, sure-footed horses, usually black but sometimes grey, brown or bay. They are on the fells all year. The fell pony originated on the moors of northwest England and is one of nine native breeds in Britain. It was used as a draught animal and packhorse since Roman times and was the

Walk 3: Roundthwaite Common and Bretherdale

Map: OL19 and OL7 (please read the general note about the walks in the Introduction).
Starting point: Roundthwaite, where the bridleway to Borrowdale swings southwest (609033).

This is a walk over the area that might have been sacrificed for the Whinash Wind Farm. Follow the bridleway southwest and immediately after the gate, take the path half left directly up the slope to Jeffrey's Mount. Continue beyond the small pile of stones at the top for a little way in order to rest while watching the busy motorway traffic far below.

When you are ready, head west along the ridge over half a dozen gentle rises, including Casterfell Hill, Belt Howe, Winterscleugh and the highest point, Whinash (471m). In places there is a path but it doesn't matter much as there are no fences and it is easy going on grass, with good views into Borrowdale. Almost certainly, Lunesdale fell ponies will be seen on the common.

When you reach Breasthigh Road, an ancient, deeply grooved track over the ridge, follow it to the right. At Bretherdale Beck you might like to detour north briefly to see the derelict Bretherdale Head. Follow the quiet road to picturesque Midwath Stead, with its small bridge.

Continue along the road (very little traffic) past Bretherdale Hall, and then take the footpath through Bretherdale Foot and Dyke Farm (where the owner assured me that there will soon be signs to help you locate the path) to Pikestone Lane. Turn right on the lane and walk for 2km to Roundthwaite.

main form of transport during the Border conflicts. The passing of these roles led to a severe decline in numbers, only arrested recently by its popularity for leisure and competitive riding, although it is really a working breed. The fell pony is still listed as endangered by the Rare Breeds Survival Trust.

Tucked between the M6, railway and A685 bridges is the first distinctive bridge across the Lune, Lune's Bridge. A document of 1379 refers to a "Lonesbrig" here but the present bridge is of the 17th century or later. This attractive bridge is perched across rocks where the Lune narrows. There are two arches, the smaller one so high that the Lune can surely never reach it. Today, the bridge leads to a memorial stone for four rail track workers who were killed near here in 2004 by a runaway trailer from Scout Green.

The Lune runs through a calm, open section that once was a quiet haven between steep hills, and is joined from the west by the sizable tributary of Borrow Beck.

Right: Lune's Bridge.

The Lune below Jeffrey's Mount

Borrow Beck

Borrow Beck runs for 10km east from between High House Fell and Bannisdale Fell through Borrowdale, the most beautiful valley in Loyne despite being split in two by the A6. Upper Borrowdale is within the Lake District National Park and has some of the character of Lakeland valleys. Unfortunately, there is no footpath in upper Borrowdale, which therefore can only be appreciated by walking the long, grassy ridges on either side.

Just below High Borrow Bridge, Crookdale Beck joins Borrow Beck. This junction illustrates the difficulty of determining the source of a watercourse. Upper and lower Borrowdale are aligned so well that it seems obvious that the same beck, Borrow Beck, flows through them both. But Crookdale Beck has a much higher and more distant source, below Harrop Pike (637m), than Borrow Beck and at the junction ought to be regarded as the senior partner.

Perhaps aesthetics play a part because Crookdale is such a dreary valley that no beck would want to be born there. There are twelve million visits to the Lake District National Park each year and approximately none of them involve an outing to Crookdale. Above Hause Foot, there is little of interest to a visitor not fascinated by varieties of grass and herb, only the modest crags of Great Yarlside breaking the monotonous, peaty slopes.

Hause Foot is on the turnpike route before the A6 was built in the 1820s. A steep curve up the northern slope can be traced, reaching 440m, with the route continuing north over Packhorse Hill and south to High Borrow Bridge. This route played a key part in the 1745 incursion of Bonnie Prince Charlie. When his army began to retreat, bridges such as High Borrow Bridge were demolished ahead of it to hamper its struggle over the Shap summit, after which the Scottish army was defeated in its last battle on English soil.

Right: Borrowdale Head from High House Bank.

Above: The wall from Great Yarlside to Little Yarlside. Right: lower Borrowdale, with Low Borrowdale farm.

Walk 4: Upper Borrowdale, Crookdale and Wasdale

Map: OL7 (please read the general note about the walks in the Introduction).
Starting point: A lay-by at the A6 summit (554062).

As we have Loyne becks from the Lake District, we must have a walk within the Lake District! This is a long, arduous, isolated walk over grassy and sometimes boggy ridges.

Go west through a gate and under two lines of pylons to reach the old turnpike route. Go south through two gates and at the third follow the wall down to Crookdale Beck. Cross it and head up High House Bank. At a small cairn there's a good view into Borrowdale.

Follow the ridge west. A faint path becomes clearer after Robin Hood, where a good cairn marks another viewpoint. Continue to Lord's Seat. Sadly, there is no sight from here of the fine cairn on Harrop Pike to inspire you, but make your way northwest around crags and peat-mounds (there is no path). Keep well to the left so that you can use the fence to guide you to the top.

After all this effort, the view of the Lakeland hills is disappointing. Only Black Combe, the Coniston range, and a glimpse of Harter Fell and High Street can be seen beyond the nearer hills. There's also a view into Mosedale and Sleddale, where you may be lucky to see red deer. No lakes can be seen apart from a bit of Wet Sleddale Reservoir to the northeast. The view eastwards is better: a panorama from Morecambe Bay to Cross Fell, with the Howgills prominent.

From Harrop Pike, follow the fence east to Great Yarlside (easy walking here). At the junction follow the fence left, not the wall right. Follow the right fence at the next junction. After a short while, a plantation comes into view half right. Make a beeline (no path) across Wasdale, with Shap Pink Quarry to your left, to the right hand corner of the plantation and then across the field to the lay-by.

Most of my walks have obvious shorter alternatives but not this one. You could forgo the pleasure of reaching Harrop Pike by contouring round from Lord's Seat to Great Yarlside – but don't cut directly across Crookdale, as it's a bog. From Great Yarlside, you could avoid walking in Wasdale by following the wall over Little Yarlside.

The reward for this walk is that you can afterwards boast to Lake District fans that you did Borrowdale and Wasdale in one day.

Walk 5: Lower Borrowdale

Map: OL19 and OL7 (please read the general note about the walks in the Introduction).
Starting point: Where a side-road leaves the A685 for Borrowdale (607014).

Walk west along the road that skirts Borrowdale Wood until it becomes a track and after a further 0.5km (at 594014) take a path leading south up through a sparse, old woodland. Eventually, views into Borrowdale open out and the repeater station, with the aerial to the left, comes into view.

From the repeater station, walk to Whinfell Beacon (good view over Kendal), Castle Fell, Mabbin Crag and Ashstead Fell. The cairns on the peaks can be seen ahead and the footpath is clear except for a short section in the plantation below Mabbin Crag. From Ashstead Fell, drop down towards the A6 and take the path northeast to Borrow Beck. Walk east on the south bank for 2km and cross the bridge leading to High and Low Borrowdale. Continue back by Borrowdale Wood.

Variations of this walk present themselves. Those of boundless energy may extend the walk into a ridge horseshoe by walking up Breasthigh Road (by fording Borrow Beck or, if that is not possible, crossing it at Huck's Bridge) to the ridge above Borrowdale Edge, dropping down the bridleway to Low Borrowdale.

Shorter walks can be devised by noting carefully the positions of the two bridges, the plantations and the other footpath (from Roundthwaite) into the valley, and the extent of CRoW land. There are crags on the valley slopes but, if necessary, they can be negotiated with care.

Walks may equally well start at the A6 end, where there are two lay-bys close by Huck's Bridge.

In a lay-by on the A6 there is a memorial to drivers over the A6 Shap summit, but the A6 is far from forgotten and unused today. There is no memorial to the souls who tackled the turnpike route. It too is not unused as it forms part of the 82km Kendal to Carlisle Miller's Way footpath, opened in 2006.

Below High Borrow Bridge, Borrow Beck enters lower Borrowdale, a serene valley enclosed by steep, grassy slopes, with occasional rocky outcrops, the ridges on both sides undulating over a series of gentle summits reaching almost 500m. The farmstead of High Borrowdale was derelict for many years until bought in 2002 by the Friends of the Lake District, perhaps as a ploy to help prevent the building of wind turbines on Whinash. Many saplings have been planted beside the beck and the barns have been restored but the farmstead

itself remains a ruin, now tidy rather than derelict. Low Borrowdale continues to farm the lower valley in splendid isolation.

It is a merciful mystery that Borrowdale has escaped change. The Romans and the drovers did not find use for an east-west path through Borrowdale but it is surprising that a road joining the Lune valley and the A6 was never contemplated. Although the planners' suggestion that Borrowdale become a reservoir and the recent Whinash Wind Farm proposal were both thwarted, the southern ridge, Whinfell, has been less successful in avoiding modern intrusions. Historically, Whinfell had a beacon to warn of Scottish invasions and it is perhaps to be expected that the ridge should now be adorned with its 21st century equivalents, a repeater station and aerial. I actually rather like them.

Left: Whinfell aerial and repeater station.

CHAPTER 3:
Western Howgills and Firbank Fell

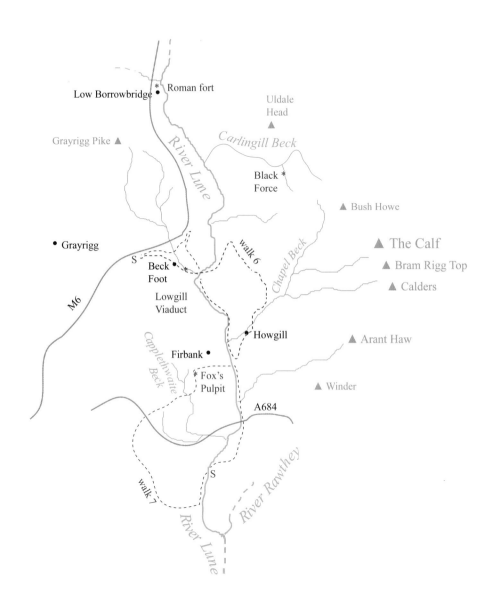

Scale: 1 cm to 1 km

0   5 kilometres

The Lune from Borrow Beck ...

Just beyond the Borrow Beck junction at Low Borrowbridge there is a flat, green field that seen from the fells on either side looks like a sports arena, which in a way it was because until the late 19th century a large sheep fair used to be held here, with associated sports and other activities. But long before that, from the 1st to the 4th century, this was the site of a Roman fort.

Somehow this fact became forgotten, despite the reminder of Borrow (or burgh) Beck, until it was rediscovered in the early 19th century. This is especially surprising since the site has been relatively undisturbed by later building. The fort measures 130m by 100m, adequate for five hundred soldiers. It lies on the Carlisle-Chester route and is the first of three sites of Roman forts that we will meet. Excavations in the 20th century have confirmed the layout of the fort but seem to have uncovered few remains. More has been found at the cemetery to the south, including a tombstone with the touching inscription (not in English, of course): "Gods of the underworld, Aelia Sentica lived for 35 years. Aurelius Verulus erected this stone for his loving wife". Although the outline of the fort is clear, there is not much to see on the ground, only ramparts along the line of the old walls and on the west side a few ditches. Some claim that, ignoring the railway, motorway and A685 (quite a feat), the line of an aqueduct can be made out running towards the fort from the slopes below Grayrigg Pike.

Grayrigg Pike is seen by many but noticed by few. The steep crags and slopes around Great Coum and Little Coum make them the most scenic cliffs we have met so far but the rebounding noise of M6 traffic lessens their appeal to walkers.

The Lune passes under Salterwath Bridge. We have met a few 'wath's already and, as you might suspect, it is an old word (Viking, in fact) for a ford. The bridge itself was last rebuilt in 1824. At about this point, the drove road that followed the Lune from Greenholme swung west to skirt Grayrigg and climbed to the Lune watershed, which it more or less followed south to Kirkby Lonsdale.

Beyond Low Carlingill farm, the Lune meets the most dramatic beck of the Howgills, Carlingill Beck.

Previous page: Chapel Beck, looking to Bush Howe. Below: Low Borrowbridge.

Carlingill Beck

Carlingill Beck and the River Lune mark the northwestern boundary of the **Yorkshire Dales National Park**. Today this seems anomalous. A boundary has to be somewhere but there seems no discernible reason for it to include the southern part of the Howgills but to exclude the northern part, as they are the same in terms of geology and scenery. The boundary is here simply because the old Westmorland-Yorkshire county border lay along Carlingill Beck at the time the Yorkshire Dales National Park was established in 1954.

Carlingill Beck is an excellent site for students of fluvial geomorphology (that is, of how flowing water affects the land), providing some intriguing illustrations of post-glacial erosion. The beck arises as Great Ulgill Beck below Wind Scarth and Breaks Head, on a ridge that runs from The Calf, and then curves west at Blakethwaite Bottom, a sheltered upland meadow below Uldale Head. It enters an increasingly narrow gorge, with contorted rock formations exposed on the southern side, giving us our first real view of the Silurian slate of the Howgills. The beck then forms The Spout, which is as much a water shoot as a waterfall, as it tumbles steeply over 10m of tilted rocks. To the north are steep screes and further exposed contorted rocks and below

The **Yorkshire Dales National Park** occupies some 1760 sq km and is the third largest of Britain's twelve National Parks. The part we encounter in the Howgills is uncharacteristic of the Dales, which are normally pictured in terms of spectacular limestone scenery. The Yorkshire Dales are no longer all in Yorkshire: the Howgills, Dentdale and Garsdale are in Cumbria.

As we will see, only a few of the Dales lie within Loyne – Dentdale, Garsdale, Kingsdale and Chapel-le-Dale. The Lune itself is the western border for about 12km and is not sensibly regarded as one of the Yorkshire Dales.

Like all British National Parks, the Yorkshire Dales National Park is not state-owned but consists of privately owned estates and farms administered by an authority responsible for conservation and recreation. It is therefore both a tourist attraction and a working area, which even includes some large quarries.

to the south looms the deep, dark gash formed by Little Ulgill Beck.

Here is Black Force, the most spectacular scene of the Howgills: not one force but a series of cascades, deep within a V-shaped ravine that has remarkable rock formations exposed on its western side. Our journey through the northern Howgills showed us little to hint at the striking degree of erosion hidden within this gill.

Beyond admiring the awesome sights, we might wonder about causes and effects. The benign, smooth slopes of the Howgills do not suggest the convulsions needed to form the contorted rocks seen by Carlingill Beck. Are these contortions limited to Carlingill Beck, or are there similar rock formations hidden elsewhere? If the latter, why have they been so dramatically exposed only here, in such deep gullies, from such relatively small becks? Or did

Left: upper Carlingill Beck, with The Spout middle right.
Right: Black Force (the scale may be judged by the two walkers and a dog on the path top right - you can't see them? - precisely).

The exposed rocks on the western slopes of Black Force, with Carlin Gill and Grayrigg beyond

the contortions cause weaknesses that the becks have exploited?

Below Black Force, Carlingill Beck begins to calm down. It still runs in a narrow valley, with small waterfalls and eroded sides, but, as becks tend to do, it eventually levels off and opens out. The lower parts of Carlingill Beck and its tributaries, especially Grains Gill, still show fine examples of post-glacial erosion, in the form of deep gullies, alluvial fans and cones. The relative absence of human and animal disturbance and the frequency of heavy flooding enable the study of hillside erosion, the changes of flow directions, and the dynamics of debris flow and deposition. Even to the non-expert, the scenes provide remarkable evidence of the continuing impact of erosive forces.

The beck passes under the old Carlingill Bridge. Being on a county border is a problem for any self-respecting bridge: in 1780, when Carlingill Bridge was dilapidated, Westmorland quarter sessions ordered a contract to rebuild half of it. Happily, the bridge is now all in Cumbria. Unhappily, it was still in need of repair when I last visited. There is a final burst of energy as Carlingill Beck runs through the narrow gorge of Lummers Gill to enter the Lune but, under normal conditions, it still seems far too demure to have caused the effects seen upstream.

Any walkers who have strolled in Bowderdale and Langdale and are wondering about an outing along Carlingill Beck should be warned that this is a serious undertaking. Walking by the beck itself involves a fair amount of rough scrambling and, if the beck is high, may be impossible. Black Force cannot be walked up, although it is possible to clamber up the grassy slope to the east. The path to The Spout is increasingly difficult and it likewise becomes impassable, although there is a challenging escape to the north. The public footpath from the south past Linghaw, which can be continued to Blakethwaite Bottom, provides no view into the Black Force ravine.

The Lune from Carlingill Beck ...

According to a generally accepted theory, long ago the Lune used to begin about here. It is believed that the Lune was then formed from the becks that drain south from the Howgills, with all the becks we've met up to now (Bowderdale Beck, Langdale Beck, Borrow Beck, and so on) at that time flowing north within the Eden catchment area. The Lune watershed was then south of what is now the Lune Gorge. In time, the headwaters of the Lune eroded northwards to capture Borrow Beck and then all the other becks to divert their flow southward. The evidence for this is complicated, involving the 'open cols' to the north through which no water now flows, or much less water than the size of the valleys would suggest; the fact that the flow of the northern becks is discordant to the underlying rocks; and the history of geological uplifts and tilts. The more recent glaciation has obscured most of this evidence for the untutored eye.

Above the Lune is Gibbet Hill, where the bodies of miscreants were displayed and where alleged eerie noises are now drowned by the M6. The small road to the east of the Lune, Fairmile Road, is along the line of the Roman road that led south from Low Borrowbridge. A part of the Roman road that diverges from the present road was investigated in 1962. At Fairmile Gate, the road crosses Fairmile Beck, which runs from the hills by Fell Head and Linghaw, which are good vantage points for the Lune valley. Fell Head is one of the more identifiable

hills of the Howgills, having a covering of heather and hence a dark appearance.

The Lune reaches the Crook of Lune Bridge, which is the quirkiest of all the Lune bridges. It is a sturdy yet graceful 16th century construction, with two 10m arches and a width of about 2m. Being a little upstream of the two lanes that drop down to it, it makes a tricky manoeuvre for vehicles. It's as though the 16th century builders wanted to ensure that no 21st century juggernaut could cross.

At the bridge we meet the Dales Way at exactly the point that it leaves (or enters) the Dales. The Dales Way is a 125km footpath between Ilkley and Bowness-on-Windermere, passing through many of the most attractive dales, especially, if I may say so, this stretch of the Lune.

Just beyond the bridge, Lummer Gill joins the Lune, having run from Grayrigg Common, through Deep Gill, under the motorway and railway (where, thankfully, they veer away from the Lune valley), past the village of Beck Foot and then under the magnificent curved Lowgill Viaduct. The eleven red arches stand 30m high and seem so thin as to be flimsy but for over a hundred years (1861 to 1964) they carried trains on the Lowgill-Clapham line, a central part of the Loyne railway network. A failure of railway politics meant that it was never used as originally intended, that is, for Ingleton to Scotland traffic – until the winter of 1963 blocked

Right: the Lune from Linghaw.

Crook of Lune Bridge

the Settle-Carlisle line. Today, the viaduct is an aerial arboretum, with shrubs and trees sprouting from the track. It is to be hoped that someone is responsible for maintaining this structure, to avoid irreparable decay.

The Lune accompanies the Dales Way for 2.5km. This is a gentle, bubbling stream in summer, but a torrent after heavy rain on the Howgills. Debris in the tree branches shows that the floodplains are indeed occasionally under water.

This is a good stretch along which to spot the dipper, the bird that best represents the spirit of the becks. It is the only passerine (that is, perching bird) that is adapted to aquatic life, in being able to close its ears and nostrils under water, having no air sacs in its bones, and in being able to store more oxygen in its blood than other passerines. It uses its wings to swim under turbulent water in its search for insect larvae. It will be seen bobbing on a rock or flying fast and direct, low over the water.

The presence of dippers along any beck is a measure of the health of that beck. Sadly, the number of dippers

The Top 10 birds in Loyne

1. Dipper: for its spirit
2. Curlew: for its call
3. Lapwing: for its flight
4. Kingfisher: for its colour
5. Skylark: for its song
6. Oystercatcher: for its bill
7. Heron: for its style
8. Black grouse: for its rarity
9. Sand martin: for its nest
10. Swan: for its grace

Honourable mention: the snipe.

seems to be declining along the Lune and its tributaries, probably because of the damage to riverbanks, where it nests, and the building of weirs for flood control, which reduces the turbulence that dippers need.

Ellergill Beck, running from Brown Moor past Beck House, and the more substantial Chapel Beck next supplement the Lune. Chapel Beck is the largest beck of the western Howgills. The western slopes below Arant Haw, Calders, Bram Rigg Top, The Calf, White Fell Head and Breaks Head all contribute to it. Its slopes also have two of the clearest paths in the Howgills, on either side of Calf Beck, providing an excellent walk to The Calf. On this walk you would see the Horse of Bush Howe, a natural (it seems to me) rocky outcrop in the vague shape of a horse. One legend is that it was created as a signal for smugglers in Morecambe Bay. One can only smile at the misguided attempts to add a touch of glamour to the Howgills, and move on.

After Castley Wood, Chapel Beck passes through what is, if anywhere is, the centre of the scattered parish of Howgill, which gives its name to the whole area. The Holy Trinity Chapel, built in 1838, presents an unreasonably pretty picture, with its narrow windows and its neatly shaped bushes and with the old mill, school and cottages nearby. Below the chapel we see an example of the work of the **Lune Habitat Group**.

The maturing Lune runs deep below grassy slopes, passing under the Waterside Viaduct, which is notable for being the highest bridge across the Lune, 30m above the heads of walkers on the Dales Way. Like the Lowgill Viaduct, the Waterside Viaduct used to carry the Lowgill-Clapham railway and is a fine structure, although here the seven arches are of irregular size and the middle section is of metal.

The Lune accepts the tributary of Crosdale Beck, which runs off the slopes of Arant Haw, and moves

Lowgill Viaduct

Walk 6: Lowgill and Brown Moor

Map: OL19 (please read the general note about the walks in the Introduction).
Starting point: The roadside verge by the railway before the road drops down to Beck Foot (610964).

This walk includes the best stretch of path beside the Lune and a taste of the Howgills, without going to the highest tops. The initial noise of the motorway and railway perhaps adds to our appreciation of the serenity of the Lune valley.

Walk east to the B6257 (with Lowgill Viaduct directly ahead) and pass under the viaduct, noticing the packhorse bridge dwarfed under it, to Crook of Lune Bridge. Immediately after the bridge, turn left, taking the path above Nether Fields Wood to Brunt Sike. Then double back, walking across fields to Gate House.

Continue to Beck House and Beck Houses Gate, beyond which you are on the open fell. Walk up Brown Moor (412m) and stop to admire the view, from Fell Head on the left to Brant Fell on the right. There's a good view of the so-called Horse of Bush Howe but better is the sight of the neatly interlacing ridges up the various valleys.

Walk south to Castley Knotts, drop down to the footpath, and follow it through Castley to Gate Side. Walk south on the road and turn right after Chapel Beck, past the Holy Trinity Chapel, and take the track to Thwaite, where the path is rather hidden behind the barn to the left. Continue towards Hole House but don't go that far: at Smithy Beck drop down to the Lune. Now you follow the Dales Way back to the Crook of Lune Bridge. Route finding is no problem, so you may concentrate on spotting dippers, kingfishers, herons, and other riverside birds.

From the bridge you could return the way you came or, trusting the OS map (for there is no signpost), turn right across fields to Nether House, which although marked on the map is just a small pile of rubble. Walk up its old drive and detour right along the road for 400m to view the neat, red Railway Terrace. Return past Lowgill Farm, turn left on the B6257 and right through Beck Foot back to the starting point and the noise of modern transport.

> The **Lune Habitat Group** was formed in 1997 to help protect watercourses, regenerate habitats, and encourage the bioversity of the Lune - and its tributaries, for of course the Lune cannot be healthy if its tributaries are not. The aim is to improve landscapes, reduce erosion and safeguard water quality. The Group is an informal partnership aiming to develop coordinated programmes of action involving farmers, land-owners, national parks, government ministries, angling clubs, and anyone else with a concerned interest in the Lune.
>
> Some of the Lune's problems are attributed to the damage that sheep and cattle cause to riverbanks. Therefore, as at Chapel Beck, the Group has carried out a programme of fencing and tree planting in order to stabilise the banks. So far, some 60kms of riverbank have been protected, to benefit wildlife such as otters, voles, kingfishers and dippers, as well as fish populations. The Group won the Best Environmental award of the Lancashire Environmental Fund in 2005 (although we are still in Cumbria here).

towards the 17th century Lincoln's Inn Bridge. Sadly, Mr Lincoln and his inn are no longer with us, and some might wish the same of the bridge, as it makes a narrow, awkward turn on the busy A684. Like most bridges, it forms a better impression from the riverside.

Here we detect some pride in being next to the Lune, for as well as the farm of Luneside there is, just along the A684, a Vale of Lune Chapel, now called St Gregory's. This was built in the 1860s, whilst the railway line was being constructed, and, judging from its unusual, robust design, it may have been built by rail workers. Opposite Luneside, Capplethwaite Beck enters the Lune from the west.

Capplethwaite Beck

Capplethwaite Beck and its tributary Priestfield Beck run from Firbank Fell behind the ridge to the west of the Waterside Viaduct. This unprepossessing moor is known only for two things: **Fox's Pulpit** and its magnificent views of the Howgills.

From the plaque at Fox's Pulpit there is a view south along the Lune valley to the Ward's Stone ridge of Bowland Fells, 35km away. However, there is no view of the Howgills, which is strange. One of the Quaker beliefs, as noted in Fox's journal, is that "the

Left: looking towards Arant Haw and Brant Fell.

steeplehouse and that ground on which it stood were no more holy than that mountain". Surely Fox would have positioned himself about 200m east so that when expressing such a sentiment he could gesture towards the Howgills. That would convince anyone, and I could even imagine listening to a three-hour sermon myself if I could look at the Howgills at the same time. There is still a graveyard by Fox's Pulpit but the church that Fox disdained has left in a huff, demolished by a gale in 1839.

Capplethwaite Beck runs past the 16th century Capplethwaite Hall, which was the home of the Morland family, one of whom, Jacob, was painted in 1763 by George Romney before he became so obsessed with Emma (later Lady) Hamilton that he painted her sixty times. This portrait is now in the Tate Britain gallery, and a grand figure he looks, although not as grand as the Howgills behind, which unfortunately he is obscuring.

> **Fox's Pulpit** marks one of the few events in Loyne to be considered of national importance. Here on June 13th 1652 George Fox preached to one thousand people for three hours, according to his own journal, an event nowadays often regarded as establishing the Society of Friends (or Quakers).
>
> The Quaker movement has been particularly influential in the Loyne region. No doubt the emphasis on equality and on the spirituality within people, rather than churches, rituals and sacraments, appealed to independent, poor northerners.
>
> The mid 17th century – Oliver Cromwell, Civil Wars, and so on – was a fertile, if challenging, time for non-conformist religious movements but Quakerism was a social movement as well, because the promotion of equality naturally upset the privileged, powerful members of society who did not receive from Quakers the respect or deference they expected. This partly explains the years of persecution suffered by Quakers. Fox himself was imprisoned seven times.
>
> It also explains the large number of 'meetinghouses' that we will pass. Quakers did not build churches, as it was against their beliefs and would have been asking for trouble. To begin with, they met within one another's houses. In some Loyne valleys almost every farmstead may be described as an old Quaker meetinghouse – that is, an old farmstead within which Quakers met. After the Restoration of the monarchy (1660), matters gradually improved for Quakers but the laws under which they had been persecuted were not ended until the 1689 Act of Toleration.

Walk 7: Fox's Pulpit and the Waterside Viaduct

Map: OL19 (please read the general note about the walks in the Introduction).
Starting point: Killington New Bridge (623908).

Walk south by the Lune to Bowersike and take the track up to Greenholme, where there's a good view back to Winder, Baugh Fell and Middleton Fell. Through Greenholme, follow the wall on the right that swings north. Across a small beck, the track turns west towards a plantation where there's a reassuring footpath sign. It's quiet here, among the bracken and heather, but from the corner of the plantation you see, a few kilometres away, reminders of the 21st century – Killington Service Station and the Lambrigg wind turbines.

Beyond the plantation the path drops down to a white gate, where you turn right to another white gate, from which there is a view of the Howgills from Winder to Fell Head. Note the prominent white building 2km ahead (New Field), which is your next objective.

Cross the A684. There is no clear path on the CRoW land but make your way across to Ghyll Farm, which is on Capplethwaite Beck. There seem to be no signposts at Ghyll Farm, so be careful to turn left off the drive, before a barn, heading north. After 500m you reach the white building you noted before.

From New Field, walk 1km along the road to Fox's Pulpit. By now, you might appreciate that Fox did well to attract a thousand people up here. Walk east across the CRoW land of Knotts and, when the view ahead is revealed, pause to relate the panorama to your map – in particular, identify the large farm of Hole House, 1km northeast. Head in the general direction of Hole House until you reach either a wall or a clear footpath running north-south (between Stocks and Whinny Haw). In the former case, follow the wall to the right until the footpath is reached.

Walk to Stocks and continue on the road north but before Goodies turn right over the old railway line and cross the Lune footbridge. Walk up by Smithy Beck to Hole House. You are now on the well sign-posted Dales Way. Follow this for 3km past the Waterside Viaduct, Lincoln's Inn Bridge and Luneside. Where the Dales Way turns left to The Oaks, turn right to the Lune, which you follow back to Killington New Bridge.

The Lune from Capplethwaite Beck ...

Paddlers (in a canoe, that is) feel the adrenaline rising as they and the Lune approach the next section, which includes a narrow rapid called the Strid that drops 2m into a large pool. This is the liveliest part of the whole Lune, as it tumbles through and over sloping rocks and into deep pools, and one of the most challenging canoeing stretches in northwest England. It may be viewed from a footpath that leads north from Killington New Bridge. The bridge has a single 18m arch and is not new. A proposal to build holiday chalets in the field southwest of the bridge would, if accepted, enable many more visitors to enjoy, or spoil, the scenic tranquillity of the region.

At the bridge there is a notice: "SAA No canoeing". I expect that SAA is the Sedbergh Angling Association but I am unsure of the legal status of their notice. The SAA presumably owns the banks and can insist upon private fishing. Does it own the Lune too? Can it prevent others using the Lune? Obviously, they would prefer canoeists not to tangle their lines and disturb their fish. Indeed, I would prefer canoeists not to disturb the dippers, kingfishers, and other wildlife (and anglers not to disturb salmon, come to that). Nevertheless, canoeists do tackle the Lune and its tributaries, with or without permission, and good luck to them.

Canoeists will, I imagine, be less happy with the dangerous-looking weir that follows at Broad Raine. Further south, at Stangerthwaite, the public bridleway and ford seem impenetrable, at least to horses and vehicles. It used to link two tracks, one of which leads up to Four Lane Ends, the other three old lanes now forming the A683 and B6256.

After this turbulent stretch, the Lune swings west to meet the largest tributary so far, the River Rawthey.

Previous page (left): Waterside Viaduct.
Previous page (right): the western Howgills from Dillicar.
Above: the Lune at Killington New Bridge.

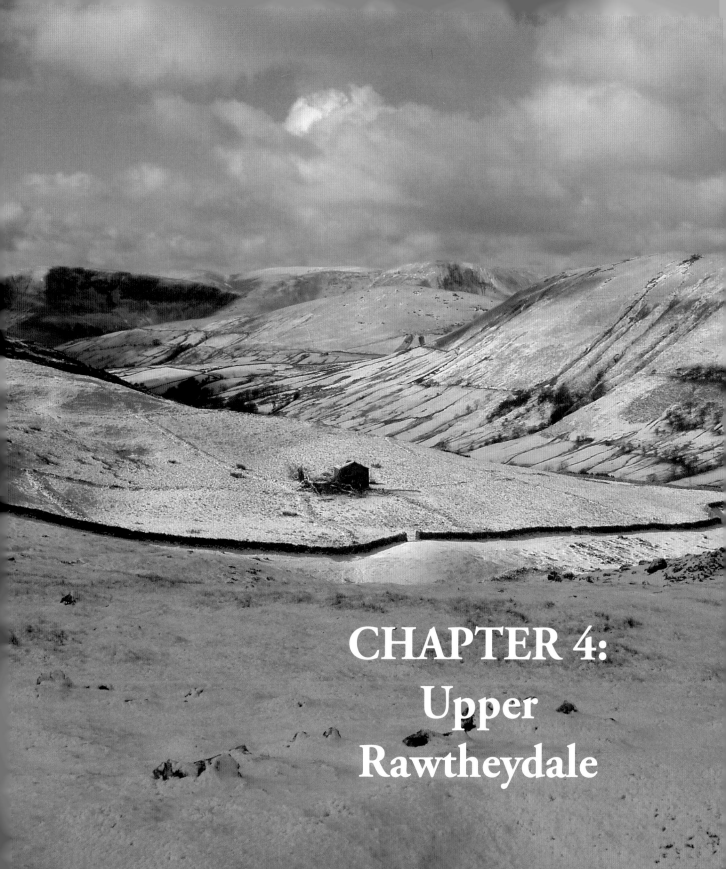

CHAPTER 4:
Upper Rawtheydale

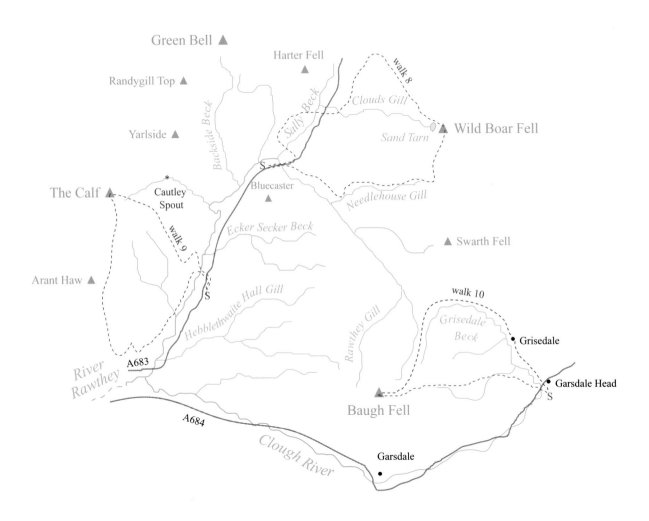

Green Bell ▲

Harter Fell ▲

Randygill Top ▲

walk 8

Clouds Gill

Wild Boar Fell ▲

Backside Beck

Sally Beck

Yarlside ▲

Sand Tarn

The Calf ▲

*

Cautley Spout

Bluecaster ▲

Needlehouse Gill

Ecker Secker Beck

▲ Swarth Fell

walk 9

Arant Haw ▲

S

Hebblethwaite Hall Gill

Rawthey Gill

walk 10

Grisedale Beck

• Grisedale

River Rawthey

A683

• Garsdale Head
S

A684

Baugh Fell ▲

Clough River

Garsdale •

Scale: 1 cm to 1 km

0   5 kilometres

The River Rawthey ...

Like the Lune, the Rawthey first flows north (as Rawthey Gill off Baugh Fell) and then swings west and south. Baugh Fell is the largest mountain of Loyne, in terms of volume, that is, not height, occupying the huge expanse of high ground between the A683, the A684 and the Grisedale-Rawthey valley. It is one of the least visited of the peaks of the Yorkshire Dales and understandably so, because it is surrounded by many more attractive challenges.

It is pudding-shaped, with the unappealing characteristic, for a walker, of being relentlessly uphill from whichever direction you tackle it and of having a top that is always over the horizon. There is little of interest above 400m. And when you reach the top, you cannot be sure that you are there. The trig point at Knoutberry Haw is, according to the OS map, 2m lower than the unmarked, gentle summit at Tarn Rigg Hill (678m).

Some would say that Baugh Fell is pudding-textured too but that is an exaggeration. Yes, it tends to be wet and there are peat mounds to negotiate but there's plenty of grass and the top is a rough, stony plateau. Still, it is one of those mountains best tackled when the ground is frozen solid and there's a layer of snow to hide the desolation.

Baugh Fell is not the most exciting fell but it does provide a magnificent view in all directions: circling from the north Wild Boar Fell, Mallerstang, Great Shunner Fell, Pen-y-Ghent, Pendle, Ingleborough, Whernside, Great Coum, the Lakeland Peaks, and the Howgills. The views of Whernside and Great Coum are particularly striking. From other directions they appear unremarkable but from here they have majestic profiles.

After 3km Rawthey Gill turns a left angle, becoming the River Rawthey, to run through a limestone gorge and over a series of waterfalls, one of which at least deserves a distinctive name. Some call it Uldale Force but Uldale seems to be the area north of Holmes Moss, with Uldale Gill further north still. What's wrong with a simple Rawthey

Force? Anyway, the 10m waterfall is quite the equal of more illustrious waterfalls that we will meet later.

Whin Stone Gill, Blea Gill and Needlehouse Gill (which begins as Uldale Gill) join the Rawthey off the western slopes of Swarth Fell, which is one of those underrated hills that suffer by comparison with a near neighbour (no, not Baugh Fell – Wild Boar Fell to the north). At 681m, Swarth Fell is higher than the Howgills and Baugh Fell and, with a flattish top and crags to the east, has the characteristic shape of the peaks of the Yorkshire Dales, although it is only half within the National Park.

Needlehouse Gill runs in a narrow valley, over waterfalls and past caves, by Needle House, one of a line of farmsteads among the small conifer plantations on the northern slopes of the Rawthey. There are actually two rather fine houses at Needle House and surely the only barn we'll see with a belfry.

Previous page: from Fell End Clouds towards Cautley Crag.
Right: Rawthey (or Uldale) Force.

Above: Needle House barn (spot the dog).
Left: lower falls of the Rawthey near Needle House.

Rawthey Cave, in which have been found the remains of humans from about 1500 BC, is on the south bank of the Rawthey, on the slopes of Bluecaster. The track across the flank of Bluecaster drops down to the river, where, as you would expect, there used to be a bridge – a bridge of some importance, it would seem, since in 1586 Queen Elizabeth wrote to those responsible for its upkeep saying that "she marvels at their negligence in the execution of her former orders concerning the rebuilding of Rawthey Bridge." Perhaps the word 'execution' spurred some action.

The old bridge is no more but there's a fine newer one 50m downstream, built in 1820 with a single semi-circular arch. There's a minor puzzle here. It is said that two children's faces were carved in the bridge. There seems to be space for a rectangular display on the two sides of the bridge but perhaps the displays have fallen out. On the west side there is a face, but that of a bewigged gentleman, it seems to me. On the east side, there are what, if viewed generously, could be two eyes and a nose. What it means, if anything, is a mystery.

Just below the bridge the nicely named Sally Beck enters the Rawthey.

Sally Beck

Sally Beck arises 4km north in the fields above Studfold. Under normal conditions, it receives numerous becks flowing from Harter Fell on the west but nothing at all from Fell End Clouds on the east. This is because the Clouds are formed of limestone, into which rainwater disappears.

The limestone does not really form terraces like we saw on Orton Scar because it is too distorted. It occurs as small cliffs and scattered, rocky outcrops. There are two well-preserved limekilns, with evidence of old mine workings, and in the middle of the Clouds there's an intriguing enclosed field containing the ruins of old walls. The Clouds have been made a Site of Special Scientific Interest, mainly because of their flora, which, because the Clouds are heavily grazed, is largely restricted to the recesses of the grikes. There are, for example, seventeen species of fern, including the rare rigid buckler fern, holly fern, and green spleenwort.

To the south of Fell End Clouds, Clouds Gill makes a brave effort to cross the limestone to reach Sally Beck. Most of the time it fails but sometimes, judging by the erosion, it succeeds with a vengeance. It flows from Sand Tarn, a perhaps unexpected oasis just below the Wild Boar Fell trig point.

At 708m, Wild Boar Fell is the highest hill we have met so far – and the most dramatic, although admittedly most of the drama is on the eastern slopes, which are within the Eden catchment area. The broader, western slopes drain to the Lune, via the Rawthey.

Wild Boar Fell has a flat top, with many cairns. Those on the eastern rim provide marvellous views into Mallerstang and across to the hills of the Yorkshire Dales. The trig point is on the western edge and provides a unique viewpoint down onto the Howgills, giving a wonderful impression of the rolling contours.

Wild Boar Fell is so called because the last English wild boar fell here, or so it is said. In case you should be sceptical, we are given a date and perpetrator for the deed: 1396 and Sir Richard Musgrave of Hartley Castle. If doubts still remain, then we're told that his tomb in Kirkby Stephen church was found to contain a boar's tusk. But your clinching counter-argument is that there are wild boars in England now.

As Clouds Gill passes the limestone it reaches an appealing high-level road that was the original road but is now a quiet by-way above the A683. It is open to the fell, has wide grassy verges, and has a line of farmsteads most of which are being revitalised as holiday homes. Cold Keld, for example, offers guided walking holidays. To the south is Fell End bunkhouse, which is owned by the Bendrigg Trust, a charity offering outdoor activities for disabled people. Foggy Hill, however, is a tractor outlet, judging by the score or more shining new in the yard. By the road there is a paddock with a signpost announcing "Quaker Burial Ground". It is completely empty (on the surface). This takes the Quaker's unfussy approach to burial close to its logical conclusion, which it would reach if the signpost were removed.

A farm name of Streetside and one further north of Street Farm and the name of Bluecaster will provoke speculation that this is the line of a Roman road. As far as I know, there is no evidence on the ground for this, but on the other hand it is certain that the Romans had major and minor roads, as we do, and it would be surprising if they did not take a short cut through Rawtheydale to get between their forts at Brough and Burrow.

On the fell opposite there's a rougher track that goes up to Sprintgill and Murthwaite, home of the Murthwaite fell ponies, except that, being semi-wild in the Howgills, they hardly have a home.

Sand Tarn from Wild Boar Fell, with Harter Fell (with its Five Gills) beyond, and beyond that Green Bell, with Randygill Top, Kensgriff and Yarlside to the left, and with the Lake District hills in the distance

The Top 10 lakes in Loyne

(Are there 10 lakes in Loyne?)
1. Sand Tarn, Wild Boar Fell
2. Greensett Tarn, Whernside
3. Sunbiggin Tarn
4. Whernside Tarns (could count as four?)
5. West Baugh Fell Tarn (a good view, at least)
6. Kitmere (but can hardly see it)
7. East Tarns, Baugh Fell (another five or more?)
8. Terrybank Tarn
9. Island Pond, Quernmore
10. The Lake, Clapham Beck (but it's artificial)
(Only just.)

As Sally Beck makes its way to the Rawthey we might pause to reflect on the significance of what we have seen on Baugh Fell, Swarth Fell and Wild Boar Fell. The craggy tops differ from the rounded hills of the Howgills. They are of millstone grit, below which is a layer of shale and sandstone above a limestone base. The limestone gives rise to caves and potholes, which are absent from the Howgills. Clearly, the geology of Baugh Fell, Swarth Fell and Wild Boar Fell is different to that of the Howgills. As we concluded when we similarly reflected at Orton, we must be on the line of a geological fault. In fact, this is the line of one of Britain's most well known faults, the **Dent Fault**.

The Rawthey from Sally Beck ...

As the Rawthey swings south it passes Murthwaite Park, the only sizable area of ancient woodland in the Howgills. The scrubby birch, hazel, ash and alder are still home to red squirrels although perhaps for not much longer as on two recent occasions I think I glimpsed grey squirrels as well.

Many becks from the eastern Howgills and West Baugh Fell join the Rawthey as it continues south through luxuriant green pastures. Wandale Beck runs from Adamthwaite, an isolated farmhouse that has the honour of being the habitation nearest to the Lune's source, just 2km southeast of Green Bell. The next significant tributary, Backside Beck, runs, appropriately, from the back side of Green Bell. All the Howgills, therefore, except for a small part northeast of Green Bell, is within the Lune catchment area. Wandale Beck and Backside Beck are notable for exposures of fossil-rich Ordovician and Silurian rocks along their beds, of great interest to geologists. The farmstead of Mountain View, above Backside Beck, is abandoned, but what can you expect of a place called Mountain View? It has to be something like Cobblethwaite to survive up here.

Within the Rawthey valley there are a few farmsteads, a garage and the Cross Keys Inn. The inn was originally a farmstead called High Haygarth (Low Haygarth continues nearby as a horse-breeding farm). It is older than the date (1730) newly installed over its door. An earlier owner's wife, Dorothy Benson, a Quaker who had been imprisoned in 1653, was later buried under what is now the dining room. High Haygarth became an inn in the 1800s, probably after the road was re-aligned in 1820 to run past it rather than over

The **Dent Fault** is the most important geological feature of the Loyne region. It runs north south for some 30km roughly between the two Kirkbys (Stephen and Lonsdale), splitting the northern half of Loyne in two. To the west are the rounded Howgills of Silurian rock (about 420 million years old); to the east are the horizontal limestone scars of the Dales (some 100 million years younger).

The line of the Dent Fault is, of course, not a hypothetical line like the equator that one might imagine standing astride. It is a line of weakness in the earth's surface that, over a long period about 300 million years ago and with tumultuous forces, caused the rocks to the west of it to rise about 2km compared to the rocks to the east. It is considered the best example in England of a reverse fault (as opposed to a normal fault, where rocks move down). In the eons afterwards the western rocks have been eroded to roughly the same level as the eastern rocks. But along the fault-line there were and remain complex distortions of the rocks. This explains also the line of quarries along the fault, as various exposed minerals were mined.

We will cross the line of the fault again later as we follow the Clough River, the River Dee and Barbon Beck.

Right: Yoadcomb Scar on Wild Boar Fell.

Walk 8: Fell End Clouds, Wild Boar Fell and Uldale Gill

Map: OL19 (please read the general note about the walks in the Introduction).

Starting point: A large lay-by on the A683 near Rawthey Bridge (712978).

Cross the bridge, walk 400m along the A683, take the footpath left up to Murthwaite and continue to Sprintgill (with views of Wild Boar Fell to the right). At Low Sprintgill, drop down to cross the A683 and take the track past the ruins of Dovengill to reach the by-road. Walk north and 200m past Cold Keld take the track passing between two prominent limekilns. Continue up the track past the enclosed fields to Dale Slack to reach the fell above the limestone.

Now it is a long, pathless walk to the top of Wild Boar Fell, gently sloped apart from the sharp climb above Sand Tarn. Aim to the left of the two cairns on the horizon.

From the trig point there are views across the rolling Howgills to the Lake District peaks. Stroll over to the cairns on the precipitous eastern edge and admire the breath-taking view into the Eden valley of Mallerstang. To the right, you can see Pen-y-Ghent, Pendle, Ingleborough and Whernside.

From Wild Boar Fell head south to the saddle below Swarth Fell, with a small tarn. Turn west to follow Uldale Gill down, keeping high on the northern bank, to avoid too much up and down. Cautley Crag is straight ahead. Just before Grain Gill joins, a beck can be seen issuing from a cave halfway up the south bank of Uldale Gill.

After crossing Grain Gill, keep to the right of the wall that takes you southwest. Follow the wall to the right of a small plantation to reach the road. Turn left and follow the track across Needlehouse Gill. As the path swings down among trees, look out to the right for a footbridge across Needlehouse Gill (there seems not to be a footpath sign). Cross the footbridge and follow the footpath that goes through Needle House, New House, Tarn and Wraygreen. Follow the road back to Rawthey Bridge.

Sally Beck (centre) joining the Rawthey (running from right to left)

Wandale Hill from the slopes of Yarlside

Bluecaster. It was converted to a temperance inn in 1902 and left to the National Trust in 1949.

Below the Cross Keys Inn, Cautley Holme Beck joins the Rawthey from within the great bowl of Cautley Crag and Yarlside. The becks that run east from The Calf create Cautley Spout, a cascade of 200m in all, with a longest single fall of 30m. Some guides assign various superlatives to Cautley Spout – for example, that it is England's highest waterfall. It would take an odd definition for any such objective claim to be sound. It is safer to be more subjective, by saying that Cautley Spout provides the best long-distance view of any English waterfall – from Bluecaster, for example. However, from afar, you see only the last of a series of cascades. The full set can be seen only from the slopes of the unnamed hill south of Yarlside. Dominated by grass, the Howgills are generally of little botanical interest but the Cautley Spout ravine, well-watered, sun-facing and protected from grazing, has a number of unusual plant species, such as alpine lady's mantle, otherwise restricted in England to the Lake District.

Cautley Spout is at the northern end of the 1km cliff face of Cautley Crag, formed by the erosion of an Ice Age cirque. The crag face is too unstable to be walked upon or climbed but it is the most impressive cliff in the Howgills. At close quarters, the cliff face is less fearsome than it seems: it is not as vertical as it looks from a distance and the ominous dark is due to heather, not rock, which is a pale grey, as the scree slopes show.

The tributary of Ecker Secker Beck, like all the becks that drain west off West Baugh Fell and cross the Dent Fault, has eroded deep ravines and formed a series of small waterfalls as it crosses tilted, fissured rocks. The unusual exposed rock formations in Taythes Gill are well worth a visit, even for the amateur geologist. For the professional, they are essential; for it is here that the

Cautley Spout (centre, to the right of Cautley Crag) from Foxhole Rigg

The Top 10 waterfalls in Loyne

1. Cautley Spout, Howgills
2. Black Force, Howgills
3. Rawthey (Uldale) Force
4. Thornton Force, Ingleton
5. Gaping Gill, below Ingleborough
6. Force Gill, Whernside
7. Ibbeth Peril, Dentdale
8. Docker Force, Birk Beck
9. Taythes Gill, Baugh Fell
10. Clough Force, Grisedale

fine detail of upper Ordovician rock (420-440 million years old) may be unravelled. The trilobite fossils first found here are used as the standard by which the same layers are identified elsewhere.

Some expertise is also required to appreciate Ecker Secker Beck's other notable feature, the meadows near Foxhole Rigg that have been made a Site of Special Scientific Interest because they are a rare example of unimproved, traditionally managed grassland. The list of herbs and grasses that grow here reads like the index to a botanical encyclopedia. If you can tell a hairy lady's mantle from an opposite-leaved golden saxifrage, then this too is worth a visit. Lacking geological or botanical

Cautley Crag - and beyond Cautley Spout, Bowderdale

expertise, we may simply enjoy the views across to the eastern Howgills, with Cautley Crag centre stage, and count the great spotted woodpeckers, which, on a bright November day, seemed plentiful.

Further south, where Hebblethwaite Hall Gill crosses the Dent Fault, the line of the fault is indicated by a series of shakeholes. As these form in limestone, the fault must run just to the west of the line of holes. To the east of the fault, on a plateau between the rough sheep grazing land and the green cow pastures, some of the exposed rock strata are almost vertical, indicating the geological stresses of long ago.

Hebblethwaite is an ancient name for the district. A Richardus and Agnes de Hebletwayt are listed in the Poll Tax of 1379 and a will of 1587 refers to "the Mannor or Graunge of Hebblethwaite". Hebblethwaite Mill was built in the 1790s and was one of the first to use the new wool carding machines, powered by a water wheel. The Woodland Trust now manages Hebblethwaite Hall Wood, which is a narrow 1km long strip of ancient oak and ash woodland alongside the beck that tumbles in a deep, dark ravine over many small waterfalls. A permitted path by the beck provides a short walk, best appreciated on a winter's day, when the leaves have fallen.

Walk 9: The Calf via Great Dummacks

Map: OL19 (please read the general note about the walks in the Introduction).
Starting point: A lay-by opposite St Marks Church (691946).

We have nearly completed our circuit of the Howgills and I have not yet provided a walk to its highest point, The Calf (676m). Since The Calf is at the centre of the radiating ridges, many walks are possible. The two 'tourist routes' (not that there are many tourists) are from Sedbergh over Winder and from Cross Keys past Cautley Spout. Our expedition is intended to provide a greater variety of walking than is usual on the Howgills.

Before setting off, note the ridge on the western horizon: that is your immediate objective. Walk 200m north along the A683, cross the footbridge at Crook Holme, and take the higher of the two paths north to reach the CRoW land. Walk north for a short distance, past gorse bushes, and then cut diagonally back to reach Fawcett Bank Rigg.

Now it is relentlessly uphill along a grassy ridge but not too steep for comfortable walking. There is no hurry: stop often to admire Rawtheydale below and Wild Boar Fell beyond. Continue to the edge of Cautley Crag, and not one step further: the best view in the Howgills is suddenly revealed. Skirt the edge a little distance and then make your way across to the Calf trig point, visible 1km to the west. This involves a little scrambling up, down and over grass tussocks.

From The Calf follow the main ridge south for 3km to Arant Haw, below which you swing south off the path to Crook (1km distant), where there is a large cairn. Descend the slope south: it is steep but not too difficult. Look at the fields below and compare carefully with your map to identify where the public footpath begins: there's a stile in the corner of the field (666931).

Then take the path northeast through Ghyll Farm, Stone Hall, Hollin Hill, Ellerthwaite, Thursgill and Fawcett Bank (noting the fine bridge over Hobdale Beck). A further km beyond Fawcett Bank you reach the path back to Crook Holme, the footbridge, and the starting point.

If you follow the path down from the hall you may need to rub your sheep-sated eyes as you approach the farmstead of Ghyllas. What you see are not sheep at all but alpaca. Ghyllas is leading a Why Not Alpacas? campaign – and, if the farmers are happy, why not indeed? Alpacas certainly have more spirit and charm than sheep. They make a soft humming noise and if in the mood they orgle (an orgle is a kind of orgasmic gargle). More to the commercial point, alpaca fibre is valued for the lightness and warmth it brings to winter clothing.

Shortly after the Hebblethwaite Hall Gill merger, the Rawthey passes under Straight Bridge and after a further 200m, the major tributary of Clough River joins the Rawthey.

Alpaca at Ghyllas, with Knott and Fawcett Bank Rigg beyond.

Pen-y-Ghent (far left), Ingleborough and Whernside (to the right) from East Baugh Fell

Clough River

Clough River begins to adopt its name at Garsdale Head, 15km east of Sedbergh, after gathering the becks that flow off East Baugh Fell and south Swarth Fell through the secluded valley of Grisedale. We can regard the westernmost of these becks, Grisedale Gill, to be its source. Grisedale Gill and Haskhaw Gill set off north from Tarn Hill on East Baugh Fell a few metres apart before going their opposite ways, Haskhaw Gill joining the Rawthey. Their waters then complete semi-circuits of Baugh Fell, before re-uniting near Sedbergh.

The only feature on East Baugh Fell is Grisedale Pike, where a dozen or so cairns form a prominent landmark at an excellent viewpoint into Grisedale and upper Wensleydale. A cairn usually stands alone, as a guide to shepherd or walker, and so when they occur in a cluster and presumably had some function beyond that of mere guide, it is natural to wonder what that function might have been. The cairns are very old but they seem not to have had any function such as has been proposed for standing stones such as Stonehenge. Their position, at this precise location, surely reflects aesthetic values of long ago, which are not so different from our own.

As Grisedale Gill swings east it enters *The Dale that Died*, as Grisedale was called in a book and television

documentary of that name in the 1970s. In the previous few decades all but one of the farmsteads in the dale were deserted and left to fall into ruin, the families there no longer able to cope with the economic hardship of farming life. Abandoned and derelict, Grisedale no doubt enabled a romantic tale to be told of human struggle against adversity.

But the funeral rites were premature. Not only does the one remaining farm appear to be flourishing, but also many of the ruins have been, or are being, revitalised. For example, Fea Fow is in fine fettle: it is a grade II listed traditional farmhouse, built in the 17th century and renovated to retain many original features, now with a new role as a holiday cottage.

One may lament the passing of a time when a family could live off a small patch of land in such an isolated location. On the other hand, Grisedale is much too fine a valley to be forgotten. Its fields, all above 350m, provide a sheltered haven – or even heaven, for those who like the quiet becks and limestone crags within the high moors. As long as the new developments are in keeping with the traditions of Grisedale – as they appear to be – they must surely be welcomed as Grisedale evolves into a new role.

After gathering a few more becks from East Baugh Fell, Grisedale Beck becomes Clough River and passes over Clough Force, a neat, curved waterfall only 3m or

Dandrymire Viaduct from Grisedale Pike

so high. Just below the A684 the Clough is joined by Black Gutter, which leaves Garsdale Low Moor heading purposefully towards Wensleydale only to swing west at Dandry Mire. According to experts, all the becks that flow east off Baugh Fell used to join the River Ure but were blocked by glacial debris and so were diverted west. At the watershed of Dandry Mire there's an impressive 12-arched viaduct, which provides our first encounter with the famous **Settle-Carlisle railway line**. It is a mire indeed for the original plan to build an embankment had to be abandoned when the earth tipped here just sank into the bog.

The Clough heads west through the valley of Garsdale, perhaps the least highly regarded of all the Yorkshire Dales, at least, by tourists. It is a narrow valley so enclosed by the steep, grassy, featureless

The **Settle-Carlisle railway line** is the most spectacular in England. It runs for nearly 120km, with 325 bridges, 21 viaducts and 14 tunnels, on a route through some of the finest scenery of northern England. It was completed in 1876, after 6½ years building, at a cost of £3.5m and many lives. It is regarded as the last great Victorian railway engineering project.

The 15km of the line that is within Loyne includes four dramatic viaducts and two long tunnels and is all at a height of 300m or more, providing fine views of the dales and hills (except when in the tunnels, of course).

In the 1980s there were plans to close the line: freight traffic was diverted, passenger services were withdrawn, and the infrastructure was allowed to decay. However, after a long, high-profile campaign the line was reprieved, which pleased tourists and also freight operators, who came to value it as an alternative to the crowded west coast main line. In 2005 it found an additional role: to carry six trains a day bringing coal from Scottish mines to Yorkshire power stations.

slopes of Baugh Fell and Rise Hill that in winter the sun can barely reach. The busy A684 runs by the Clough, crossing it eight times in all.

There are a few footpaths in the dale but they cannot be linked to make a good long walk. Many of them appear unwelcoming and under-used, giving the walker the feeling of trespassing. Although the slopes of Baugh Fell and Rise Hill are CRoW land they are tantalisingly out of reach above the pastures: a walker must enter at the eastern or western end and it must be rare indeed for anyone to find the incentive to walk the slopes from one end to the other. On a recent occasion when I walked in Garsdale the A684 was closed because the Clough had washed some of it away, which was much appreciated. The footpaths, by-roads and quiet A684 could be combined to provide a rare, blissful experience: an indication of what Garsdale once was and could be.

There is little to cause a tourist to linger, although rural architecture is always interesting. Some houses are converted long barns but many follow the standard design of three windows up, two down, with a door and porch between. Dandra Garth, by the bridleway to Dentdale and now rather enclosed, has character. Swarthgill House is startlingly white.

The village of Garsdale consists of little more than a row of cottages. There's a Primitive Methodist Chapel (1876) at Garsdale Head, and in the village another Primitive Methodist Chapel (1841) and the Church of St John the Baptist, and a little further on a Wesleyan Methodist Chapel (1830), and at Bridge End another Wesleyan Chapel (1868), now a barn, and at Frostrow yet another Wesleyan Chapel (1886). Methodism, like Quakerism, had and has a particular appeal to non-conformist northerners. It is a more visible presence in Loyne because, clearly, Methodists, unlike Quakers, believed in their chapels and the 19th century was a safe time to build them. Even in the remotest regions we come across sometimes tiny chapels, to which itinerant preachers came to give enthusiastic sermons.

A considerate warning on the footpath into Grisedale

At Danny Bridge, as the Clough emerges from the confines of Baugh Fell and Rise Hill, it runs beside the Sedgwick Trail across the Dent Fault. A detailed leaflet should be obtained from Sedbergh Tourist Information Centre in order fully to appreciate the significance of the viewpoints but even without it the transition across the Dent Fault, from the contorted Carboniferous limestone to the older Silurian rocks, should be clear: roughly where the wood opposite ends there is an abrupt change from a rocky gorge within sloping limestone to a shallow, broad valley with rocks 100m years older.

The Clough runs between the gentler slopes of Dowbiggin and Frostrow and, just before it enters the Rawthey, passes Farfield Mill, an arts and heritage centre in which a range of artists (such as weavers, furniture makers and textile workers) work in open studios. Built in 1836, it had functioned as a woollen mill until it closed in 1992, after which it was bought and restored by the Sedbergh and District Buildings Preservation Trust.

A once-fine but now derelict homestead in Garsdale

Walk 10: Grisedale and East Baugh Fell

Map: OL19 (please read the general note about the walks in the Introduction).
Starting point: Near Garsdale Station (787917).

Cross the A684 and take the clearly signposted path to Blake Mire. Continue to Moor Rigg and then follow the road to East House and the track past Fea Fow to Flust. At Flust take the higher of the two paths, continuing on the contour west. The path gradually becomes less distinct, as it passes lines of shakeholes.

Note the deep gully of Rawthey Gill ahead: your aim is to reach between the two gullies east of it, Haskhaw Gill and Grisedale Gill. At that point, it becomes clear that the former flows west and the latter east. There is a cave marked on the OS map at the strategic point but don't worry unduly about locating it – it refers to one of the many shakeholes.

So far, it has been a pleasant stroll through the hidden valley of Grisedale but now you must summon the energy to walk up the watershed between the two gills. Eventually, a cairn will come into view on your right. Keep to the left of the cairn, proceed to the wall and follow it to the top of Tarn Rigg Hill. The panorama is wide but note especially the view of Whernside, 10km south.

Return east by the wall for 1km and continue in its line, leaving it as it bends to the right. This takes you directly to the cairns of Grisedale Pike, with a view of Dandrymire Viaduct and upper Wensleydale.

Aim towards the viaduct and, keeping to the CRoW land, reach Double Hole Bridge. Keep on the right bank of Stony Gill to pass Clough Force and then, after reaching the road at Clough Cottage, walk back towards Garsdale Station.

CHAPTER 5:
Lower Rawtheydale and Dentdale

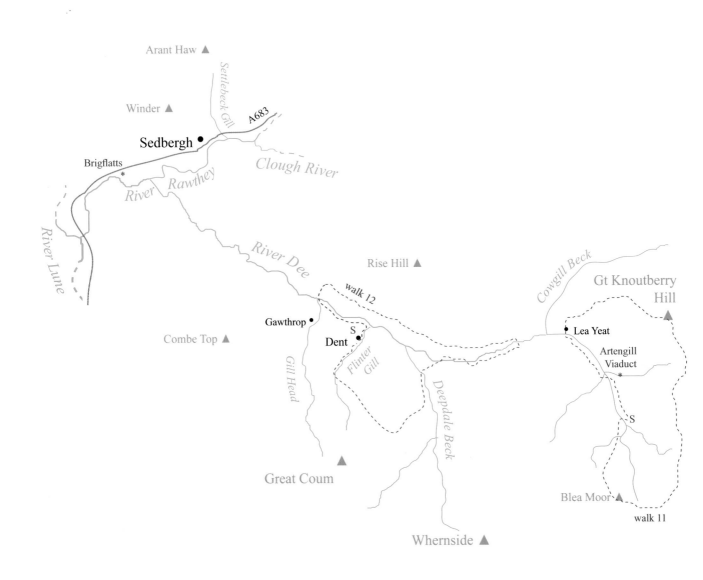

Scale: 1 cm to 1 km

0   5 kilometres

The Rawthey from the Clough ...

The Clough, having travelled much the same distance as the Rawthey up to this point, almost doubles the size of the Rawthey, which now changes character and relaxes into a double bed, as it were, some 50m wide. On the outskirts of Sedbergh the Rawthey is joined by Settlebeck Gill, which runs past the earthwork remains of the Castlehaw motte and bailey. The motte, at 9m high, must have been a good observation post. The remains are on private land but seem in good shape, as can be best seen from the slopes of Winder.

Sedbergh oozes contentment, and why not? Basking below Winder, it gains strength from its one thousand years of history, serenity from the playing fields of the five-hundred-year-old school, and self-confidence from its newfound status as a 'book town'.

Sedbergh was mentioned in the Domesday Book of 1086 and Castlehaw confirms its strategic importance, lying near the meeting of four rivers, the Lune, Rawthey, Clough and Dee. A market charter was granted in 1251. St Andrews Church has a Norman doorway and lists vicars back to 1350 but was largely rebuilt in 1886 (although the clock has a date of 1866, for some reason). Within the church are several plaques to local notables, including John Dawson, an eminent mathematician, born in Garsdale and "beloved for his amiable simplicity of character." My favourite is that of the Rev. Posthumus Wharton, who was headmaster of Sedbergh School from 1674 to 1706.

Sedbergh School was established as a chantry school in 1525 by Roger Lupton, provost of Eton and born in the parish of Sedbergh. After the Dissolution of the Monasteries (1539), it was re-established as a grammar school in 1551. The school has not always flourished: in 1865, when it had only ten pupils, an inspection considered that "it simply cumbers the ground". Amongst recent alumni are the rugby stars, Will Carling and Will Greenwood. Although Sedbergh School is not in the top division of independent schools, it is central to Sedbergh's image.

This image perhaps helped Sedbergh to persuade itself to become England's first book town in 2005 (the pioneering book town, Hay-on-Wye, being just in Wales). Book town status is not formally defined: what makes a place a book town is simply a decision to proclaim itself one. By convention, a book town is a small town in which little else happens apart from the selling of old books. This description may deter non-bibliophiles but presumably Sedbergh hopes that overall a boost will be given to the local economy and culture.

Sedbergh's self-image is also reflected in its participation in 2004 in the BBC TV programme *The Town that Wants a Twin* in which, over twelve long episodes, Sedbergh auditioned four towns for the honour of becoming Sedbergh's twin. The citizens of Sedbergh duly voted for Zrêce of Slovenia. This one-way process does not seem to reflect the spirit of twinning as an equal partnership.

There are pleasant, well-used paths on both banks of the Rawthey. At Millthrop Bridge we rejoin the Dales Way, which follows the Rawthey for 4km before veering north to join the Lune. As you might expect of a village whose sign proudly calls it a "hamlet", Millthrop itself is a set of cottages too pretty for words – at least, any words of mine.

After a further kilometre, the Rawthey goes over a weir that was used to power Birks Mill for cotton spinning and then, after a bend, is joined by the River Dee from the south.

Previous page: Deepdale and Dentdale.
Right: Stone Hall, near Sedbergh.

Sedbergh, with Winder, Arant Haw and Crook behind

The River Dee

The River Dee rises on Blea Moor and runs 20km through Dentdale, many people's favourite of the Yorkshire Dales, even though it is now in Cumbria. Only the very highest of the headwaters of the Dee on Blea Moor are in North Yorkshire.

There is only one feature of note on Blea Moor and that we cannot see: the tunnel that runs for 2.5km under it. This is for the Settle-Carlisle line, which continues on the flanks of Wold Fell and Great Knoutberry Hill over the impressive viaducts at Dent Head and Arten Gill, built from 1870 to 1875. They have ten and eleven arches, respectively, and are both over 30m high. Their construction, in this high and remote terrain, was difficult and hazardous. On one occasion, a flood caused by 6cm of rain in 45 minutes drowned two people, buried a horse and wagon in debris, and washed away several bridges. Earlier, according to David Boulton's leaflet *Discovering Upper Dentdale*, in 1752 an avalanche killed seven people, which, I believe, makes that the second worst avalanche in the United Kingdom. So,

although it is likely to be pastoral tranquillity when we visit, the weather can be wild here.

The two viaducts are built of 'Dent marble', which is actually a dark limestone. The marble was mined locally until the 1920s and prepared at Stone House, near Arten Gill. It was valued for ornamental masonry, such as luxury fireplaces – indeed, being so valued, it seems strange that such huge volumes were used in the viaducts. No doubt, the convenience of being to hand was the main factor. The previously rough track by Arten Gill has recently been renovated to form part of the 350-mile Pennine Bridleway National Trail.

Dent Station is 2km north of Artengill Viaduct and is a tribute to the engineer's faith in the energy of the residents in Dentdale. It is 7km from Dent itself and the final kilometre up from Lea Yeat is very steep. The station platform has a notice saying that, at 350m, it is "the highest mainline station in England". It is pleasing that someone at least regards the Settle-Carlisle line as a main line. The station is surprisingly neat, considering the weather conditions, painted dark red, and gives fine views into Dentdale. The old station building can be rented for holiday accommodation, so you could enjoy the view through its windows, obscured a little by "eciffo tekcit" and "moor gnitaiw seidal".

The road passing Dent Station is called the Coal Road and the stretch on Galloway Gate is pockmarked with disused coal pits. Coal mining stopped as soon as the railway existed to deliver coal more cheaply. The name of Galloway Gate tells us that it used to be a drove road. It is hard today to imagine this clamour of activities high up, at over 500m, on the now lonely and quiet moor.

Cowgill Beck runs from the area of the coal pits, through Dodderham Moss, one of the conifer plantations that disfigure Dentdale, past the entrance to Risehill Tunnel on the Settle-Carlisle line, to join the Dee at Cowgill. The foundation stone of Cowgill Chapel was laid in 1837 by Dentdale's most famous son, **Adam Sedgwick**, who, although living in Cambridge, continued to keep a fatherly eye on his chapel. Thirty years later,

Sedgwick led a campaign to parliament to have the name of Cowgill Chapel restored when the curate changed it to Kirkthwaite Chapel. He preferred the unpretentious 'Cowgill' and was angry at the misspelling of Kirthwaite, the old name for the region. The curate, however, was not to blame: the 1852 OS map has "Kirkthwaite".

In the valley the River Dee gathers the waters than run steeply off the fells through deep gorges and cascades, and proceeds serenely down its upper reaches from Dent Head to Cowgill. The riverbed is mostly flat rock, which the river seems to shimmer over, with occasional ledges producing little waterfalls and, at Scow, a reasonably large one.

As the Dee turns west, it enters a more turbulent phase. If you investigate the river closely – for example, around the Ibbeth Peril waterfall and along the stretch between Lenny's Leap, where the river narrows to run in a gully 50cm wide, and Tommy Bridge – you may

Artengill Viaduct

The Top 10 people of Loyne

Before you complain, yes, they are all men. Nominations of women are very welcome.

1.   Adam Sedgwick (1785-1873), Dent, geologist.
2.   John Fleming (1849-1945), Lancaster, electrical engineer.
3.   Richard Owen (1804-1892), Lancaster, palaeontologist.
4.   John L. Austin (1911-1960), Lancaster, philosopher.
5.   William Whewell (1794-1866), Lancaster, philosopher and scientist*.
6.   Reginald Farrer (1880-1920), Clapham, botanist.
7.   James Williamson (1842-1930), the son, Lancaster, businessman.
8.   John Lingard (1771-1851), Hornby, Catholic historian.
9.   William Sturgeon (1783-1850), Whittington, physicist.
10. Laurence Binyon (1869-1943), Burton-in-Lonsdale, poet.

*Whewell is said to have invented the word 'scientist'.

Adam Sedgwick (1785-1873) was born in Dent and spent much of his youth scrambling over the fells collecting rocks and fossils. From Sedbergh School he went to Trinity College, Cambridge, where he became a fellow. He was ordained in 1817, thus following the family tradition, as evidenced by the many memorials in the Dent church. In 1818, despite having no recognised experience of fieldwork, he became Professor of Geology.

He duly set out to become a proper geologist. His studies of the complex geology of the Lake District led to a pioneering publication in 1835. He discovered the Dent Fault, and the Sedgwick Trail in Garsdale is named after him. He became president of the Geological Society of London and organised many scientific activities.

Inevitably, he became embroiled in scientific debates of the time, such as the Great Devonian Controversy, concerning the mapping and interpretation of various geological strata. Of more resonance today is his disagreement with his ex-student Darwin over his theory of evolution. To the author of *Origin of Species*, Sedgwick wrote "I have read your book with more pain than pleasure. Parts of it I admired greatly; parts I laughed at until my sides were sore; other parts I read with absolute sorrow; because I think them utterly false and grievously mischievous". What grieved him was the removal of the guiding hand of God from the process of natural selection, which he could not accept. This view endears him today to creationists, although unlike many of them he did, as a geologist, accept that the Earth was extremely old.

Sedgwick retained the warm-spirited generosity attributable to his Dentdale upbringing. Although he lived in Cambridge all his working life, he maintained his links to Dent and in 1868 wrote *A Memorial by the Trustees of Cowgill Chapel* that gives one of the best pictures of Dentdale life at the time.

Ibbeth Peril

notice that the volume of water does not always increase as it flows west. Some of the clefts and holes that can be seen in the limestone walls and bed of the gorge are large enough to form caves, through which the river tends to disappear. As you walk on the north bank towards Tommy Bridge, water can be seen entering the Dee from below the south bank, with no beck apparent in the fields above.

The area forms the Upper Dentdale Cave System, a Site of Special Scientific Interest. It is one of the best examples of a cave system that had developed beneath the valley floor and that has been broken into by the modern river eroding its bed. The system extends for 1.7km in a narrow band under the present river and includes a 30m by 60m chamber. Under normal conditions, most of the

Walk 11: Upper Dentdale and Great Knoutberry Hill

Map: OL2 (please read the general note about the walks in the Introduction).
Starting point: By Dent Head Viaduct (777845).

Some of this walk is on roads, but they are quiet ones and the easy walking there compensates for the difficult going elsewhere. From Dent Head Viaduct walk on the road 200m northwest to Bridge End Cottage and then take the footpath opposite that leads back to Dent Head Farm and past the entrance to Bleamoor Tunnel. Once out of the plantation and past the air shaft cut across to the trig point on Blea Moor (535m) for a good view of Whernside and of the Settle-Carlisle railway line far below behind you.

Make your way east as best you can (there is no path) to join the Dales Way north to reach the road. Turn right and take the path north that continues past Wold Fell (resist the temptation to conquer Wold Fell: there is no identifiable top and walking is unpleasantly uneven, being on grassed-over limestone clints) to reach the bridleway at the top of Arten Gill at the point opposite the track that leads to the Galloway Gate.

Turn right for 200m to take the waymarked path that follows the wall to the top of Great Knoutberry Hill (672m), from where the peaks of Pen-y-Ghent, Ingleborough and Whernside are wonderfully arrayed and the outline of Wild Boar Fell is impressive. Widdale Tarns can be seen to the north. Continue west by the fence past a family of cairns to the recently-improved bridleway.

Follow this track for 600m north and then take the Coal Road west, having a look at the neat Dent Station on the way. At Lea Yeat Bridge note the Cowgill Institute, a Quaker meetinghouse from 1702. Many farmsteads here served as meetinghouses in the years after George Fox visited in 1652, on his way to speak at Fox's Pulpit. Cross the River Dee and turn left to follow the road back to Dent Head Viaduct, past (or not, if you wish) the Sportsman's Inn, a 17th century establishment that regards grouse shooters as sportsmen. If energy permits, a detour to look at Artengill Viaduct is worth it.

---

river is now underground and is modifying pre-existing caves. The cave system is complex and needs experts to investigate and interpret but, on the surface, we see holes and caves, with water flowing into or out of some of them.

Above the level of the floodplain Dentdale is lined with farmsteads every 200m or so on both sides. Most of the farmsteads are still actively farming, giving a predominantly rural feel to the valley. Some have been converted to holiday homes and some are derelict. The most interesting of the latter is Gibbs Hall – a ruin now surrounded by its offspring: Gibbs Hall Cottage, Little Gibbs Hall and Gibbs Hall Barn. From the road two windows with chamfered mullions and arched lintels can be seen.

On the opposite bank is the imposing Whernside Manor, originally and more properly called West House, as it is not a manor house. It was built by the Sill family, who not only became rich by exploiting slaves in Jamaica but also employed slaves in Dentdale, a practice continued long after they were supposed to be emancipated. This is now a matter of shame for locals although I overheard one in the Sun Inn who was either proud that Dentdale had had the last slaves in England or had imbibed too much of the esteemed local ale from the Dent Brewery at Cowgill.

The name of Whernside Manor reminds us that the Dee has been flowing around the broad northern slopes of Whernside, the highest point (736m) of the Yorkshire Dales, and gathering the becks that flow north from it. Despite its height, there are few impressive views of Whernside, the one from Dent across Deepdale being as good as any. It is a ridge rather than a plateau or peak and has few of the high-level cliffs that provide such distinctive profiles to other Dales peaks.

It is usually assumed that Whernside's name derives from the querns, or stone mills for grinding corn, that were extracted from its slopes. However, Harry Speight, in his 19th century guides, says that it comes from the Anglo-Saxon word for 'warn', since anyone on the ridge, which separated the Anglo-Saxons to the east and the Norse to the west, could give warnings. At least this draws attention to the differences east and west of Whernside: the Anglo-Saxons were arable farmers and lived in small villages; the Norse were sheep farmers who preferred isolated farmsteads.

Deepdale Beck is a substantial tributary of the Dee that drains the basin that lies north of the ridge separating Deepdale from Kingsdale. Deepdale itself is a rarely visited dale, quieter even than Dentdale and with, as the name would suggest, a deeply incised valley. Its hay meadows are a Special Area of Conservation under

The Megger Stones

European law. The road over to Kingsdale is not often travelled but those who do tackle it are rewarded with a roadside view of Lockin Garth Force.

The Craven Way, an ancient track linking Dent and Ingleton, leads around Whernside, reaching a height of 540m. The walk from the Craven Way past the surprisingly large Whernside Tarns provides a good ascent of Whernside. Combined with a drop down to the Kingsdale road and then a walk through Deepdale, it gives an excellent all-day expedition from Dent.

The River Dee begins to behave itself, flowing steadily over an even bed, as it passes south of Dent, the centre of Dentdale. The Domesday Book records Dentone, which became Dent Town, and now plain Dent – although it is far from plain: its narrow, cobbled streets and whitewashed walls provide a distinctive, attractive character.

The Church of St Andrews has Norman foundations and was largely rebuilt in the 15th and 17th centuries. The floor around the altar is paved with Dent marble, both the black and grey versions. Next to the church is the old grammar school (now a private home), built in 1604 from funding provided by Dentdale benefactors. The school closed in 1897 but the governors still meet for the enjoyable task of distributing money from the still-existing charities to local pupils.

Like all grammar schools, Dent's existed to educate young men in the delights of Latin and Greek grammar. Young women were trained in more practical skills, amongst which knitting was the most renowned in Dentdale. Girls were sent, not always willingly, to Dent from around the region to learn the art. The activity peaked in the 18th century when socks and gloves were supplied to the army. The narrow streets then appeared narrower still because the houses had over-hanging galleries where people sat to knit and chat.

On the streets today is the Sedgwick Memorial, in honour of Adam Sedgwick. The Dent Fault that runs through Dentdale partly accounts for the differences between east and west Dentdale. To the east, becks cut deep gills in the V-shaped valley and the fields are large and walled; to the west, the slopes are gentle with fields hedged and with deciduous trees.

In 2006 the Flinter Gill Nature Trail and the Dent Village Heritage Centre were opened, the latter helping immensely to clear the attics of local farmsteads. In fact, the leaflet for the nature trail existed before the trail did, showing it to be a fine piece of creative literature, with waulking, deiseal, sniggin, Dancing Flags and a Wishing Tree. Its wishful thinking is symptomatic of a problem with the tourist industry, upon which Dent now depends: it is liable to ruin the very things that appeal to tourists in the first place.

Self-defeatingly, Dentdale sells itself as 'the hidden valley'. It can be entered by the railway and by five narrow roads (from Rawtheydale, Garsdale, Ribblesdale, Kingsdale and Barbondale), all of which feel like back entrances. It should be a green, restful haven but the more we are persuaded to visit it the less hidden it will become. In the summer the cobbled streets are already thronging with people and cars. There seems little need for artificial trails or for the air of desperation that pervades Dent's publicity.

Flinter Gill provides a pleasant stroll along a stony track by small waterfalls but if the crowds are encouraged there it will soon need litter bins, barriers (to stop people slipping on the dangerous 'dancing flags'), and so on. The 1km trail ends at a "magnificent viewpoint" where a toposcope tells us what we can see, leaving the fells above still empty for those with a little more energy.

Above this point, Flinter Gill runs from the northern slopes of Great Coum (687m), an underrated hill that displays its great coum or cirque towards Dentdale. All three north-facing slopes of Dentdale have their cirques, gouged out in the Ice Age (Middleton Fell has Combe Top and Combe Scar; Whernside has Combe and Combe Bottom) but Great Coum is the most impressive. The southern ridge of the cirque, past the old quarry where Dent marble was also mined, is the best ascent. The view is excellent, from Whernside nearby to the Howgills and the Lake District in the distance and to the south the lower Lune valley.

Below Great Coum, on a rise overlooking Dentdale, stand the Megger Stones, a group of ten or so cairns showing varying degrees of competence at cairn-building. The Megger Stones are just above the Occupation Road or Green Lane, as the OS map calls it. It is named from when the fells, used for common grazing, were enclosed or occupied in the 1850s. It may be assumed to be an ancient track, like the Craven Way, but it is not marked on an OS map of 1853. It reaches a height of 520m around the head of Deepdale and, although rutted and muddy, provides a fine high-level walk.

From the Occupation Road we have a good view of Rise Hill, which some call Aye Gill Pike, although there is nothing pikey about it. Its rises gently and uniformly north of Dentdale like an enormous backcloth, to reach 556m. It is nearly all CRoW land but it can only be entered at the eastern and western ends, 8km apart, and few bother to venture into the central part. Although the

Rise Hill

Whernside from the Occupation Road

Dentdale from Combe Scar, with Great Knoutberry Hill in the distance

Walk 12: Middle Dentdale

Map: OL2 (please read the general note about the walks in the Introduction).
Starting point: Dent (704872).

The character of Dentdale is best appreciated in the valley, so this walk is on the lower slopes, with an optional extension to a medium height, to provide good views of the dale.

Walk through Dent, keeping left past the church, to Church Bridge and then turn left to follow the Dales Way west for 2km to Barth Bridge. At Barth Bridge take the footpath north to High Barth and then follow this path that winds its way east through a series of farmsteads (including High Hall, Scotchergill and Peggleswright) to Bankland. You will become well practised at the art of locating and passing the various stiles.

Now walk east for a little over a kilometre on the quiet road past Gibbs Hall to Ibbeth Peril waterfall. Cross the footbridge (behind the lay-by just east of the waterfall) and then take the equally quiet road west for 1km to Rise View, where you drop down to the footbridge over the Dee and then continue on the north bank to Tommy Bridge.

Cross the bridge and continue southwest to Bridge End, at which point you have a choice. If the pubs in Dent beckon, continue along the Dales Way to Church Bridge and Dent.

Otherwise, cross Mill Bridge over Deepdale Beck and immediately take the footpath (signposted "Deepdale Road 1/4m") south to Scow (about 1km). Turn right to Peacock Hill and then take the wide path of Nun House Outrake that leads up to Green Lane, which gives good views of Dentdale and of Rise Hill opposite. Take this track west and after 2km turn down by Flinter Gill, to return to Dent.

ridge now has stiles over the many walls, it is no great pleasure to walk its boggy length.

The Dee flows west to Barth Bridge, below the small village of Gawthrop, and by the Helmside Craft Centre to the north and Combe Scar to the south, and on to Rash Bridge. Here, we pause to point out a general problem concerning the maintenance of bridges. Bats like to roost in crevices under bridges and they are protected by law, it being illegal to damage or destroy bat roosts. Fifteen roosts were found under Rash Bridge in 1994, so delaying repair work. The bats subsequently returned, although they did not after similar repair to Barth Bridge upstream.

By Rash Bridge is an old woollen spinning mill. There was an even older corn mill here, as there are records of one being demolished in 1590 after a dispute over whose land it was on. Before food was readily transported, cereals were grown locally, as oats were part of the staple diet. The ownership of corn mills was, therefore, an important matter. The Normans required all grain to be ground at the lord of the manor's mill and not within individual households, which obviously gave power to the lord and his manor. The custom gradually lapsed and the corn mills that survived into the 18th and 19th century were often converted for textiles and other uses.

After a further 2km, the Dee joins the Rawthey, by the narrow Abbot Holme Bridge.

The Rawthey from the Dee

Beyond a bridge for the old Lowgill-Clapham railway line, the Rawthey passes near Brigflatts, a building invariably described as the oldest Quaker meetinghouse in northern England (a rather odd claim as ordinary farmhouses were used as meetinghouses). Brigflatts was built in 1675, when Quakers were still being persecuted and meeting surreptitiously. Whether Brigflatts was overtly declared to be a Quaker meetinghouse in 1675, I don't know, but as George Fox stayed there in 1677 its function could hardly have been a secret. Today its peaceful sturdiness seems to embody some of the tenets of Quakerism although the earlier Brigflatts probably did so better, as until 1881 there was a soil floor across which water from the nearby pond flowed.

Brigflatts inspired the greatest work of the Newcastle-born, modernist poet Basil Bunting (1900-1985), who described himself as having been "brought up entirely in a Quaker atmosphere" although not a Quaker himself. The poem *Briggflatts*, written in 1966, is described by the *Oxford Companion to English Literature* as "long, semi-autobiographical and deeply Northumbrian" (although Brigflatts was never in Northumbria).

After passing another Hebblethwaites and the Holme Open Farm, the Rawthey is joined by Haverah Beck, which runs past Ingmire Hall in the narrow finger of land between the Rawthey and the Lune. Ingmire Hall was the seat of the Otway family from the 16th century or earlier. Sir John Otway was an eminent lawyer during the Civil War (1642-51) and, as a Roman Catholic, was sympathetic to the problems of the Quakers and provided them with valuable legal advice. The hall passed through the female side to the Upton family of Cornwall. After acquiring two hyphens, a descendant, Mrs Florence Upton-Cottrell-Dormer, became a benefactress to Sedbergh, donating Queen's Gardens and the cemetery.

Beyond Middleton Bridge, the Rawthey, at last, reaches the Lune.

Above: Brigflatts.
Below: The Rawthey, approaching the Lune.

CHAPTER 6:
Middleton Fell

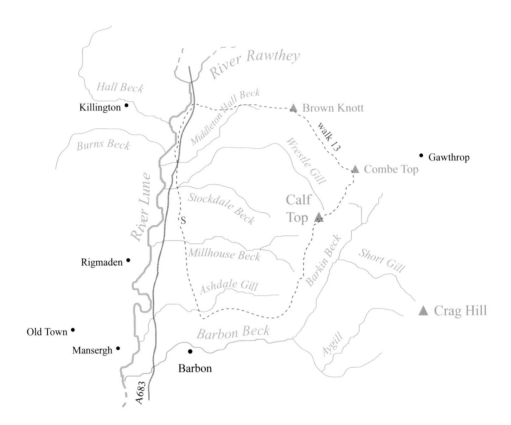

Scale: 1 cm to 1 km

0   5 kilometres

The Lune from the Rawthey ...

The Lune and the Rawthey meet as the arms of a Y to form a deep pool and then proceed south. The rivers are of comparable size, as the catchment areas of the Lune up to this point and the Rawthey are much the same. The headwaters of the Rawthey on Baugh Fell, Wild Boar Fell and Whernside are higher than those of the Lune on Green Bell but the western branch took precedence because, I assume, it was the obvious continuation of the lower Lune for early Britons travelling north towards what we now call the Lune Gorge. At all events, the Lune is now established as a mature river and flows more sedately as the valley opens out. Beyond a wide curve, the Lune is joined by Hall Beck from the west and Middleton Hall Beck from the east.

Hall Beck begins life in the marshes on New Park near Lily Mere and runs beside the Old Scotch Road, the drove road that left us at Low Borrowbridge, and by Three Mile House, a drover's service stop. It then drops down through Springs Wood to Killington, a village whose size today does not reflect its past importance.

Not long ago, Killington had a school and a pub, as well as the still-active All Saints Church. Killington Hall half-survives. The older part is in ruins but the part dated 1640 (and 1803 and 2003) is still occupied. It used to belong to the Pickering family and also passed through the hands of the Morlands (of Capplethwaite) and Uptons (of Ingmire). The front door bears the black horse of the Ingmire coat of arms. Today, the road to Killington from Three Mile House has grass in the middle, which is always a good sign.

Killington Park to the north and Killington Common to the south are no longer on the map but the name remains familiar through the Killington Reservoir and the M6

Previous page: Middleton Fell at Brown Knott.
Above: The Rawthey (from the right) joins the Lune (from the middle distance).

Killington Hall

Orchid on New Park, Killington

service station. The old common, now called Park Hill, provides scenery untypical of Loyne, with hummocky little hills and rocky outcrops. It is noticed only because of its prominent aerial and is rarely visited although much of it is CRoW land providing good views of the Lune valley and the Howgills. You could explore it from the disused Hills Quarry, south of Three Mile House, but wait for a dry spell out of late summer in order to avoid the bogs and bracken that otherwise make it difficult terrain.

Across the road from Hills Quarry is a gate giving access to a footpath around Burns Beck Moss Nature Reserve, owned by Cumbria Wildlife Trust. Up to 6m of peat now fill an old upland tarn, providing a raised mire habitat, with areas of grassland, reed bed and willow shrubs. These support a large variety of plants (including sixteen species of sphagnum moss), insects and birds (such as reed bunting and sedge warbler). Despite man's determined efforts to ruin the site – by cutting the peat, straightening the beck, digging drainage channels, planning to create a reservoir, building dams and weirs to slow the beck, removing them, putting them back – the reserve now appears to be a natural habitat, in safe hands.

Middleton Hall Beck is also named after a hall but unlike Hall Beck has the courtesy to tell us which one, which is as well as there are two halls on its short length. The higher, Beckside Hall, was the birthplace of the Sir John Otway of Ingmire Hall we met earlier. The lower, Middleton Hall, is the more interesting. From the 14th to the 17th century it was the manorial home of the esteemed Middleton family. Their manor was large and dispersed (like the the parish of Middleton today). The Middleton men distinguished themselves mainly through their military activities and in due course also extinguished themselves. The male line died out, leaving a sister with the familiar name of Mrs Hebblethwaite as the last surviving heir in the 1690s.

The extinction of the Middletons was hastened by the Civil War, which wrought havoc along this stretch of the Lune. Like all the halls and castles along the valley, Middleton Hall was a royalist stronghold but was unfortunately not strong enough. After the war, Middleton Hall was never rebuilt. As a result, the remains of Middleton Hall provide a good illustration of medieval, fortified, domestic architecture. The high, 1m thick wall used to enclose an inner and outer courtyard. The damage to the wall is supposed to have been caused by Cromwell's cannon balls. There was also a gatehouse and probably a chapel.

Middleton Hall

Stockdale Beck

Stockdale Beck gathers much of the water from the hinterland of Middleton Fell, via Luge Gill, Wrestle Gill and Thirnbeck Gill, running from Calf Top (609m), the highest point of the fell. Middleton Fell is, like the Howgills, west of the Dent Fault and has similar topography. It has rolling grassy slopes but with more heather, higher up, and bracken, lower down, than the Howgills. The bedrock seems closer to the surface, judging by the exposures on paths and the occasional outcrops.

Above the pastures, Middleton Fell is all CRoW land but, although the slopes in Dentdale and Barbondale have their excitements, in the 15 sq km to the west of the ridge wall the OS map marks nothing apart from two sets of grouse butts and, by the western wall, seven sheepfolds. Nonetheless, Middleton Fell is excellent walking country because of the terrain and the views it affords of the surrounding hills. As you walk the ridge heading southwest and then southeast, the Howgills, Wild Boar Fell, Baugh Fell, Rise Hill, Great Knoutberry Hill, Whernside, Crag Hill and the top of Ingleborough parade before you. To the west there is the Lakeland skyline and from Calf Top the Lune estuary and Morecambe Bay glints ahead.

Cairn on Middleton Fell

The Lune at Low Waterside

Walk 13: Middleton Fell

Map: OL2 (please read the general note about the walks in the Introduction).

Starting point: The corner east of School House (626858): there is space for one car. Otherwise, start from the lay-by on the east side of the A683, just north of where it swings away from the line of the Roman road (631892), starting the circular walk at (*) below.

This is a long walk but on easy paths and quiet roads, with a continuously evolving panorama of hills. Walk north for 2km over High Stockdale Bridge (a Scheduled Ancient Monument) to Middleton Hall Bridge, with the hall to your right. Cross the A683 and take the path across the field and between Low Waterside and the Lune. Continue on this path, which eventually rises through a wood to the A683.

(*) Walk south a short distance and cross a field to join the track east to Fellside (demolished and rebuilt in 2007). Beyond Fellside you are on the open fell and will probably see nobody for the next three hours or so. There are many tracks but follow one east to reach the ridge near Brown Knott, for a view of Sedbergh and the Howgills beyond.

Follow the ridge wall southeast. Above Combe Scar there is a new slab stile in the wall that is worth crossing for a short detour to peek at the scar and gain a bird's-eye view of Dent. Return by the stile.

Continue round the ridge, now heading southwest, to reach Calf Top. From Calf Top continue over Castle Knott and Eskholme Pike to Eskholme. Take the track and road to join the quiet High Road, which you follow north for 3km to the corner near School House.

In case you are tempted to take a short cut west from Calf Top to Mill House, its owners will appreciate me pointing out that the apparent exit from the CRoW land shown on the OS map does not exist because there are a few metres of adamantly private land separating CRoW land from the public footpath. Which is a pity.

The Lune from Stockdale Beck ...

On a hill south of the Church of Holy Ghost (that's what its sign says) stands a column 2m high carved with the letters M P LIII. This is a Roman milestone indicating that this point is 53 Roman miles from, it is presumed, Carlisle. This provokes speculation. Was this apparently unremarkable point special in some way? Did it mark a junction in the Roman highways? Or were there perhaps 52 other milestones, now all lost, between here and Carlisle?

Also carved on the column (in Latin) are the words "Unearthed and restored William Moore 1836", which seems a clear admission to an act of vandalism, for the said William Moore obviously knew the significance of what he had found. For some reason, he re-erected the column 200m west of where he found it, where the Roman road is thought to have run.

After a long meander the Lune is joined beyond Treasonfield by Black Beck, which is the product of many becks that hurry off the western slopes of Castle Knott before crossing the quietest High Road in the country and then flowing gently over green pastures to the Lune. Ashdale Gill is the largest of these becks, running in a deep gully past the Three Little Boys, which are upright slabs about 1m high.

There are remains of an ancient homestead near Borwens, with roughly circular ramparts 30m in diameter. Borwens itself has an interesting old barn, ornately dated 1718. These datestones, usually placed above main entrances, were fashionable when stone buildings began to replace impermanent dwellings in the 17th and 18th centuries. Apart from the date, there is usually a triangle of letters: husband and wife initials below and family name initial above.

Meanwhile, on the anonymous but rich, green slopes above the west bank are two of Loyne's rural estates, Rigmaden and Mansergh. The architect George Webster of Kendal built Rigmaden Park in the 1820s for Christopher Wilson, a banker of that town. Wilson was known as a breeder of turf ponies, which are derived from fell ponies and intended for racing. His grandson, Christopher Wyndham Wilson, continued the tradition so successfully that the breed became known as the Wilson Pony (it is now called the Hackney Pony and considered the world's best harness pony). He was also High Sheriff of Westmorland and a noted wrestler, which sounds a useful combination.

Above Rigmaden Park is Kitmere, a reservoir for Rigmaden Farm. The lake and its boathouse are difficult to see for they are shrouded by hundreds of thick, high rhododendrons. These led to an interesting test case. At first, the Kitmere region was mapped as CRoW land but, after appeal, it was agreed that the rhododendrons meant that the land did not meet the legal definition of 'moor'. (As is their custom, the rhododendrons are spreading over the surrounding land so perhaps it too will need to be excluded soon.)

Directly below Rigmaden Park is the relatively new, metal Rigmaden Bridge. This is a favourite put-in spot for canoeists, who can paddle 10km downstream, round sweeping bends, by shingle islands and beaches, and over relatively gentle rapids to Kirkby Lonsdale. Before attempting this, you should read the long list of conditions helpfully displayed at the bridge by the

The Roman milestone near Hawking Hall

British Canoe Union: the first, for example, says that it must be within the months from November to March.

Christopher Wilson took over the manor of Mansergh, a name that appears in the Domesday Book and that is still the parish name. St Peter's Church was built in 1880, with an oddly shaped tower, to replace an old chapel in an isolated location overlooking the Lune valley and Middleton Fell. It is directly below the village of Old Town, on the Old Scotch Road.

The largest building in Old Town is the gaunt Terry Bank, which bears an enigmatic datestone reading "EC 1542-1910". The Westmorland Church Notes record the death of an "Edward Conder of Terry Bank" seven times between 1542 and 1843. It is unlikely that any of the building dates from the 16th century: the central part shows a date of 1846. The nearby Terrybank Tarn used to provide water to power Kirkby Lonsdale's mills.

Mansergh Hall, which is a farm specialising in organic lamb and sausages, is to the south, and directly below the hall the Lune is supplemented by the substantial tributary of Barbon Beck.

Barbon Beck

Barbon Beck flows for 10km through the magnificent valley of Barbondale, with the steep scree and grass slopes below Calf Top to the west and the less steep, peaty moorland below Crag Hill (682m) to the east. The beginnings of Barbon Beck are interesting to explore although what exactly is seen depends upon the amount of recent rain. Normally, the beck appears to arise hesitantly as Barkin Beck, 3km within the Yorkshire Dales boundary, beside the road to Dentdale. Before reaching the boundary it usually disappears and restarts a few times. Our suspected explanation for this is confirmed by an examination of the Short Gill tributary, which forms the Dales boundary from Crag Hill.

Short Gill runs contentedly in a deep gorge of grey slate, stained brown with peat, over a series of waterfalls until, 100m above Barkin Beck, it crosses a clear ridge of limestone and enters a canyon that is eerily silent. All the water disappears through the limestone. The line of limestone continues on the eastern slopes of Barbondale but there is no limestone to be seen on the western slopes, the grey scree being of the Silurian slate that we saw in the Howgills. The transition from limestone to slate can be clearly seen in the walls by the roadside, from the white-grey limestone to the north to the dark-grey slate to the south.

We are on the continuation of the Dent Fault, as you may have anticipated. Here, the upheavals of 300m years ago turned the limestone beds into a roughly vertical position and today Short Gill provides the best examples in England of caves formed in vertical limestone. About 200m south of Short Gill Bridge, a large resurgence from under a limestone outcrop joins Barkin Beck, which is usually dry at this point. This I assume to be the lost waters of Short Gill, which therefore ought to be regarded as the major source of Barbon Beck, which is at last properly established.

The beck here is a favourite haunt of the wren, which we tend to think of as a bird of the garden and woodland. They delight in flitting in and out of the crevices around the rocks at the beck's edge.

To the east, above the limestone outcrops, not visible from Barbon Beck but prominent from Calf Top, a large area has been set aside for heather, to provide a home for grouse. This appears to have been successful because black grouse are still resident. Black grouse have become extinct in many counties of England, including, it is believed, Lancashire, which is only a few kilometres away. In 1998 there were only 800 breeding males left

Above: Kitmere.
Right: Barbondale from Barbon Low Fell.

The head of Barbondale

in England, although conservation efforts are thought to have led to a slight increase since. The male black grouse or blackcock is much too fine a bird to shoot, with its glossy, purple-black plumage, red eye patches, and colourful mating displays.

Running north to south across the heather and moor of Barbon High Fell is a line of disused coal pits, barely detectable on the ground. This again indicates that Barbondale crosses a geological line. Below the popular picnic site at Blindbeck Bridge, Barbon Beck is joined by Aygill (or Blind Beck), which has a mildly curious property. As it crosses limestone, some of its water falls into the Aygill pothole: the water underground runs south to emerge on Leck Fell; the water above ground runs north to join Barbon Beck.

Barbon Beck then runs through woodland, where there is a pleasant footpath passing below Barbon Manor. The path provides no glimpse of the manor but from afar it can be picked out as a white island within the dark plantation. This is one building that cannot be said to blend unobtrusively into its surroundings. Barbon Manor was built in the French Renaissance style for the Kay-Shuttleworth family in 1863. James Kay was a doctor and social reformer known for his treatment of cholera in Manchester in 1832, after which he wrote an influential book, *The Moral and Physical Condition of the Working Classes Employed in the Cotton Manufacture in Manchester*. In 1842 Kay married Janet Shuttleworth, daughter of Robert Shuttleworth of Gawthorpe Hall, Burnley, who had long owned land in Barbondale. Sir James Kay-Shuttleworth, as he became, retired here in 1872 after his wife died.

Since 1910 the curving drive up to Barbon Manor has been the site for the Barbon Sprint Hillclimb, which is part of the British Hillclimb Championship. The aim is to drive a vehicle up the 800m course as fast as possible. While no doubt a challenge for mechanics, it seems to be a sport of great simplicity and (I imagine) great noise.

Crag Hill from Calf Top, with a glimpse of Whernside to the left and Ingleborough to the right

Below the manor Barbon Beck passes behind the neat village of Barbon. Barbon is ancient, being listed in the Domesday Book as Berebrune, but hides its heritage. St Bartholomew's Church was built in 1893, on the site of a 17th century chapel, all sign of which was thereby removed. It was built in the perpendicular style by the Lancaster-based firm of Paley & Austin, which had a national reputation for its ecclesiastical buildings.

There is a distinctive quality about the buildings of Edward Paley and Hubert Austin, featuring majestic towers, recessed spires and well-lit naves, but, according to *The Victorian Society,* "The later work of the Austin

The wood near Barbon Manor

and Paley era took on a squared-off Gothic look and became stereotyped and conventionalised … There was a loss of zest though still much to admire". Since Paley died in 1895 this may be thought to apply to the Barbon church. But probably the quotation is referring not to the afore-mentioned gentlemen but to the firm of Paley & Austin, which continued, through their sons, until 1942.

More recently, new buildings have hidden traces of the Lowgill-Clapham railway line and station, which only closed in 1966. The 17th century Barbon Inn still survives, however, and the sheep still graze, if rather tweely, in the paddock by the memorial cross.

Below Hodge Bridge, Barbon Beck passes under no less than four functional footbridges that enable golfers to get from one part of Kirkby Lonsdale golf course to the other. These bridges lack the charm and, I am sure, the durability of the narrow packhorse bridge by Beckfoot Farm. It is natural to wonder where the packhorses were heading: did they use the two bridleway fords across the Lune marked on the map? Today the fords seem usable only very rarely.

CHAPTER 7:
Middle Lunesdale and Leck Fell

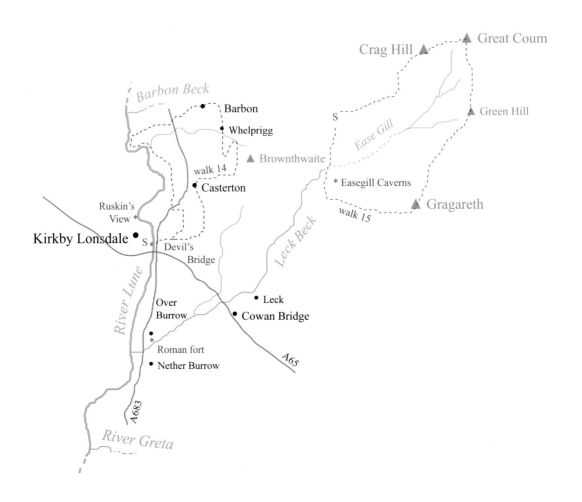

Barbon Beck

• Barbon

• Whelprigg

▲ Brownthwaite

walk 14

• Casterton

Ruskin's
View *

Kirkby Lonsdale •   S *

Devil's
Bridge

River Lune

Over
Burrow

*
Roman fort
• Nether Burrow

A683

River Greta

• Leck
• Cowan Bridge

A65

Leck Beck

Crag Hill ▲   ▲ Great Coum

S

Ease Gill

▲ Green Hill

* Easegill Caverns

walk 15

▲ Gragareth

Scale: 1 cm to 1 km

0   5 kilometres

The Lune from Barbon Beck ...

A kilometre from the Barbon Beck junction the Lune passes a badly eroded west bank, just before Underley Bridge. The inordinate ornateness of this bridge reflects its limited functionality, for it was built in 1872 (or 1875, depending which datestone on the bridge you believe) to enable gentry and their lady folk to travel in their coaches from the Underley estate to the Barbon railway station. The bridge was built for Lord Bective, MP for Westmorland, whose father, if not already rich on his own account, became so by marrying the daughter of William Thompson, a Lord Mayor of London and previous owner of the Underley estate. The bridge is adorned with battlements, gargoyles and a motto – consequitur quodcunque petit, that is, one attains whatever one seeks (Barbon railway station, I assume).

Before the Lune sweeps south under a dramatic cliff the small beck of Grove Gill enters on the left. This has run off Barbon Low Fell past Whelprigg, another of Loyne's fine country houses. The Whelprigg estate belonged to the Gibson family, for whom Whelprigg was built in 1834, in an imposing Victorian style. In the fields by the drive to the house is an ancient cross, on the line of the Roman road, and to the north six trees that seem uniquely honoured by having their types specified on the OS map (four ash and two oak), presumably because they mark the parish boundary.

To the south of Whelprigg runs the old track of Fellfoot Road, where it is difficult to turn a blind eye to the **Goldsworthy Sheepfolds** (as we have done so far): there are sixteen of them, all created in 2003.

The Lune next runs by the elegant mansion of Underley Hall. This was rebuilt in 1826 in the Gothic style and later embellished and enlarged by Lord Bective. Lord Bective and his successor at Underley, Lord Cavendish-Bentinck (MP for South Nottingham), and, of course, the Ladies, lived in the style that befits such names. At one time, the estate employed twenty-six gardeners. In the 1980s Underley Hall became a residential school

Previous page: View from Brownthwaite.
Below: Underley Bridge.

The **Goldsworthy Sheepfolds** were created between 1996 and 2003 by the environmental sculptor Andy Goldsworthy during a project funded by Cumbria County Council. The 46 folds were built from existing folds that were derelict or built anew where they were indicated on old maps. Goldsworthy uses natural materials to create his art forms and "feels the energy from nature and transcends that energy into art form". Each sheepfold was thus reinvigorated by this new energy and re-connected to the farming traditions of Cumbria. Inspiration, however, seems rather thin along Fellfoot Road: all sixteen folds are similar, with a large boulder enclosed in a small fold.

It is more in the spirit of the project if the sculptures are appreciated by encountering them serendipitously and by being momentarily confused by the strangely modern, possibly functional, structures. (On our journey so far we have passed Goldsworthy Sheepfolds at Raisbeck (see page 22), Scout Green, Bretherdale, Cautley Crag, and Barbondale.) However, now that the project is complete and the folds are listed in leaflets and on websites, inevitably people will set out purposefully to tick them off. Whether they warrant such explicit attention I leave art-connoisseurs to judge.

for boys with emotional and behavioural difficulties but the estate is still owned by relatives of the Cavendish-Bentincks, the Pease family.

To the east is the old village of Casterton. It may not be as old as its name suggests since there is no evidence of a Roman castle on the site but it is old enough to have been included in the Domesday Book. It is a small village of class, with scarcely a house lacking style. It has all the essentials of life: a school, a church, a garage-cum-shop, a pub and a golf course.

Casterton School is an independent boarding and day school for 320 girls (with 20 lucky? boys as day pupils). The school began in the 1830s when Low Wood School, which the Rev. William Carus Wilson had established at Tunstall to train girls to be servants, and the Clergy Daughters' School (of which, more shortly) that he'd started at Cowan Bridge were both transferred to Casterton. To help the clergy daughters feel more at home, he had the Holy Trinity Church built. And to help himself feel at home, he moved into the neo-classical Casterton Hall, which had been built in 1812 for his father.

Underley Hall

Ruskin's View is the only point along the Lune that the Ordnance Survey considers worthy of a viewpoint symbol. I'd prefer that OS maps kept to matters of fact rather than opinion. For what it's worth, my opinion is that the view is OK, but neither high enough to provide an extensive view of the Lune valley, with its fine surrounding hills receding into the distance, nor low enough to enable an appreciation of the sights and sounds of the riverside. Instead, we see one bland bend of the Lune, with a backdrop of Brownthwaite and Middleton Fell, among the least impressive of Loyne's hills.

The viewpoint is called Ruskin's View, in thanks to the art critic and thinker John Ruskin, whose opinion was that "Here are moorland, sweet river and English forest at their best ... [the view is] one of the loveliest in England and therefore in the world". According to the *Cumbrian Directory*, Ruskin said this in the 1870s after seeing J.M.W. Turner's 1818 painting of the view. One might query Ruskin's status as an art critic if he really considered this view comparable to the one from his own window at Brantwood, looking over Coniston Water.

Ruskin was a fervent promoter and protector of Turner's reputation. So much so that art historians had always believed his statement in 1858 that he had destroyed a set of erotic paintings by Turner, not wanting his reputation to be sullied. However, the paintings were found in 2005. Ruskin himself was fond of young girls. So that's two reputations sullied.

My point is that we should not just follow the opinions of others – eminent aesthetes such as Turner or Ruskin, or the OS, or, certainly, me. It is better to form your own judgements about this and other views of the Lune.

Below Casterton Hall stands the 17th century Kirfit Hall, with what looks like a peel tower but is apparently a staircase tower. Because of a planning dispute, one of its barns has been garishly painted, in order to enliven **Ruskin's View**, which is a viewpoint at the top of a steep bank of the Lune 1km south.

Near Ruskin's View is Cockpit Hill, a 40m diameter, overgrown mound that is thought to be the site of an old motte and bailey castle, and behind it is Kirkby Lonsdale's Church of St Mary the Virgin, a substantial edifice with many notable features. For most old settlements, the church is the largest and most important structure and it therefore becomes a focus for passing visitors, even for those who rarely venture into churches. Here, there is much of non-specialist interest, both inside and outside the church. There's some fine Jacobean wood carving and on the northern side of the nave there are three large Norman arches, two of which have distinctive diamond patterns. Some doorways and part of the tower are also Norman. The church is therefore at least as old as the 12th century and is probably of Saxon origin, although there has been much rebuilding, notably in the 18th century and again in 1866. Outside the church, the visitor may contemplate the self-closing mechanism of the churchyard gates, the oddly placed clocks on the tower, the intriguing gazebo painted by Turner in 1818, and the pillar in memory of five young women burned to death in 1820.

Passing through the churchyard, we enter Kirkby Lonsdale, the most desirable location in Loyne, or so estate agents tell us. It lies by the A65, midway between the Lakes and the Dales, and does not try too hard to detain tourists travelling between the two. The narrow main street has shops and restaurants of refinement, even trendiness (as epitomised by the renaming of the Green Dragon as the Snooty Fox), and there is a profusion of hanging baskets and other floral decorations. The market square, however, has an unstylish crown-shaped structure, now serving as a bus shelter, which used to have a sort of dome with a cross atop. It was donated in 1905 by the vicar of Kirkby Lonsdale, whose generosity could presumably not be declined.

St Mary's Church, Kirkby Lonsdale

The ambience is suburban, rather than rural, for, apart from Ruskin's View, Kirkby Lonsdale is inward-looking, focused on its own business, with little outlook onto the surrounding fields. The older buildings are of limestone, which outcrops locally. Apart from the church and pubs, there are few buildings earlier than the 18th century and on the outskirts many standard 20th century houses.

Although there are few features of antiquity, Kirkby Lonsdale is old, appearing in the Domesday Book as Cherkeby Lownesdale and being granted its market charter in 1227. The manor of Kirkby Lonsdale, including the church, was given to St Mary's Abbey in York in the 1090s and after the Dissolution of the Monasteries the church rights were granted to Trinity College, Cambridge. Kirkby Lonsdale plays up to its history, without going back quite that far, by holding a Victorian Fair in September, with participants in period dress.

From the market square Jingling Lane drops down towards the Lune. Up to the 19th century there was a series of mills here, powered by water from Terrybank

Tarn. The lane meets up with the footpath that proceeds from below Ruskin's View alongside the Lune, where there was a millrace for further mills. Anyone walking along this path will notice the flood debris in the tree branches above their head, indicating the torrents that sometimes rage through this narrow valley. All the more surprising, then, that the elegant, three-arched Devil's Bridge has withstood the Lune for five centuries, or even longer. The date of the bridge is unknown but, to be on the safe side, it is a Scheduled Ancient Monument. Some think it to be Roman, but this seems unlikely; others can detect the same Norman hands as built the church; others refer to records of repairs in 1275 and 1365 (which show only that there was *a* bridge here but not necessarily this one); others consider the form of the arches to be late 15th century at the earliest.

The name of the bridge is more recent, for until the 19th century it was simply the Kirkby Lonsdale Bridge. The uncertainty about the origin of the bridge's remarkable design encourages thoughts of a supernatural agency. The legend is, in brief, that a woman entered a Faustian deal with the devil to get the bridge built and

Devil's Bridge

then sacrificed her dog to meet the conditions of the deal.

For many people, hurrying between the Lakes and the Dales and pausing at the Devil's Bridge, this is the only glimpse they will have of the Lune. It is a pity that quiet contemplation of the bridge and the scenery is difficult. There are normally crowds milling around the snack bars and over the bridge and, at weekends, motorcyclists, canoeists, picnickers, and maybe even divers off the bridge. If we could but focus upon it we'd appreciate the unique beauty and elegance of the old bridge, 12m high, with ribbed, almost semi-circular arches, two of 17m and one of 9m span. The breakwaters continue to the parapet to provide refuges

in the roadway, which with a width of only 3.5m is too narrow for modern vehicular traffic. Below, the Lune swirls through sloping crags.

The Lune runs under the A65 at Stanley Bridge, built in 1932 150m south of the Devil's Bridge. Stanley – that is, Oliver Stanley, MP for Westmorland, after whom the bridge was named – does not compete with the devil. Instead, the new bridge, with its off-yellow colouring and bold single span, provides a strong, if inelegant, contrast. Just south of Stanley Bridge the Lune enters the county of Lancashire.

From Kirkby Lonsdale the Lune is accompanied by the Lune Valley Ramble, which continues, mainly on its west bank, for 26km to Lancaster. Since the more varied and major part of the Lune valley lies to the north of Kirkby Lonsdale it should perhaps be called the Lower Lune Valley Ramble. This may seem pedantic but the Lune is often underrated because the remit of the body most concerned with its support and promotion, Lancashire County Council, ends at the county border.

The Ramble is a fine walk, the part here being best tackled on a bright morning with the sun sparkling on the rippling surface, with distant views of Leck Fell, Ingleborough and the Bowland Fells. On the riverside there may be a flock of oystercatchers, if it is outside their breeding season. These birds of the lower Lune, easily recognised by their long, straight, dark red bill,

---

Walk 14: A Loop between Kirkby Lonsdale and Barbon

Map: OL2 (please read the general note about the walks in the Introduction).
Starting point: Near the Devil's Bridge (617783).

This is a walk along country lanes and tracks, passing a variety of rural houses and reaching no great height. There is the chance to refuel in Barbon.

Head east, past the caravan park, towards Chapel House and then follow Chapelhouse Lane to High Casterton, passing the golf course on your left. After the Old Manor, cross the junction, following the sign to Low Casterton. Turn right at the Holy Trinity church towards Langthwaite.

Immediately after Langthwaite take the footpath south to Fellfoot Road, which you follow north, past some Goldsworthy Sheepfolds, until it drops down to a road. Turn left at the road and walk to Fell Garth. Take the path north past Whelprigg to Underfell, to drop into Barbon by the church. From Barbon, walk southwest along Scaleber Lane to Low Beckfoot. You could take a short detour north to see the packhorse bridge at Beckfoot Farm. At Low Beckfoot take the path west to the Lune.

At the Lune turn south to follow the long bend past Underley Bridge and then swing back to join Lowfields Lane. Walk east and take the path south, below Underley Grange, to the wood below Gildard Hill, with views on the way across the river to Underley Hall. If you should, accidentally, of course, stray west from the path in the wood, you would have a view down the steepest and highest Luneside bank.

The path continues south to Casterton Hall and then across the field to the A683, where it is best to turn left for 100m or so (take care) and follow the track (Laitha Lane) south from the Old Toll House. This returns you to the Devil's Bridge if you turn right at the end (or via a short cut through the caravan park on the right).

red legs, and black and white colouring, are more often seen in small numbers, flying fast, with a shrill call.

One kilometre from Kirkby Lonsdale the Lune passes under the 130km Haweswater Aqueduct, which transports up to 500 million litres of water every day to Manchester. It was completed in 1955, 36 years after permission for the controversial Haweswater Reservoir had been granted.

Showing excessive concern for walkers' safety, there are warnings to keep on the landward side of a small embankment for flood protection. I assume the real intention is to keep us away from fishermen, but if they are absent the river-edge is much the better place to be.

The next significant tributary is Leck Beck, joining from the east.

Leck Beck

The mature beck that gushes from the fellside at Leck Beck Head emerges after an eventful and secretive infancy. The waters that drain the southern slopes below the fine ridge that arches from Crag Hill to Great Coum and Gragareth form the becks of Aygill and Ease Gill, which proceed normally enough over the high moorland until they reach beds of limestone at about the 350m contour, at which point they begin to disappear through various potholes and caves.

We have flirted with potholes and caves in Dentdale and Barbondale but a confession is now required. My guiding principle has been to write only about what I have seen, wherever possible, and this has led me to visit every one of Loyne's 1285 sq km – but I draw the line at going under them as well. This is unfortunate because potholes are one of the few things in Loyne for which we can dust off our superlatives, as it is undoubtedly England's best potholing region. However, I cannot imagine ever standing at the entrance to a pothole and opting to spend the next few hours in the damp, dark, dangerous depths when I could be striding the hills, with fresh air in my lungs, the wind in my hair, a spring in my step, and a view in all directions. I can appreciate the physical, mental and scientific challenge of potholing but I prefer to resist it.

Therefore, apart from modest forays into cave entrances and the tourist trips into White Scar Caves,

The ridge to Gragareth from Great Coum

Ingleborough Cave and Gaping Gill, all the potholes and caves are unknown territory to me. The little that I say about them is passed on, second hand, in good faith. Those who wish to venture seriously (and there should be no other way) into potholes should consult more reliable first-hand sources.

The potholes into which Ease Gill disappears are part of the Easegill Caverns, which form, according to English Nature's description of the Leck Beck Head Catchment Area Site of Special Scientific Interest, the longest cave system in Britain and the 11th longest in the world. Some call it, or used to call it, the Three Counties System, as it stretches from Aygill (in Cumbria) across Leck Fell (in Lancashire) to Ireby Fell (on the North Yorkshire border). The caves under Casterton Fell (from Lancaster Hole, Bull Pot of the Witches and others) have 60km of connected passages and these have a flooded connection to a further 12km under Leck Fell (from Lost John's Cave and others). An additional 12km of passage under southern Leck Fell are, as yet, unconnected. An idea that there would be an eastern link to the Kingsdale caves seems to be dormant. To the west the cave system is ended by the Dent Fault.

It must be galling to the Yorkshire Dales National Park, renowned for its potholing, to find that its borders exclude Britain's longest cave system. The old county border that ran from Gragareth to Great Coum and into Barbondale neatly steals the Easegill Caverns from the Yorkshire Dales. Perhaps this will be remedied by the review of the **National Park boundaries**.

The details of this three-dimensional underworld are complex to unravel but the cause of the cave system is as we have seen before. Water runs off the shale and sandstone upper slopes to sink at the limestone boundary, to make its way underground to the impermeable lower layer and eventually re-emerge, in this case at Leck Beck Head. Normally the bed of Ease Gill is dry for 2km above Leck Beck Head but in flood conditions the caves fill and Ease Gill becomes a torrent. Leck Beck actually emerges about 100m north of the present line of the bed of Ease Gill.

On the surface there is the barest indication of the wonders underneath. At Lancaster Hole, for example, there is only a manhole cover to see, unless it happens to be raised, in which case you can peer down the 35m shaft. The discovery of Lancaster Hole in 1946, which really began the exploration of the Easegill Caverns, has entered potholing legend: a resting caver noticed the

The Lakes and Dales **National Park boundaries** are being reviewed by the Countryside Agency, which is due to make proposals in 2008. It seems likely to propose that the Dales be extended westward to include the northern part of the Howgills, Middleton Fell, Leck Fell and Wild Boar Fell and that the Lakes be extended eastward to include Birkbeck Fells – in short, that the upper Lune becomes a border between the two National Parks.

There are many factors involved in determining National Parks, as they are legal entities with administrative roles. One factor concerns their role in conservation. It is assumed that 'undesirable' developments would not be permitted within a National Park. Therefore, by extending the boundaries, the area protected from such developments would, it is hoped, be increased.

In a rational world boundaries would not be determined by politics or history but by natural properties that give a region its coherence. In our case, the Dent Fault suggests that Wild Boar Fell and Leck Fell (but not the Howgills and Middleton Fell) belong to the Dales. The characteristic areas of the Lake District are on igneous rocks that differ from Loyne's sedimentary rocks, including the Shap Fells, which are now within the Lake District National Park (but if we follow this line of reasoning we might conclude that the areas south of Windermere and Coniston don't belong in the National Park either!).

Geologically, the Shap Fells, Birkbeck Fells, the Howgills and Middleton Fell form a homogeneous region. Perhaps this region could be designated an Area of Outstanding Natural Beauty, for even the strongest supporter could not claim it equal to the two National Parks. It is, however, unlikely that areas already within the National Parks (the Shap Fells and the southern Howgills) will be excluded. Let's leave it to the experts.

grass moving more than the breeze warranted, inferred that a draught was issuing from underground, and shifted a few rocks to reveal the pothole.

As Leck Beck runs through Springs Wood, a natural wood unlike the many fir plantations in the area, it passes below Castle Hill to the east. Here are the remains of – well, what exactly? There appears to be a roughly circular ditch, 100m in diameter, with gaps to the north and south. Within the ditch, there is some unevenness and a few piles of rocks but no real sign of any building – certainly no castle. It probably enclosed a few Iron Age settlements. One thing we can be sure of: whoever lived here had an excellent view of the lower Lune valley.

Across Leck Beck at High Park are the remains of ancient settlements, visible on the ground as earthworks

1. Ease Gill runs from the slopes of Great Coum ...

2. ... and gradually disappears through limestone ...

3. ... the bed becoming completely dry in places ...

4. ... though there's usually a trickle at Cow Dub ...

5. ... below which the valley is dry and quiet ...

6. ... with eerie grottos and waterless waterfalls ...

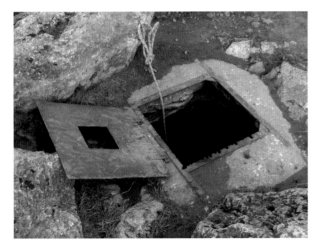

7. ... meanwhile the underground waters of Ease Gill are exploring the Easegill Caverns, as many potholers also do by, for example, entering Lancaster Hole ...

8. ... and eventually, as the waters reach the impermeable rock below the layer of limestone, they re-emerge at Leck Beck Head near Ease Gill Kirk to form Leck Beck.

Walk 15: Leck Fell, Gragareth and Great Coum

Map: OL2 (please read the general note about the walks in the Introduction).
Starting point: The track near Bullpot Farm (663815).

This expedition provides a surface exploration of some potholes of the Easegill Caverns followed by a high-level ridge walk.

From Bullpot Farm walk south 1km to cross a stile below Hellot Scales Barn. (In the very unlikely circumstance that Ease Gill cannot be forded at this point, be sensible: abandon the suggested walk. Content yourself with a walk along the north bank to view the rare sight of waterfalls in the Ease Gill valley and return to Bullpot Farm.)

Detour for 100m up the dry bed to view a chamber with a U-shaped (dry!) waterfall (see photograph left). Some people call this Ease Gill Kirk but the name is properly applied to a less accessible but larger and more spectacular amphitheatre with overhanging cliffs about 200m downstream from the stile. The Kirk (or Church, as it used to be called) is said to have been a clandestine meeting place for Quakers. Returning to the stile, cross the bed of Ease Gill (leaving Cumbria for Lancashire) and follow the footpath south. At a grassy slope a side-path allows a detour to see the real Ease Gill Kirk.

Leave the footpath before reaching a wall and head southeast across a field, viewing Big Meanie and Rumbling Hole en route. Note the Three Men of Gragareth, the central group of a set of cairns, on the horizon as you cross the field. These are your next objective. On reaching the road, take the track above Leck Fell House north for 100m and then scramble up to the Three Men.

From the cairns, take a faint path east for 1km to the Gragareth trig point, and then continue for 150m to reach a wall (peer over the wall into North Yorkshire). Walk north by the wall for 5km, passing Green Hill (628m, the highest point of Lancashire) and the County Stone (the northernmost point of Lancashire) to reach Great Coum, from which there is an excellent view of the Lakeland hills, the Howgills, the nearby Yorkshire Dales peaks, the lower Lune and Morecambe Bay.

Walk west by the wall to Crag Hill (1km) and continue southwest to Richard Man, a rather inconspicuous set of stones (a further 1km). At this point walk south for 250m to a parallel wall, which you then follow southwest for 2km to reach the Bullpot Farm track.

and jumbled lines of rocks. Archaeologists tell us that they date from 300 AD or so. Even older is the Casterton stone circle, which lies southwest of Brownthwaite Pike and dates from the late Neolithic or early Bronze Age (2000-600 BC). There are about eighteen stones, none higher than 30cm and some sunk in the grass, in a 20m-diameter circle. It is said that 1,800 finds, including drinking vessels, flint arrowheads and a bronze spearhead, have been made here. The circle is not, however, an impressive sight. In the same field are many large piles of rocks, the remains of thick walls, which are rather more intriguing.

You cannot see Kirkby Lonsdale from the stone circle, as you might have expected since the stone circle is marked on the display at Ruskin's View. However, if you climb to the prominent cairn on Brownthwaite Pike, you are rewarded with an excellent view of Kirkby Lonsdale, with Morecambe Bay behind, the Lakes skyline to the right and the middle reaches of the Lune to the left.

Leck Beck runs by the village of Leck, which is not the traditional cluster of stone cottages: it is not a cluster at all. The ingredients – an old mill, parsonage, chapel, and school – are there but they do not seem to be integrated to make a community. An ignored triangular field looks like it would make a fine village green – perhaps it once was, for many houses here were burnt down in the 1800s after a smallpox outbreak. Leck Hall, which was rebuilt in the early 19th century and bought by the Kay-Shuttleworth family in 1952, stands apart. From this outpost Lord Charles Shuttleworth serves as Lord Lieutenant of Lancashire, a post instituted by Henry VIII to deal with local defence. Perhaps the need to repel Yorkshire invaders explains all the noise of shooting heard hereabouts.

At Cowan Bridge, Leck Beck passes under an overgrown three-arched bridge for the old Lowgill-Clapham railway line. Cowan Bridge itself is bisected by the busy A65. This is an ancient road along which tolls were collected as early as the 16th century but the traffic associated with the Yorkshire and Cumbria woollen trade had died down by 1824, when the Brontë sisters came. Cowan Bridge is now most remarked upon because of its **Brontë connection**, excessively so, given that it is the grim pestilence of the place that is recalled.

South of Leck Beck, on Woodman Lane, there is a poultry farm that is surprisingly large for such a quiet rural area. Perhaps the authorities, too, are surprised, for the

The **Brontë connection** began when the Rev. Patrick Brontë sent four of his five daughters to the Clergy Daughters' School opened by the Rev. William Carus Wilson in Cowan Bridge in 1824. They were only there for a year, illness forcing them back to Haworth. Maria and Elizabeth died of tuberculosis in 1825, although Charlotte and Emily did, of course, survive to write novels. All they wrote whilst at Cowan Bridge, however, was "Dearest father, please, please get us out of this place".

Elizabeth Gaskell's biography (1857) of Charlotte Brontë painted a harsh picture of the Clergy Daughters' School (Lowood of *Jane Eyre*, perhaps derived from the Low Wood School we met at Casterton) and of the Rev. Carus Wilson (Mr. Brocklehurst), so much so that threatened legal action brought changes to the third edition. To put the Brontë's illnesses into context, child mortality in the region was so high at the time that average life expectancy was only 26 years.

A plaque on the wall of Brontë Cottage by the old road bridge commemorates the Brontë sisters' brief and unhappy time at the Cowan Bridge school.

buildings have neither planning permission nor an IPPC (Integrated Pollution Prevention and Control) licence. To avoid getting myself entangled in this legal dispute I should clarify that 'agricultural permitted development tolerances' allow a small amount of construction every two years without planning permission, which of course builds up over the years. Lancaster City Council refused a retrospective application for planning permission in 2005. Where this leaves Mayfield Chicks, I am not sure.

Leck Beck next passes under Burrow Bridge, whose two arches seem almost too low for the beck when it is in flood. In alcoves on the bridge there are acknowledgements to the work of those who built the bridge in 1733 – labourers (on the west) separated from management (on the east).

The bridge is midway between Nether Burrow and Over Burrow. If you walk to the gate at the drive of Burrow Hall and then 20m to the barn to the north and look at the wall near the north end, about head high, you will see a red sandstone block with carvings on it. This is a remnant of Roman stonework and is all that can be seen of the Roman fort that existed at Over Burrow from the 1st to the 4th century.

The rest you must imagine. The gate to the hall driveway is probably at the east entrance to the fort, midway along the east wall. Burrow Hall itself, visible up the drive, 140m away, is on the west wall of the fort. The fort was roughly square, so the south wall was 70m south of the drive, across the green field. The north wall was similarly 70m north, where there are buildings now. The fort thus enclosed about 2ha, enough space for a thousand soldiers.

How do we know this, when there is so little to see? The Roman's Antonine Itinerary listed a fort called Calacum 27 Roman miles from Bremetenacum (Ribchester) and 30 Roman miles from Galava (Ambleside) – in other words, here. In the past, Burrow was regarded as a very old place and, not so long ago, there was more evidence than there is today: William Camden, in his great work *Britannia* (1610), the first historical survey of Great Britain, wrote "… by divers and sundry monuments exceeding ancient, by engraven stones, pavements of square checker worke, peeces of Roman coine, and by this new name Burrow, which with us signifieth a Burgh, that place should seeme to bee of great antiquity."

Various excavations have been carried out, particularly in the 1950s, to confirm the lines of the walls and positions of the gates. About thirty coins have been found, from Vespasian (69-79 AD) to Constantius I (305-306 AD), but none from the 3rd century. Of course, much remains unknown and may always be so. It is assumed that a road went west across the Lune to Galava although its route has not been traced. The road from Low Borrowbridge, which we have been tracking south, runs 1km to the east of the fort.

Roman stonework in Over Burrow barn

Burrow Hall is a substantial Grade I listed Georgian mansion, best seen from the footpath to the north. After the Civil War the Burrow estate was given to a Colonel Briggs, who built the first hall in the 1650s. The estate was sold to the Fenwick family in 1690 and Robert Fenwick, Attorney General and MP for Lancaster, rebuilt the hall, as we see it now, in 1740. After passing through various hands, the estate was offered for sale in 2005 for £3.5m and so, for what it's worth, we have the estate agent's description of the interior of the building: the Baroque ceilings, the marble fireplaces, the delicate cornicing of its five grand reception rooms, the sumptuous master suite, the stunning atrium with fabulous views, and so on. The Burrow estate also includes 0.5km of fishing on the Lune, which Leck Beck joins 300m below Burrow Bridge.

The Lune from Leck Beck ...

The map shows a ford across the Lune immediately after Leck Beck has entered the Lune and I can vouch for the fact that it is indeed fordable, on foot (sometimes). If the paddling expedition is from the east and is timed properly, it is possible to sneak in on the Whittington point to point steeplechases that are held on Easter Saturdays in the fields opposite.

The Lune valley has now flattened out, giving long views to the south, east and north. An island (when the river is high) has been formed, with its shores strewn with large boulders and tree-trunks washed down in floods. The riverside fields show evidence of old river channels, with the lagoons left by the shifting Lune being favourite haunts of the heron, a bird that, unlike others, rises with graceful dignity if disturbed and with slow beats of its wings drifts off to settle in the long reeds where it can keep a better eye on you than vice versa.

This is a magnificent spot for seeing the **salmon** leap. Settle on the west bank on a fine autumn day, at a point opposite the island, where a deep stretch of Lune runs straight towards you from the north. There will be little noise, apart from the splashing salmon. If the salmon should be resting, there will be, apart from the heron, a display of bird-life such as oystercatcher, snipe and kingfisher, if you are lucky – and all this with a backdrop of the Howgills, Leck Fell and Ingleborough. This beats Ruskin's View by far!

The 1847 OS map shows that, south of the island, the Lune swept in a wide curve half the way to Tunstall,

The **salmon** is the Lune's jewel. The Lune has one of the most important populations of Atlantic salmon in England, salmon being found through much of the Lune's catchment area. The eggs are laid in autumn, with the young salmon staying in their native beck for up to three years. The mature salmon then spend two or three years in the sea before returning to their beck in early summer in order to spawn and then, usually, to die.

The Lune was once one of the best salmon fisheries in England but numbers dropped in the 1960s because of disease (ulcerative dermal necrosis, which certainly sounds bad). There may well have been other factors, such as the loss of spawning habitats, excessive fishing, poor water quality, and barriers to the salmons' swim upstream, as well as causes external to the Lune. The Lune's problems are not unique as global catches of Atlantic salmon fell by 80% in the 30 years from 1970. Although the numbers of Lune salmon have since revived they are not yet back to previous levels and the numbers of sea-trout also remain disappointing.

The Environment Agency now monitors salmon populations through automatic counters at Forge Weir, Caton and Broadraine Weir, Killington and has developed a 'salmon action plan' for the Lune. This includes giving nature a hand by releasing four-month-old salmon fry, reared from Lune eggs, into upstream tributaries.

Below: The Lune at the 'island', with Leck Fell and Ingleborough beyond.

that is, 500m from its present course. All the fields east and west of the Lune from Kirkby Lonsdale were marked as "liable to flooding". The Lune floodplain, about 1km wide and running 15km from Kirkby Lonsdale to Caton, has all the characteristics of a textbook floodplain. In normal conditions, the Lune meanders gently among wide, flat and tranquil pastures, where glacial till and regular alluvium deposits create rich soils to provide fertile grazing land for sheep and cattle. Abandoned channels and protected hollows create lagoons that are replenished by floods and heavy rain to provide important wetland habitats for birds, fish and plants. Kingfishers and sand martins are able to nest in the eroded riverbanks.

For obvious reasons, there are no human habitations in the floodplain, increasing the sense that the area is a haven for wildlife. The floodplain rises gently to its undulating fringes, where homesteads have been built and along which important lines of communication have always existed. Communication across the floodplain was more difficult, although there were several fords between settlements on opposite banks. In general, the Lune is fortunate that, although there has been some drainage and flood protection work, there has been no major urban or industrial development to affect these ecologically important areas of grassland and wet meadows.

The Lune continues south, to be joined by the major tributary of the River Greta.

CHAPTER 8:
The Greta Headwaters

Great Coum ▲

Blea Moor ▲

Force Gill

Little Dale Beck

Green Hill ▲

Whernside
▲

Yordas
Cave

Batty Moss Viaduct
*

Gragareth ▲

walk 16

Winterscales Beck

Kingsdale Beck

S

Chapel-
le-Dale
●

Park Fell ▲

walk 17

Chapel Beck

S

B6255

Thornton Force *

Simon Fell ▲

▲ Ingleborough

* White Scar
Cave

River Greta
●

Ingleton

Scale: 1 cm to 1 km

0   5 kilometres

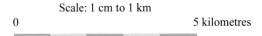

The River Greta (Chapel Beck) ...

The River Greta is formed at Ingleton by the confluence of the River Doe and River Twiss. Unfortunately, there is confusion as to which is which. The Ordnance Survey and the Ingleton Waterfalls Walk leaflet have the Doe to the east but Wainwright's *Walks in Limestone Country* and Ingleton's own leaflet have the Doe to the west. Upstream, the two rivers are called Chapel Beck (in Chapel-le-Dale) and Kingsdale Beck (in Kingsdale) and it seems simplest to retain those names down to the Ingleton junction, rather than choose between the river names.

As Chapel Beck is the larger of the two at the junction I will consider that to provide the source of the Greta, with Kingsdale Beck being a tributary. This is supported by Thos Johnson's 1872 book *A Pictorial Handbook to the Valley of the Lune and Gossiping Guide to Morecambe and District* (yes, really), which considers Chapel-le-Dale to lie in Gretadale. Moreover, he has a River Doe in Kingsdale, so if I were forced off the fence, I'd say the Ordnance Survey has it wrong.

The source of Chapel Beck is at the head of Little Dale, a liitle dale between Whernside and Blea Moor. Here, Little Dale Beck is joined by Force Gill, which has two fair-sized waterfalls and crosses the Settle-Carlisle railway line over an aqueduct. Force Gill arises in Greensett, an intriguing plateau below the high slopes of Whernside. Our obsession with getting to the tops of mountains – perhaps understandable with Whernside, as it is the highest peak of the Dales – tends to lead us to hurry past more interesting areas. Although the slopes of Whernside are now all CRoW land, at least 99% of walkers dutifully follow the signposted route, part of the **Three Peaks** walk, via Grain Head, ignoring Force Gill and Greensett.

Actually, my preferred route up Whernside is from Kingsdale Head – all grass and no people (so forget I mentioned it). But the CRoW policy does raise a question: is it environmentally better that we all tread the standard path, thereby giving up that path to erosion and decay? Or should we spread ourselves thinly across CRoW land? There seems little point in creating access land if we are not expected to access it but, on the other hand, even the occasional walker may be too much for some of the flora and fauna.

The first time we walked the Three Peaks route we came across a curlew's nest right by the path. There's

The **Three Peaks** are Whernside, Ingleborough and Pen-y-Ghent. The first two, at 736m and 724m, are the two highest peaks in the Yorkshire Dales and are wholly within Loyne. Pen-y-Ghent (694m) is the 7th highest Dales peak and is in Ribblesdale.

The Three Peaks walk of about 38km, with over 1500m of ascent, is a challenging all-day expedition. The Three Peaks fell race is even more challenging but should not take all day (only serious runners are allowed: no pantomime horses). The record is 2hr 46min for the present course and 2hr 29min for a previous course. In 2008 the Three Peaks race will be run as the World Long Distance Mountain Running Challenge. The start used to be at Chapel-le-Dale but is now at Horton-in-Ribblesdale, which has taken upon itself the role of Three Peaks centre. Of course, walkers may start at any point on the circuit.

However, it is hardly a *fell* walk or race nowadays. Much of the route has been so badly eroded that the natural fell has been replaced. It is a shame that so many people continue to follow such a worn path. Jack Sharp's *New Walks in the Yorkshire Dales* provides a score of alternative long-distance walks.

I would also suggest a Loyne Three Peaks – replace Pen-y-Ghent with Great Coum. The latter is only 7m lower and this route avoids the long trek over bog and on road from Pen-y-Ghent to Whernside and the eyesore of the Horton quarries (and it's 10km shorter).

little chance of that today. The curlew is the bird most redolent of the northern moors, with its distinctive call as it glides earthwards. Some describe it as plaintive or melancholy but it sounds bubblingly joyful to me. Never mind the swallow and cuckoo, it is the call of the curlew that is for me the most evocative of the new year (as early as January in 2006) as the curlew returns up the Lune valley to its nesting haunts.

Below the red-tinged sandstone slopes of Whernside, grey slate tumbles towards the peat of Greensett Moss. Here is Greensett Tarn, the sheltered home of black-headed gulls, and below the tarn is a line of shakeholes and caves, including Greensett Cave. Their existence at 560m, when the main potholes and caves of the valley are at about 300m, shows that there is a layer of limestone here, as well as in the valley.

Little Dale Beck absorbs Hare Gill and Foul Gutter from Blea Moor before crossing under the railway line, 1km north of the Ribblehead Viaduct, to become

Previous page: Ingleborough from Souther Scales.

Force Gill, with walkers on the Three Peaks route

Winterscales Beck. This viaduct was originally called Batty Moss Viaduct, in keeping with the tradition of naming viaducts after what they cross (Dent Head, Arten Gill and Dandry Mire). Its renaming, along with that of Batty Green Station to Ribblehead Station, is a triumph for the tourist industry of Ribblesdale.

The source of the Ribble is 8km north at Newby Head in Widdale. Standing under the viaduct, it is hard to tell whether water will flow southwest to the Lune or southeast to the Ribble, precisely because the viaduct was built over the watershed. If anything, it looks more downhill to the southwest and, certainly, the largest beck of any size that is close to the viaduct is Winterscales Beck, which flows to the Lune.

It is too late to claim the viaduct for the Lune but there is every justification for calling it Batty Moss Viaduct, as I will, not least because its actual existence here may be a little batty. The Settle-Carlisle railway line is now absorbed into the romance of the Dales and we may marvel at the skill and energy that produced the scenic section from Batty Moss Viaduct to Dandrymire Viaduct, via Bleamoor Tunnel, Dent Head Viaduct, Artengill Viaduct and Risehill Tunnel. But we might pause to ask: Why? Why was it necessary?

Imagine yourself to be a railway engineer in 1870, standing at Selside in Ribblesdale. The Settle-Carlisle line will proceed north up Ribblesdale and south below Wild Boar Fell. How would you bridge the gap? Would you go over the watershed to Dentdale and then out again to Garsdale rather than through Widdale (the present B6265 route), knowing that the line from Hawes to Garsdale, completed in 1878, was already planned? I am not a railway engineer but it seems to me that this route requires no large viaducts and no tunnels.

Anyway, let us be grateful, for if they had so decided all of the Settle-Carlisle line would be outside Loyne. However, we should always remember that the "thrilling story of this magnificent engineering enterprise", as Wainwright's *Walks in Limestone Country* puts it, involved a few thousand people working here, under appalling conditions, for six years (less for the two hundred or so who died). The Batty Green shantytown sounds jolly but it must have been a hard, tough life here in the cold, wet, muddy desolation. I hope that the workers' sacrifices were not in the cause of some vainglorious adventure.

Batty Moss Viaduct

Walk 16: Whernside from Chapel-le-Dale

Map: OL2 (please read the general note about the walks in the Introduction).
Starting point: A lay-by on the north side of the B6255 200m northwest of Hill Inn (744777).

Walk past the Hill Inn to take Philpin Lane north to Bruntscar. This is on the Three Peaks walk route but you will avoid the steep, knee-jarring slog up the reinforced thoroughfare on the flank of Whernside by taking a more leisurely uphill amble, mainly on grass.

Turn left past Bruntscar and Ellerbeck and on to the bridleway southwest. After about 1km leave the bridleway to cut across to the straight wall that runs up the West Fell ridge. Follow this wall all the way to the top of Whernside, 1km before which you rejoin the Three Peaks thoroughfare.

From the top, drop down the slope (steep but not too steep) to reach the remains of a wall 0.5km east and follow it northeast, investigating the Greensett caves and potholes, as you wish. Follow the wall down east to see the Force Gill waterfalls. Rejoin the footpath to cross the railway line and after 1km go under the railway to Winterscales and Ivescar. From Ivescar take the footpath south to Winterscales Beck. Continue on the road and then footpath back to Philpin Lane, noting the caves and potholes and the signs of damage wrought when the beck is in spate.

When planning a high-level walk, it is always worth having a low-level alternative in mind, for often on arrival we find that the tops have gathered cloud. Here there is a fine loop walk under the shelter of Whernside: from Chapel-le-Dale take Oddies Lane to Twisleton Hall, then follow the footpath across Scales Moor to Bruntscar and on to Winterscales, and then work your way back along Winterscales Beck.

Today, we may admire the results of their labours. The Batty Moss Viaduct is the most spectacular of all the engineering works on the Settle-Carlisle line and an awesome sight from Whernside and other vantage points. Its 24 arches are made from local limestone and the embankment from earth excavated from Bleamoor Tunnel. The viaduct is 32m high and 400m long and the spans are 7m wide, with each sixth pier thickened to help prevent collapse. Its gentle curve seems fully in keeping with the surroundings, now that the shantytown has long gone.

Winterscales Beck makes its way intermittently southwest, repeatedly disappearing through its limestone bed and being re-created by resurgences, of which the largest is from Gatekirk Cave. In summer much of its bed will be dry but it is obvious from the erosion that after heavy rain this is a ferocious torrent. In places, one can stand in the dry bed and see debris in the trees several metres above.

After Winterscales Beck disappears, a series of potholes and caves continues its line until the emergence of Chapel Beck below Chapel-le-Dale. Some of these potholes are described in the overblown prose of John Hutton, vicar of Burton-in-Kendal, who in 1780 wrote a 49-page pamphlet considered to be the first-ever book on caving. He considered Weathercote Cave to be "the most surprising natural curiosity of the kind in the island of Great Britain … a stupendous subterranean cataract." Hurtle Pot, however, was "one of the most dismal prospects we had yet been presented with … [and he viewed] with horror and astonishment its dreadful aspect."

Like many rural hamlets, Chapel-le-Dale is known for its pub and its church. The Hill Inn was long regarded as a rowdy base for potholers. St Leonard's Church is a more sombre resting place for the "many men, women and children … who died through accident or disease during the construction of the Settle-Carlisle railway and who were buried in this churchyard", as a millennium year memorial plaque puts it. Sadly, the plaque does not list the two hundred names given in the burial register. The church itself is neat, with mullioned windows and bellcot, built in the 17th century and restored in 1869.

Above Chapel-le-Dale soars Ingleborough, the supreme peak of the Yorkshire Dales. Although second in height to Whernside, its isolated location and proud profile make it seem higher from almost every direction. Its position at the head of the Greta and Wenning valleys

means that it oversees, and can be seen from, much of Loyne.

Its name alludes, perhaps fortuitously, to two early roles. The word 'ingle' is from an old Gaelic word for fire and no doubt, because of its domineering position, Ingleborough was often in the past the site of a beacon. The 'borough' (as we saw with Low Borrowbridge and Over Burrow) may be associated with a Roman fort that some believe to have been based on the summit. The remains of a military wall can be seen on the eastern rim of the summit plateau but most experts consider the fort to have been built in the 1st century by the Brigantes, as a defence against the Romans. Others consider it to be pre-Roman Iron Age. The remains of several ancient hut circles can also be discerned.

These remains should not be confused with the great pile of stones on the western rim. This was a hospice-cum-tower-cum-shooting-box. It was left to fall into ruin after damage was caused at a boisterous opening ceremony in 1830. Recalling this event in the Lancaster Guardian in 1897, Joseph Carr described the tower as "one of the wonders of Lunesdale" – note the Lunesdale. Still standing is the cross-shaped wind shelter erected in 1953. This provides endless entertainment for, sitting in one quarter, one cannot help eavesdropping on conversations in the other three quarters. These are often disputes over the identification of distant peaks. One can hardly intrude to point out the view indicator in the middle of the cross.

Ingleborough's distinctive profile is a consequence of its geology, which is similar to that of Whernside and Wild Boar Fell. The top 30m or so are of hardwearing millstone grit. This sits atop 250m of conglomerate rocks (the Yoredale series), mainly shales and sandstones, with a little limestone, all covered with peat except where exposed on the crags. Below this is a 200m layer of limestone (the Great Scar limestone), which is visible on the lower slopes of the mountain. These are all sedimentary rocks of the Carboniferous period that have not been distorted much from their horizontal layers. Below the 250m contour are the much older Silurian slates and grits, which have been folded and contorted. And the whole has been much shaped by glacial action.

Some of the western slopes of Ingleborough and Simon Fell form a National Nature Reserve, although at the moment it is more a matter of reversing nature than of reserving it. Previously the land had been fertilised and over-grazed, preventing the growth of wildflowers

Ingleborough from White Scars

and trees. The moorland areas are now being managed to restore lost acid-loving plants such as ling heather and bilberry, to join plants such as bog asphodel and purple moor-grass. The grazing regime on the limestone grasslands is intended to enable the flowering of different plants through the seasons: purple wild thyme, orchids, yellow rockrose, harebell, and so on. Within the grikes many woodland plants flourish but now trees and shrubs (ash, elm, hawthorn, hazel, sycamore) also have a chance to thrive.

To the north, Scar Close has been protected for longer and gives an idea of the clint-and-grike flora

The Top 10 peaks in Loyne
(to look at, not from)
1. Ingleborough
2. Wild Boar Fell
3. Great Coum
4. Grayrigg Pike
5. Calf Top
6. Whinfell
7. Whernside
8. Clougha Pike
9. Winder
10. Mallowdale Pike

before wood clearance and over-grazing. Ash, hazel and rowan trees have become established. Further north, the raised terrace of Howrake Rocks has formed a prominent rectangle of woodland, showing how different the Yorkshire Dales would look if left to revert to its natural state.

Above the limestone terraces, there is a line of caves and potholes where becks running off the fells disappear underground. Great Douk Cave and Middle Washfold Caves are popular with novice cavers. Braithwaite Wife Hole (which Thos Johnson and Harry Speight, in their 19th century guides, rendered more intriguingly as Barefoot Wives Hole) is a huge shakehole, 60m in diameter. Raven Scar Cave, only discovered in 1971, was found to be a Neolithic burial site. Meregill Hole is 170m deep, with the mere that gives the pot its name visible 12m down – or so they say. The sound of a waterfall below, when the beck above was dry, was enough for me.

There is a line of springs, particularly clearly seen after rain, in the green fields below Twisleton Scars, where the limestone meets the impermeable lower layer. Below God's Bridge, several resurgences can be seen entering Chapel Beck – or in summer creating Chapel Beck, for then the bed is dry above the bridge. God's Bridge, incidentally, is traditionally a name that denotes a natural, as opposed to man-made or devil-made, bridge but here it has been sacrilegiously cemented over.

Chapel Beck runs below Oddie's Lane, which is along the line of a Roman road that ran from Bainbridge to near Ingleton and then probably to join the road at Over Burrow. On the east bank is the site of the disused Ingleton Granite Quarry. It is, in fact, not granite at all

but greywacke, an impure sandstone with a toughness that made it a valued stone for roads.

As Chapel Beck flows gently south-east, on the left a building comes into view that delivers exactly what it says on its roof, that is, caves – to be precise, the **White Scar Caves**. By the time Chapel Beck crosses the footpath from Beezleys it is wide and docile enough to require nearly fifty stepping-stones to cross. But it is only girding its loins for a tumultuous fall through Baxenghyll Gorge, including impressive cascades at Beezley Falls, Rival Falls and Snow Falls, between which the water lies black-brown in deep pools.

The glen is a Site of Special Scientific Interest because of its geology and associated flora. It is also

Above: Ingleborough top (with no people!).
Below: Beezley Falls.

White Scar Caves are the longest show caves in England. They were discovered in 1923 when two Cambridge students, Christopher Long and John Churchill, investigated Playfair's Cave, then thought to lead only a short distance. They had previously explored the Cheddar Gorge in Somerset and Stump Cross Cavern near Harrogate and, having concluded that there was money to be made from developing a show cave, had come to Ingleborough with that specific intention.

So, wearing, according to the Yorkshire Post, an outfit that "consisted of all-leather clothes, thoroughly treated with dubbin; a helmet, with three candles and an electric lamp, served by a battery and switch attached to their belts; rock-climbing boots and a plentiful application of vaseline to such parts of their body as were exposed" (that is, most of them), Long and Churchill ventured in. They found a way beyond a pool and after crawling 200m reached the first waterfall of the cave's main stream. Subsequently they explored upstream, passing many fine formations, now bearing prosaic names such the Sword of Damocles and the Devil's Tongue, as far as the lakes now bypassed by the Bagshaw Tunnel.

Unfortunately, they were not rewarded for this endeavour because Long, a manic depressive, died of a drug overdose in 1924 and Churchill was unable to raise sufficient funds to continue the development of the cave. The cave was eventually opened to the public in 1925, with the first manager, Tom Greenwood, adding further galleries and passages in the 1930s. In 1971 the massive 200,000-year-old Battlefield Cavern, 100m long and 30m high with thousands of delicate stalactites and undisturbed prehistoric mud pools, was discovered and this now forms the climax of the present tour, 1.5km and 90 minutes from the entrance.

designated an Ancient Semi-Natural Woodland, ancient in this context being defined as pre-1600. Ancient woodland is scarce locally because of grazing but much of this glen is inaccessible to sheep or cattle, enabling oak and birch, with occasional hazel, holly and rowan, to flourish on the acidic soils that overlie the Silurian slate. The woodlands are also important for their mosses and liverworts, which thrive in dark gullies, and ground plants such as wood rush, dog's mercury and wild garlic.

The path alongside the falls provides views of several disused slate quarries, while from high to the east the stone-crushing noise of Skirwith Quarry may well intrude. This quarry continues to mine the Ingleton Granite previously mined upstream.

As Chapel Beck emerges from the wooded glen it passes through the remains of Mealbank Quarry. It contains probably the thickest coal seam within an English limestone sequence, and the sediments are rich in fossils yet to be fully understood. The quarry also has the ruins of England's first Hoffmann kiln, which operated from 1864 to 1909. This kiln had a literally revolutionary design, whereby material was burned in a continuous horizontal loop, rather than tipped into a vertical furnace.

On the outskirts of Ingleton, Chapel Beck passes an outdoor swimming pool that a plaque proudly informs us has been ranked the 52nd such pool in the world. Just before the viaduct for the old Lowgill-Clapham line Chapel Beck is joined by Kingsdale Beck to form the River Greta.

Kingsdale Beck

Most visitors to Kingsdale intend to go through or under it, which is less than it deserves. They are either using the road between Dent and Thornton-in-Lonsdale or they are aiming to tackle the potholes arrayed along the sides of Kingsdale.

Kingsdale is a fine upland valley, flanked by Whernside to the east and Great Coum and Gragareth to the west, with its limestone scars below the millstone grit tops providing superb views. It can be lonely and wild but also, on sunny summer days, balmy and serene. It would perhaps have its deserved appeal to tourists if it reverted to its full name of Vikingsdale – some of the names here (Yordas, Braida Garth) are of Norse origin, as indeed are 'beck' and 'dale'.

The valley runs straight from north to south for 7km with only 1½ farmsteads in it – Braida Garth and Kingsdale Head. The other ½ of the latter is a holiday cottage. The head of Kingsdale is 3km above Kingsdale Head, where the road between Whernside and High Pike begins to drop down steeply to Dentdale. Kingsdale Beck gathers off the boggy slopes of Great Coum and Whernside but, like Barbon Beck to the north, comes and goes a few times. It has usually gone between Kingsdale Head and Keld Head. This is convenient for it means we can follow the new 'conservation path' across the beck to investigate the Apronfull of Stones. This 20m-diameter ring of stones, with gaps to the east and west (the latter probably from beck erosion), is a Bronze Age burial cairn.

Directly opposite is Yordas Cave, which was one of the first tourist attractions in the Dales. The aforementioned Reverend Hutton said of Yordas Cave: "Having never been in a cave before, a thousand ideas … were excited in my imagination on my entrance into this gloomy cavern … As we advanced ... and the gloom and the horror increased, the den of Cacus, and the cave of Poliphemus came into my mind [sadly, our knowledge of Greek mythology is not what it was] … The roof was so high, and the bottom and sides so dark, that, with all the light we could procure from our candles and torches, we were not able to see the dimensions of this cavern [it's about 20m high and 50m long] ... On the right was the bishop's throne, and on the left the chapter-house ... [the religious terminology was in use before the reverend's visit and is still used today]. Here we could not but lament the devastation made in the ornaments of these sacred places; some Goths not long since having defaced both throne and chapter-house of their pendant petrified works, which had been some ages in forming [so vandalism is not a recent problem]."

Left (top): Gragareth and Yordas Wood from the
*   Apronfull of Stones.*
Left (bottom): Kingsdale and Whernside.
Below: Keld Head Scar in Kingsdale.

Yordas Cave has been formed from Yordas Gill dropping through the limestone, forming the waterfall in the chapter-house, and running across the floor of the cavern. After heavy rain, its present exit is insufficient and the cavern begins to fill. It is one of a series of caves and potholes that line the Turbary Road that runs above the limestone terraces. This track provided access to turbary, that is, common land where peat or turf may be cut, an important right in ancient times. Today, it provides an excellent walking track, safely guiding us between the potholes.

These potholes and those on the eastern side of Kingsdale hold a proud place in potholing history because in 1991 the route from King Pot (on the east) to Keld Head provided the then longest diving traverse in the world. The best pothole to view from the surface, Rowten Pot, can hardly be missed, although I hope it is avoided. Walking from the south, the sound of the beck will first be heard, rather scarily, from a hole barely 1m from the Turbary Road. This hole is in the roof of Rowten Cave, which can be entered 100m to the west. Rowten Pot itself is a huge chasm 10m to the east. Actually, it is two chasms, between which it is possible to walk – with care, for the southern one falls 70m. Walking from the north, it is the northern chasm, with trees sprouting out of it, which is seen first.

The Turbary Road swings west towards Masongill but there is a good path back to the Dent road, past the Tow Scar trig point. From this there's a view of Ingleborough and Whernside and across the Greta and Wenning valleys to Bowland and Pendle – a much better view, in fact, than the one afforded by the Millennium viewing station kindly provided on the Dent road, for this is dominated to the south by the nearby mast of a radio station and there is no view to the north.

Meanwhile, Kingsdale Beck (if it exists) has run along its straightened course to be replenished at Keld Head, where the becks that disappear into the potholes re-emerge. At Keld Head the waters meet the impermeable Silurian rocks that underlie the limestone and form a huge underwater cavern. At first glance, it seems that Kingsdale is enclosed on all four sides by higher ground, with Raven Ray forming a barrier to the south. It is easy to imagine Kingsdale as a glaciated valley, with terminal moraines being deposited at Raven Ray, so enclosing a large lake. But there is now a way through for Kingsdale Beck.

If you innocently follow the beck by taking the path over Ravenray Bridge you may be surprised to find yourself struggling against the flow of walkers in the opposite direction. Clearly there is something special downstream – and we soon hear and see it, that is, Thornton Force, which many regard as the most picturesque waterfall in the Dales. At 14m it is not the highest but the graceful cascade within a shrub-topped cliff face seems perfectly designed for tourists' snapshots from the footpath. It is even possible, with care, to scramble behind the waterfall to enhance the magic.

A better reason for doing so is to investigate at close quarters the geological unconformity in the cliff face. An unconformity does not just mean that there is a change in the type of rock, which is obvious to even the untrained eye, but that two rocks are adjacent when they shouldn't be: a younger rock rests upon an older rock with an expected intervening middle-aged rock missing. Here, the sediments of 350 million year old Carboniferous limestone lie above distorted Silurian slates some 100

Left: Ingleborough from Tow Scar.
Right: Thornton Force.

Walk 17: Kingsdale and Yordas Cave

Map: OL2 (please read the general note about the walks in the Introduction).
Starting point: A lay-by on the Thornton-in-Lonsdale to Dent road (692757).

This is a shorter walk than usual, to allow time for pottering about. Before I forget, take a torch with you.

From the lay-by walk 200m north along the road to take the track east over Kingsdale Beck. Continue for 1km and then take the footpath that cuts back north heading for Braida Garth, 3km away. Follow this path below limestone scars to Braida Garth and then continue across a field to the road.

At this point there is a new path alongside Kingsdale Beck to the Apronfull of Stones, 1km upstream. If Kingsdale Beck is dry, as it usually is, walk to the Apronfull and then follow a new path west to Yordas Cave, where the torch will come in handy. (If it isn't, forget the Apronfull and just walk 1km along the road to the cave). The field within which Yordas Wood is located is CRoW land, so from the cave walk above the wood to locate the line of the permissive path linking to the Turbary Road, which you follow south. Stray from the Turbary Road only with care, for example, to see Jingling Pot, Rowten Pot (and the cave above it) and as many other pots as you wish.

Now it only remains to locate the path back to the starting point: after a section where the Turbary Road runs near a wall, stay on the Road across another field, and your path, a clear track, is 200m further (at 685768), heading south. It goes past Tow Scar (worth a detour to the trig point) and then drops down to near the lay-by.

The **Ingleton Waterfalls Walk** is an 8km circular walk up Thornton Glen, across the path by Twisleton Hall and Beezleys and back down Baxenghyll Gorge, passing a series of waterfalls.

The walk was opened in 1885 and soon there were packed trains bringing multitudes from places such as Leeds, Bradford and Manchester. Inevitably, this financial windfall provoked disputes about who should benefit – the developers of the pathways, the farmers whose lands were being crossed, or the village of Ingleton itself. There was also a debate with Mealbank Quarry, the noise of which spoilt an idyllic country ramble. At one stage, there were two companies involved, one charging for Thornton Glen, the other for Baxenghyll Gorge: many visitors were so disgruntled at being charged twice for one walk that they returned home to put up notices warning others "not to go to Ingleton unless you want to be robbed".

There is obviously a difficulty in charging for a walk that has four entry points – the tops and bottoms of the two glens. The tops may be freely entered, as may the bottom of Baxenghyll Gorge. Some people resent paying for what nature has freely provided. Guidebooks agree that the fee is a bargain, authors not wishing to appear curmudgeonly or to belittle the undoubted splendour of the walk. For example, Wainwright's *Walks in Limestone Country* effuses "So small a fee! So great a reward!". But then it was one shilling (5p) in 1970. It now costs an arm and a leg, with reduces the pleasure, not to say feasibility, of the walk. The paths do need to be maintained, and they are, to a high standard, but does it cost so much to do so? Today, the Waterfalls Walk is managed by the Ingleton Scenery Company, with an address in Skipton.

million years older, with the Devonian layer missing, the whole forming a textbook illustration of severe earth movement and erosion. Between them is a narrow band of softer conglomerate limestone that has eroded to give the overhanging waterfall lip.

The region clearly has a complex geology. Chapel Beck and Kingsdale Beck are crossed by the North Craven Fault, one of several Craven Faults that run across the southern Yorkshire Dales, from Grassington past Malham Cove and Ingleton towards Barbon. The faults are responsible for some of the most dramatic Dales scenery and for the clear change from limestone to millstone grit to the south. It is less apparent that on a 2km stroll near Ingleton you may walk over the oldest sedimentary bedrock in Loyne, that is, Ordovician (Arenig), 500m years old, and also the youngest, Permian Red Sandstone, 250m years old.

Our admiration of the outcome is enhanced as we continue downstream, passing Pecca Falls and entering Thornton Glen. The gorge woodland is, like Baxenghyll Gorge, a Site of Special Scientific Interest on account of its stands of ash, hazel, wych elm and yew, with rich woodland herbs. If you follow our path down Baxenghyll Gorge and Thornton Glen then, as you emerge from Swilla Glen, an official may well challenge your innocence by demanding payment, for you have completed, in an unorthodox fashion, the famous **Ingleton Waterfalls Walk**.

CHAPTER 9:
Gretadale and a little
more Lunesdale

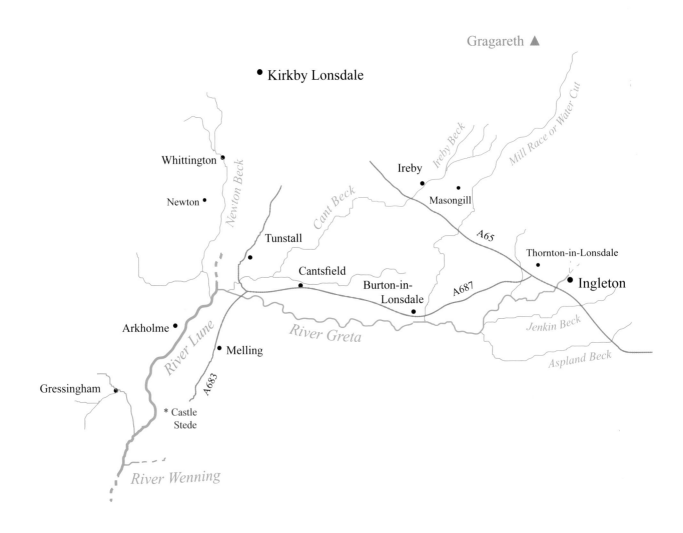

Scale: 1 cm to 1 km

0   5 kilometres

The Greta from Kingsdale Beck

Chapel Beck and Kingsdale Beck (or the Rivers Twiss and Doe, or vice versa) merge to form the Greta in the middle of Ingleton. Ingleton is always thought of as part of the Yorkshire Dales although it is in fact carefully excluded from the National Park, whose boundary detours around the northern outskirts. Perhaps the boundary makers agreed with the afore-mentioned Thos Johnson who, writing of the church in 1872, said that it "partakes of the character of the houses, being a miserable, slap-dashed building, without one redeeming feature."

No writer would dare to be so offensive today but even so it cannot be denied that Ingleton has more of an industrial nature than places we've visited earlier. Apart from the tourist industry, which dominates today, there is still quarrying nearby, although on a lesser scale than previously, and an industrial estate, close to the site of the old Ingleton Colliery. In 2004 a monument was erected near the A65 to help ensure that Ingleton's coal mining history is not forgotten. Small-scale coal mining, as in Dentdale and Barbondale, existed here since the 17th century, although the seams were of poor quality and thin, as indicated by their being called the 'four feet' and 'six feet' seams. Numerous pits are shown on the OS map, all marked as disused, which they became once the railways made local coal mining uneconomic. In 1913, however, a 'ten feet' seam was found deeper underground (quite why anyone went to the trouble of looking is unclear). The Ingleton Colliery operated until 1936, employing up to 900 people. There is no sign of the colliery now but it is not inconceivable that, with new technologies and changing energy policies, coal mining will return to the region.

The Greta passes under the 1861 Ingleton Viaduct (for the Lowgill-Clapham line) of eleven arches nearly 30m high. Tourists heading for the waterfalls disembarked at the station to the east (where the information centre now is) and were led by guides to the start of the walk, averting eyes from the slap-dashed church, at least until 1896 when St Mary's was rebuilt. Inside the church there's a 12th century font with intriguing carvings. Ingleton is ancient, appearing as Inglestune in the Domesday Book, but, as Thos Johnson warns us, there are few old buildings of interest. Around the viaduct and the entrance to the waterfall walk, the main streets are lined with cafés and shops and in summer the pavements are jostling with the booted backpacked brigade.

The regions to the east and west of Ingleton drain to the Greta, from below Tow Scar by becks flowing through Thornton-in-Lonsdale and from Ingleborough Common, south of Ingleborough, by Jenkin Beck and Aspland Beck. Thornton-in-Lonsdale is the place furthest from the Lune to acknowledge in its name an association with it. A website for its Marton Arms says that "together with historic St Oswald's Church, they form the charming hamlet of Thornton-in-Lonsdale." There is a little more to Thornton-in-Lonsdale than the pub and church, but not much. The church is surprisingly large for such a location and has a distinctive pyramid, too short to be a steeple, atop its tower. It was rebuilt in 1933 after being burned down in a blizzard, which sounds an event worth seeing.

Jenkin Beck forms the waterfall of Easegill Force in a secluded gorge, falling behind a natural arch. The beck dawdles across flat land to join the Greta 2km south

Previous page: Barn near Burton-in-Lonsdale.
Left: Ingleton Viaduct.

The Greta near Barnoldswick

of Ingleton and is followed shortly after by Aspland Beck, which similarly runs uneventfully west from Cold Cotes. Here, the bed of the Greta is adorned with multi-coloured stones, reflecting the varied geology upstream, and the banks are heavily eroded, revealing interesting strata.

As the Greta approaches Burton-in-Lonsdale it passes Waterside Pottery, which it isn't but which reminds us that potteries thrived here from the early 18th century until after the Second World War. At one time there were fifteen potteries. The only evidence today is the pockmarked appearance of the fields, from which the shale was dug. Burton-in-Lonsdale was called 'Black Burton', in reference to the earthenware produced, or to the coal and shale used, or to the smoke from the kilns. Or perhaps to distinguish our Burton from the other Burton, Burton-in-Kendal, just 12km west in limestone country, although I can find no record of the latter being called 'White Burton'.

On the outskirts of Burton-in-Lonsdale, the Greta is joined by a millrace that runs from the old corn mill at Bogg Bridge. On the 1850 OS map this bridge is called Mill Race Bridge and the watercourse, for the 10km from its origins on the slopes below Gragareth to the Greta, is the "Mill Race or Water Cut". This indicates the considerable efforts that were made to control the

flow of water in order to power mills. In this case there were several mills on the route of the millrace. Today the watercourse looks entirely natural below Masongill Fell Lane. Perhaps it was only the section to harness Gragareth's water that was man-made.

The beck, if we may call it that, runs past Masongill Hall, on the east of the village of Masongill. This is a quiet cul-de-sac, with most residences being conversions of traditional long-houses. Masongill is responsible for another of Loyne's tenuous links with celebrity: in 1883 the mother of Sir Arthur Conan Doyle (who was then 27) moved here. Literary sleuths, who earnestly seek the inspiration for the creator of Sherlock Holmes, know that he regularly visited his mother and was sufficiently part of the region to be married in 1885 at St Oswald's Church in Thornton-in-Lonsdale, where a certificate in the porch names the bride as Louisa Hawkins. Some of them are convinced that Masongill House is Baskerville Hall, minus the hound. Others are intrigued that a Randall Sherlock, brother of the Rev. Sherlock, vicar of Ingleton and Bentham, was killed by lightning at Ingleton station in 1874. I can find no contemporary, local comments on this 'coincidence' after Sherlock Holmes made his appearance in *A Study in Scarlet* in 1887.

From Byber Mill the Water Cut seems not to follow its old line but supplements Threaber Beck, which joins Moor Gill from Westhouse near Low Threaber. Westhouse is a distributed hamlet, with Higher, Lower and Far Westhouse satellites. Its lodge, recently renovated, has been given a new datestone of 1676. The Wesleyan Chapel bears three dates, 1810, 1890 and 1912.

In 2002 over ten thousand native trees were planted in fields north of Far Westhouse to create Edith's Wood, managed by the Woodland Trust. It is open to the public, with benches from which to survey the growing trees, with Ingleborough beyond. As the wood is a memorial, we should remember to whom: Edith Bradshaw of Ingleton, a teacher at Casterton School.

The Greta reaches the three-arched Burton Bridge, with the sizable, ancient village of Burton-in-Lonsdale on its northern slopes. It appeared as Borctune in the Domesday Book and is the site of another motte and bailey castle. In 1174, the de Mowbrays were ordered to demolish the castle after an unsuccessful rebellion against the king. A later stone castle stood until about 1350, since when the site has been abandoned. The motte, at 10m high, is a prominent landmark, and remains of the bailey and defensive ditches can still be seen.

Also prominent is the nearby steeple – a rarity in Loyne – of the All Saints Church, completed in 1870. The steeple is surfaced with wooden slats. There is also a Methodist church, built in 1871. Like many Loyne communities, Burton-in-Lonsdale joined in the general questioning of the established church that began in the 17th and 18th centuries and, unlike nearby Bentham, it came to side more with the Methodists than with the Quakers. Maybe John Wesley's visit in 1764 played a part in this. So the churches are not particularly old and neither are the houses. Most of those of any age have been renovated, so that the neat Low Street, off the A687, presents a parade of Smithy House, The Old Ropery, and so on.

Motorists driving west through Burton-in-Lonsdale will see a blue sign saying "Richard Thornton's Church of England Primary School". When Richard Thornton died in 1865, having amassed a huge fortune of over £3m from his shipping business, he left £10,000 for a school for poor children in Burton-in-Lonsdale. He also left £1m to his nephew Thomas Thornton, who duly had the All Saints Church built. Behind the School is the Old Vicarage, which has a plaque in its porch that cannot be read without trespassing (I assume that it is to the poet **Laurence Binyon**).

Below Burton-in-Lonsdale, the south bank of the Greta is wooded, with two of the woods, Memorial Plantation and Greta Wood, having recently been acquired by the Woodland Trust. The former is typical of 19th century small plantations on land that cannot be farmed, with pine, beech and sycamore. Greta Wood is an older ash and oak woodland, designated an Ancient Semi-Natural Woodland. A riverside walk follows the Greta west for 1km – and then stops. Perhaps it is more for fishermen, who have given names to the various stations along Blair's Beat: Long Pool, Tommy's Run, The Dubs, and Black Hole.

The Greta runs west through secluded wooded gullies, crossing the county border and the Roman road. At Wrayton, the Greta passes under Greeta Bridge (as it calls itself), which has been washed away a few times but is now in more danger from the traffic on a difficult junction of the A683 and A687. Just before the Greta reaches the Lune, Cant Beck joins it from the north.

The Greta at Scaleber Woods

Laurence Binyon is a poet from whom, if not of whom, everybody will have heard. He wrote the words intoned at Remembrance Day events:

They shall grow not old, as we that are left grow old;
Age shall not weary them, nor the years condemn.
At the going down of the sun and in the morning
We will remember them.

The words are part of *For the Fallen*, which he wrote in September 1914.

However, Burton-in-Lonsdale's claim to Laurence Binyon is a little weak. He was born in Lancaster in 1869, moving a year later to Burton-in-Lonsdale, where his father had been appointed vicar. But in 1874 the family left for Chelmsford. Later, working at the British Museum, he became an authority on oriental art.

We might imagine that the brief time in Burton-in-Lonsdale made little impression upon him but for his own recollections of his first memories, which were of views of Ingleborough from the vicarage windows. Ingleborough inspired his poem *Inheritance*, which began "To a bare blue hill" and ended "Beautiful, dark and solitary, the first of England that spoke to me."

Cant Beck

Cant Beck is a surprisingly modest beck considering that it drains the broad parishes of Ireby, Cantsfield and Tunstall between Leck Beck and the Greta. It loses the momentum gained in flowing off Ireby Fell, as Ireby Beck, in a sluggish meander across gently undulating pastures to Tunstall.

Ireby Beck begins life uncertainly on the southern slopes below Gragareth, hovering around the county border and seeming to disappear into various potholes. The most impressive on the surface is Marble Steps Pot, which is enclosed within the only cluster of trees on Ireby Fell. It drops 130m. Along the line of the beck, 400m south, is Low Douk Cave and across the county border is Ireby Fell Cavern, a large depression with at least two holes into which water disappears and one hole, a pipe cemented into place (is planning permission needed for these mutilations?), into which potholers disappear.

I have been carefully vague in the preceding paragraph because I read that, contrary to superficial appearance on the map, the water falling into these holes does not join Ireby Beck at all. The water in Marble Steps resurges at Keld Head in Kingsdale; that of Ireby Fell Cavern at Leck Beck Head (probably). Of course,

flows may have differed in the past and may differ in the future. I leave this all to experts – as far as fell walkers are concerned, the potholes mentioned can be conveniently viewed together, above the head of Ireby Beck.

Once Ireby Beck is incontrovertibly established it heads for Ireby past Over Hall, a tower house dated 1687 and recently smartened up, with a cairn-like structure in the drive. As a rule of thumb, any village with a beck flowing through its centre is at ease with itself. It soothes and adds a timeless quality. In Ireby, the old-style red telephone box, the only public amenity, enhances this feeling. The houses, some of the 17th century, have been tastefully renovated and given countrified names – all very nice but perhaps without the character to detain a visitor.

The fields west of Ireby Hall Farm form pleasant and peaceful farming country, with fine views of Ingleborough and Leck Fell. The Roman road that we have been following cuts across here, but you would not notice it on the ground without being told. Cowdber Farm is so isolated that it feels it needs to put a "you are nearly there" sign on the track to it. But the quietness has its benefits: in the plantation near Churchfield House is the largest heronry in Loyne. Most farms here have been converted, partially or wholly, into homes for holidaymakers. Laithbutts has gone further: it provides a home for holidaymakers' homes. If you wish to put your caravan into storage, there are large barns for it at Laithbutts.

To the south, Cantsfield is a small community on the A687. The rather fine Cantsfield House, dating back to the 16th century or earlier, has an oddly appealing asymmetric frontage that was built by the Tatham family in the early 18th century.

A visitor's impression of a place can be unfair. I noticed a sign saying "This bridleway is over private land and is for the sole purpose of making a journey to Tunstall and Tunstall Church. It is not a dog loo. Please keep out unless you intend to complete the full journey." The map says that this is a *public* bridleway. It runs through land for cows, horses and sheep and at Abbotson's Farm I had just plodded through their contribution (much more substantial than a dog's) to the countryside aroma. And why must I complete the full journey and not turn back?

As it happens, I had no wish to return to Cantsfield. I pressed on to Tunstall's St John the Baptist Church, on the site of a chapel recorded in the Domesday Book.

It escaped the 19th century renovations that 'improved' most Loyne churches and as a result is mainly of the 15th century, with some parts thought to be pre-Norman. A Roman votive stone from the Over Burrow fort was built into an eastern window during a 1907 restoration. Despite all its merits the church is best known for the fact that some girls used to come here in 1824. The Brontë sisters ate their packed lunches here and it became the Brocklebridge Church of Charlotte's *Jane Eyre*.

Tunstall itself is 1km to the west, past the Old School House of 1753. The Post Office bears a date "circa 1640", which is refreshingly honest and a warning to treat other dates (of which there are several in Tunstall) with some suspicion. Especially, perhaps, Marmaduke House, with a plaque "Sir Marmaduke Tunstall 1506-57", which I take to be the date of Sir Marmaduke, not the house. As this indicates, we are nearing the historic Tunstall family home, Thurland Castle, by which Cant Beck flows. Thurland Castle is open to the public only in the sense that if you have half a million or so to spare you can buy a flat and live in it – which is a shame for Loyne is short of castles with pedigree.

Sir Thomas Tunstall, knighted at Agincourt, was granted a royal licence to fortify the site in 1402. The most famous of the Tunstalls was Sir Brian, who was

The Top 10 pubs in Loyne

On their ambience and ability to provide sustenance after a walk:
1. Lunesdale Arms, Tunstall
2. Cross Keys Inn, Tebay
3. Golden Ball, Lancaster
4. Game Cock, Austwick
5. Redwell Inn, Gressingham/Arkholme
6. Barbon Inn, Barbon
7. Marton Arms, Thornton-in-Lonsdale
8. Sun Inn, Dent
9. Stork, Conder Green
10. The Head, Middleton

slain at the Battle of Flodden Field in 1513 – the 'stainless knight' described in Scott's *Marmion*: "Tunstall lies dead upon the field, His life-blood stains the spotless shield".

The Tunstalls sold the castle in 1605 to the Girlingtons and they were the owners when it was razed to the ground during the Civil War. It was restored in the old style in 1809 and rebuilt again in the 1880s after a fire. It has, no doubt, been tastefully renovated for the present tenants. The castle can now only be glimpsed from afar through trees. It consists of a circuit of walls and towers, enclosed in a moat, with a drawbridge into a courtyard but with no keep.

The estate agents try to give the castle some prestige by asserting that "in 1809 the architect James Wyatt, who was working on Windsor Castle at the time, was commissioned to restore the castle." James Wyatt (1746-1813) was the principal architect of the day and was notorious for taking on more commissions than he could manage. His nephew Jeffry Wyatt (1766-1840), later Wyattville, was probably more involved with Thurland

Left: St John the Baptist Church, Tunstall.

The Greta joins the Lune

Castle and it was he who later (1824 to 1836) carried out a major renovation of Windsor Castle. Thurland Castle does not feature highly in either architect's portfolio.

A short distance after Cant Beck has joined, the Greta reaches the Lune, which it enters in a straightened westerly channel, as old maps show the Greta entering the Lune in a long curve to the south of its present course. Then, unnoticed (almost), Newton Beck sidles into the Lune from the west.

Newton Beck

Like most becks on the west bank of the Lune, Newton Beck begins in desultory fashion among the low, rolling hills and never really gets going. It runs alongside the Lune for 5km from High Biggins, just south of Kirkby Lonsdale. At High Biggins there are three halls of strikingly different architecture: Biggins Hall, a white Georgian mansion; Biggins Home Farm, a black-and-white, seemingly half-timbered house with a red-tiled roof; Sellet Hall, a more vernacular stone building. In 2006 the farm was put up for sale in six lots. Sellet Hall is the home of a forestry management company. Loyne has no stately mansions like, say, Chatsworth House, but it has many halls for the landed gentry of the Middle Ages and later. The story of these halls, and the attempts, of mixed success, to find them a role in the 21st century, would make a fascinating contribution to the social history of the region.

Sellet Hall Beck and Pinfold Beck converge in the village of Whittington, near an even more impressive

hall, Whittington Hall. It was designed in 1831 for the Lancaster MP, Thomas Greene, by George Webster, four of whose halls we have already met: Ingmire, Rigmaden, Whelprigg and Underley. It is similarly in the Elizabethan revival style, in this case with medieval features, such as a peel tower. The best view of Whittington Hall is to be had on the path north from Outfield, where a walk is in silence apart from the screech of disturbed pheasants. The hall is seen, from a distance admittedly, with the Howgills and Barbon Fell behind.

East of the Hall is St Michael's Church, which was probably founded as the chapel within the bailey of a motte and bailey castle. The tower, of 1600 or so, is the oldest part of the present church, which was rebuilt in 1875. In the graveyard is a headstone that reads "In memory of Edward Baines of Whittington who died of Asiatic cholera on board the ship Brutus midway to America and was buried at sea June 3rd 1832". Historians of Lancashire will be familiar with Baines's Gazetteer, that is, *The History, Directory and Gazetteer of the County Palatine of Lancaster*, written by Edward Baines in 1824 – which contains details of Whittington's illustrious history. They are, however, not the same Edward Baines and, as far as I can determine, were unrelated.

According to Baines (of the Gazetteer), before the Norman Conquest, Tostig, Earl of Northumbria and brother of Harold II, owned six carucates (over 2 sq km) in Whittington, which was regarded as the capital of the region between Sedbergh, Ingleton and Gressingham. Tostig owned a further 20 sq km within this region. After

Tostig's death at the Battle of Stamford Bridge, the estate was broken up and by 1090 Whittington had passed into the hands of Roger of Poitou, who eventually owned all of what was to become Lancashire. At Baines's time, Whittington was one of five parishes in the deanery of Lonsdale (the others being Claughton, Melling, Tatham and Tunstall).

Some of this heritage may be appreciated by a stroll around the village, where several houses bear 17th century dates. The Manor House and T'Owd Rose Tree, both 1658, share the prize for oldest house (subject to appeal). Croft House in Main Street was the birthplace in 1783 of William Sturgeon. As with other Loyne notables, the response is probably: Who? Well, in 1802 he escaped from working as a shoemaker's apprentice in Whittington to join the army and there taught himself enough science to be able to build the first practical electromagnet in 1825 and to invent the galvanometer.

The becks merge to form Newton Beck beyond Newton, which, like Whittington, is old enough to be in the Domesday Book. The beck eventually makes it way past the flood embankment to join the Lune near Higher Broomfield. The finger of land beyond the footbridge over Newton Beck is not publicly accessible and is therefore a haven for birds, such as snipe.

The Lune from Newton Beck ...

The Lune passes under the bridge for the Wennington-Carnforth railway line. To be precise, it passes through the second of the six arches, which, although the largest, seems not large enough for the Lune to be channelled through. Is there an explanation?

There are, 500m east, a further sixteen arches. The 1847 OS map shows the Lune flowing there, with the present course of the Lune, by Arkholme's Chapel Hill, then being a backwater marked as "old Lune", indicating that before 1847 the Lune had followed its present path. Moreover, there is a second "old Lune" marked, near Melling to the east, indicating a third Lune channel. In short, the Lune has changed course frequently within relatively recent times. It is thought that when the bridge was built in 1867 the embankment between the two sets of arches was on an island in the Lune. Today the Melling Viaduct, which would form the longest bridge across the Lune if only the Lune were still to run under it, stands over ponds in green fields.

The railway line was built to link Furness Railway's eastern station at Carnforth with Midland Railway's 'little North Western' line from Leeds to Lancaster, and hence to link the growing port of Barrow with the industries of Yorkshire. When the Wennington-Lancaster line closed in 1966, the Wennington-Carnforth line became part of the Leeds-Lancaster route.

There were stations at both Arkholme and Melling but they were closed in 1960. There is no footpath on the railway line, the ferry across the Lune ended service in the 1940s, and the ford has fallen into disuse, leaving the two villages, only 1km apart, more separated now than ever.

By fortune or foresight, the road in Arkholme runs from the old ferry (from the Ferryman's Cottage, in fact) west for 1km to meet the Kirkby Lonsdale road at right angles and is therefore a peaceful cul-de-sac. In summer, colourful gardens face the road and there is a

The Melling Viaduct

The old Arkholme station

prettiness and cheeriness, due to the relative absence of traffic. The houses are strung out higgledy-piggledy, no two alike, some old (17th century), some new (21st century).

Most of the older houses have names indicating their previous lives, although I noticed none that refer to the industry for which Arkholme was best known, the making of baskets, from about 1700 to 1950. This activity was typical of many Loyne industries, being based on some local resource (here, osiers in the Lune floodplain), intended to meet local needs (of, for example, potato growers in Fylde), and passed on as a family trade, but then succumbing to competition from larger, more commercial ventures, especially after the advent of the railways.

On the other bank, its sister Melling lies mainly along the busy and narrow A683 and as a result its doors and windows are shut, its gardens are away from the road, and people do not linger by the noisy and dangerous traffic. The future of Melling Hall, an 18th century manor house, more recently a hotel and now a listed building, has been the subject of a planning debate that is an interesting example of the difficulties of conservation policies. The building is a key part of the Melling Conservation Area, and the Lancaster District policy is that no pub or hotel will be converted to residential use unless it can

be demonstrated to be no longer viable, even if, as in this case, it was originally a residence. No buyer could be found to sustain it as a hotel and, after some controversy, it is being converted into flats.

Arkholme and Melling are listed in the Domesday Book as Ergune and Mellinge, respectively. The parish boundary between them lies near Melling, where the Lune once flowed. Both Arkholme and Melling had their motte and bailey castles and in both cases a church has been built, as at Whittington, within the bailey. Arkholme's St John the Baptist Church is tucked below, almost into, the motte, which is 30m in diameter. Melling's St Wilfrid's is a larger church, with a long nave and square tower, and is a Biological Heritage Site because of the lichens on its gravestones. The Melling motte is now a feature in the garden of the Old Vicarage.

The Arkholme motte is close to the Lune Valley Ramble, which the Lune has accompanied from Kirkby Lonsdale, and below Arkholme the Ramble shares footsteps with the Lunesdale Walk, a name that is even more of an exaggeration than the Ramble since its 59km cover only 6km of the Lune. The walk traces an elaborate figure of eight route from Carnforth to Roeburndale.

The Lune runs by flat, green pastures on the east, where the old Lune has created many ditches and where enormous logs have been left stranded by floods. Bank erosion continues apace, and the Lune shifts between various channels, running by pebble beaches and new islands. To the west, there are gentle hills, on the horizon of which can be seen the turrets of Storrs Hall, which was rebuilt in 1850, and from which minor tributaries such as Bains Beck and Thrush Gill enter the Lune. The hills are not high, reaching only 142m at Cragg Lot, but nevertheless there is an application to put five 125m wind turbines on them. This proposal is ominous for the Lune valley, for if turbines are built in such a location then no field and no view within the Lune valley is safe.

The Lune reaches Loyn Bridge, which was built in 1684 or before – it is known that an earlier bridge was reported as dangerous in 1591. The bridge is built of sandstone blocks and has three arches, the outer ones of 16m and the inner of 19m. The piers have pointed cutwaters that provide alcoves on the 4m-wide carriageway. The bridge provides the only vehicular crossing of the Lune for about 8km in either direction. It is clearly sturdy enough to withstand Lune floods but no doubt its builders knew that when the Lune is high it takes a short cut across the fields to the west, as damage to the hedgerows shows.

Above Loyn Bridge to the east is Castle Stede, the remains of a motte and bailey castle (our eighth, if you are counting). When Castle Stede was abandoned as a castle, later buildings did not engulf it, so the original structures are well preserved. We can see the 15m-high motte and the bailey, with its defensive ramparts and ditch, and appreciate the strategic position overlooking the Lune valley. Strictly, it is off the public footpath but it is tempting to wander over the causeway (probably where the original entrance was) into the bailey and transport oneself back to the 12th century by imagining the bustle of activity – kitchens, stables, maybe a chapel – below the lord's hall on the motte.

At Loyn Bridge we enter for the first time the **Forest of Bowland** Area of Outstanding Natural Beauty, although we are still some distance from typical Bowland country. The ambivalent regard for the Bowland region

Erosion of the Lune bank near Arkholme

is indicated by the inclusion of "Bowland and the Lune Valley" (where they mean the lower Lune valley) as one of twelve projects within the Culture 2000 European Pathways to Cultural Landscapes programme, funded by the European Union. This sounds like an honour indeed – until we read that the project is "dedicated to 'marginal'

Loyn Bridge

landscapes, border regions and landscapes whose image is one of poverty and historical insignificance".

The Lune passes below Priory Farm, which is on the site of an old Premonstratensian priory, that is, one belonging to the order of 'White Canons' (from the colour of their habit) founded at Prémontré in France. Shortly after, the small Gressingham Beck enters from the west. This beck gathers the waters from the rolling green hinterland beyond the western ridge and, with High Dam Beck (which runs from the 'high dam' that used to power the mill), channels them through the ancient village of Gressingham.

Gressingham is another of Earl Tostig's holdings that was listed in the Domesday Book (as Ghersinctune) but nothing much has happened here since. The small triangle of homesteads and the line of dwellings by the beck are quietly attractive, as is the church with its 12th century arch in the doorway, but the village does little to draw attention to itself. As far as I am aware, it does not even claim an association with the one thing that makes its name famous, the Gressingham Duck, which features on the best menus. However, assiduous research (I asked the producers of the duck) revealed that "the chap who first bred the duck is called Peter Dodd, [who] lived in the village of Gressingham in Lancashire … the breeding stock [was moved to] Suffolk in 1990".

Next, the River Wenning joins the Lune from the east.

The **Forest of Bowland** was designated an Area of Outstanding Natural Beauty (AONB) in 1964 and its 800 sq km make it the 11th largest of the 41 AONBs in England and Wales. An AONB designation recognises a region's scenic qualities and implies a commitment to conserve its flora, fauna and landscape features, consistent with the needs of residents. Only the northern third of Bowland lies within Loyne. The remainder, reached by the two bleak roads to Slaidburn or through the Trough of Bowland, drains to the Wyre or Ribble.

The Forest of Bowland is a forest in the historical sense of an unenclosed, outlying region of little use except for hunting. Bowland was originally a Royal Forest, although no sovereign is known to have hunted here. However, Henry VI was himself hunted, when in 1465, during the Wars of the Roses, he hid in Bolton-by-Bowland. Traditional hunting has long gone, to be replaced by grouse shooting, mainly on land owned by England's richest aristocrat, the Duke of Westminster. Until the Countryside and Rights of Way Act took effect in 2004 (launched in Bowland), this was England's largest area without public access.

Lower Bowland consists of rolling green pastures with picturesque grey stone buildings. The upland areas are of millstone grit, with thin layers of sandstone and shale on the slopes, giving rise to open and wild upland areas of blanket bog and heather moorland that are incised by fast becks to form steep cloughs and wooded valleys. The wilderness areas of Bowland remain largely unspoilt by exploitation, with the works of the water authorities and the Forestry Commission lying mainly outside Loyne. The higher fells have been maintained in a relatively natural state for the sheep and grouse and, since 2004, humans.

The Norman doorway of Gressingham church

CHAPTER 10:
The Wenning Headwaters

The River Wenning ...

The Wenning has the most dramatic birth of all the Lune's tributaries. It springs forth at Swine Tail just below Ingleborough's plateau, gathers a few more becks to form Fell Beck, and then plunges headlong into the awesome chasm of Gaping Gill, Britain's most famous pothole.

The waters fall 111m, making it Britain's largest unbroken waterfall, according to the Guinness Book of Records. The hole was first descended (intentionally) in 1895 by the French caver, Edouard Martel. He mapped the main chamber, which is 130m long and 30m high and wide – large enough, it is said, for York Minster to be fitted in (I'd like to see them try).

You can judge for yourself by taking the winch that local potholing clubs fit up at bank holiday weekends. It is often said that it is free to go down ... but there's a charge to come up. In fact, they insist that you pay at the top, in case you should disappear forever underground. No, I must be fair: they are most solicitous about our well-being and careful to count us all down and count us all up again.

It is certainly an unforgettable experience, as you sink slowly in the cage below the diminishing skylight, past the green, then grey, then black, walls of the cavern, in the shower of Fell Beck. On the floor of the cavern, the water largely percolates away through the boulders and it is possible to scramble around searching into various crannies of the chamber. After a while, non-troglodytes would like to escape – and then a problem becomes clear: what goes down must come up. On the surface, a numbered-ticket queuing system enables you to lounge around, having a picnic, smiling as people return drenched and blinking, as you wait your turn. Below, there isn't: you must stand in line. And if you waited 45 minutes in the sun on top, you will have to wait 45 minutes in the cold, dark Fell Beck shower below (or even longer, as potholers tend to enter the cavern from elsewhere and lazily take a ride out).

I see that there is now a leaflet advertising these bank holiday treats and that the winch now operates for a week. It'll be a permanent tourist attraction soon, with a snack bar and souvenir shop nearby, and umbrellas for the queue below.

The geology of Gaping Gill is as we have come to expect. Water streams off the gritstone on the eastern slopes of Ingleborough and then disappears into the limestone layer. Faulting has occurred at Gaping Gill to enable such a large chasm to form. The Fell Beck water then makes its way underground over the impermeable slate and eventually emerges in Clapdale at the cave spring of Beck Head to become Clapham Beck.

Potholers have found a difficult and dangerous way through from Gaping Gill to Beck Head but over ground we must make our way through the more appealing Trow Gill. This is a dry gorge, with boulders heaped at the top, between steep limestone cliffs. There are two theories about the formation of Trow Gill: either the roof

Previous page: Austwick and Norber.
Below: Gaping Gill.

of an underground cavern collapsed or it was caused by a flood of meltwater after the Ice Age.

Below Trow Gill we enter Clapdale. On its eastern side runs Long Lane, which is part of an ancient track from Ribblesdale. From it, Thwaite Lane, an equally ancient track that used to lead to Fountains Abbey, heads east. As Long Lane approaches Clapham it passes under two dank tunnels, built to protect the privacy of Ingleborough Hall.

On the west bank of Clapdale is Clapdale Drive, which provides the most gentle of Dales walks. The **Farrer family** created the drive for the carriages of guests at their Ingleborough Hall in Clapham and, later, tourists arriving by train at Clapham Station. Below a gate, the drive becomes an artificially delightful environment of trees, shrubs and lake, forming the Reginald Farrer Nature Trail. As was the fashion, a grotto was added to provide a romantic character that was presumably perceived to be lacking. You may test your skill at identifying trees and shrubs by ticking off ash, beech, box, chestnut, European silver fir, larch, laurel, holly, holm oak, Norway spruce, red oak, rhododendron, Sitka spruce, Scots pine, and no doubt several others. Do not, however, stray from the trail in your search, as there are many warnings of "hidden dangers", which I think mean that you will be mistaken for a pheasant and shot.

By the cross in Clapham there is a footpath sign informing walkers that it is 102m to the Brokken Bridge. Clapham tries hard to be perfect. The natural valley of Clapham Beck has been transformed with alien species to provide a parkland stroll; the old village of Clapham was redesigned by the Farrer family; St James Church, which lists vicars back to 1160, was rebuilt in 1814 by the Farrers; and now Clapham Beck runs from the waterfall outlet of the lake through the village under several unreasonably pretty bridges. Clapham's tourist leaflet lists the various attractions and services but does not mention the **Cave Rescue Organisation**, presumably not wishing to alarm tourists.

Two kilometres south of Clapham, a tributary from the east joins Clapham Beck, which now becomes called the River Wenning. The tributary has been formed 1km east by the merger of Austwick Beck (from the north), Fen Beck (from the east) and Kettles Beck (from the south).

The Farrer family are largely responsible for the attractiveness that we see today in Clapham.

Oliver Farrer, a rich lawyer, bought the estate in the early 19th century. His two nephews, James and Oliver, re-planned the estate, including the building of the tunnels and the replacement of much of the old village. They created the drive and in 1837 opened Ingleborough Cave, the first show cave in the region. It is apparent that Clapham Beck used to flow through Ingleborough Cave. Today, visitors may explore the floodlit passages for 1km underground to see the 300m-year-old stalagmites and stalactites.

Reginald Farrer (1880-1920) was a botanist and plant collector, particularly of exotic species from Asia, many of which he introduced to Europe and especially to the Clapham estate. He was also a painter and novelist but he is most remembered for his books, such as *The Garden of Asia*, *Alpines and Bog Plants*, and *My Rock Garden*. His name has been given to many of the plants he introduced, such as gentiana farreri. He died in the mountains of Burma, where, as the Buddhist he had become, he was buried.

The Farrer family still own much of the estate around the parish of Clapham.

The falls from the lake at Clapham

The **Cave Rescue Organisation** (CRO) is a charity run by volunteers to provide a rescue service around the Three Peaks region. The emphasis on cave rescue in the title reflects its history and the fact that these incidents are the most demanding in terms of time, expertise and equipment but nowadays over 80% of CRO's call-outs are to non-caving incidents.

In the six years 2000-2006 (excluding the foot-and-mouth year of 2001) the CRO was called out to 295 incidents, which is nearly one a week. Although some incidents involved more than one person (for example, when a group got lost in mist), these can be classified as: walker (128), caver (57), animal (51), climber (12), cyclist (11), runner (9), and other (27). The 'other' includes a motley collection of incidents, involving a foolhardy diver off Thornton Force, someone who fell out of a tree, the rescue of cars stuck in mud on the Occupation Road, the investigation of abandoned canoes, and so on.

To assess the severity of incidents we can further classify them as: fatal/involving injury/becoming lost, exhausted or trapped. The caving incidents are 4/18/35, although this 4 includes an elderly man who collapsed and died in Ingleborough Cave. Climbing incidents (1/10/1) are usually serious. Although injuries are usually minor, walking incidents (10/64/54) seem worst in terms of fatalities. The 10 fatalities include 4 heart attacks, 2 drownings in a flood, 2 falls over a rock face, and 2 unspecified. (Don't have nightmares: these incidents are still rare.)

Austwick Beck

At the head of Crummackdale a sizable beck emerges from a couple of gashes in the fell-side. This is called Austwick Beck Head but we are alert to this situation now. The beck emerges after percolating through the limestone fells above it and reaching the impermeable lower layer at this level. The OS map shows becks flowing off Simon Fell in this direction only to disappear into potholes such as Juniper Gulf. Tests show that this water emerges several days later at Austwick Beck Head.

Austwick Beck Head is in an amphitheatre surrounded by limestone scars. Its sheltered setting and supply of fresh water no doubt encouraged the medieval or earlier settlements, traces of which in the form of field outlines can still be seen. Documents of the 13th century show that farming was at that time active in Crummackdale. It is entirely livestock farming now but this has only been so since the essentials of life (bread and beer) could be transported from elsewhere. There was arable farming in Crummackdale until the 19th century.

Opposite Crummack farm on Studrigg Scar is a clear geological unconformity, with Silurian slates at 60 degrees below horizontal beds of limestone. The cliffs

Studrigg Scar

on the eastern edge of Crummackdale rim the extensive limestone plateau of Moughton, from which there are splendid views of Pen-y-Ghent. The flora of Moughton is surprising, for there are shrubs of juniper and heather. The juniper is a rare remnant of the woodlands that covered the region thousands of years ago. Heather does not grow on soil derived from limestone but somehow here sufficient soil has become raised high enough not to receive the alkaline water draining from the limestone. The heather has apparently attracted enough grouse to encourage the construction of shooting butts, an unusual feature on limestone terraces.

Before exploring Moughton, ensure that you are fully familiar with a way off because it is surrounded by quarries, steep cliffs and high walls. In the north the footpath that runs from Crummackdale past Moughton Scars is safe. In the south a high stile can be seen on the horizon from the path that leads north from Wharfe. However, it is in a state of disrepair, so it may be wise to check before relying on it to get off Moughton.

Wharfe is a community of a dozen or so houses, the owners of which have agreed not to waste money on surfaced roads or exterior paint. So the cottages lie along narrow, stony tracks and are of grey stone that seems at one with the cliffs behind.

Across the valley from Wharfe lie the famous Norber erratics. These are so well known that few people today will reach these fields completely unprepared for the sight of dark boulders scattered incongruously on white limestone but the number and size of the boulders will surely astonish anyone. Their presence here must have been a great mystery, until it was all explained to us.

As is now described in many textbooks, Ice Age glaciers transported the boulders here from the Silurian slate that underlies Austwick Beck Head and outcrops in Crummackdale. The highest boulders now lie at about 340m. Austwick Beck Head is at 280m. The immense forces at work during the Ice Age are indicated by the fact that these huge boulders were lifted not just along but also up the valley.

Opposite: Ingleborough from Moughton.
Below: Moughton.

Above: Robin Proctor's Scar and Norber. Opposite: a Norber erratic.

When the ice melted, the Silurian slate boulders were left above the younger Carboniferous limestone rocks. As we know, the latter is eroded by rainwater but here the limestone under the boulders has been protected and, as a result, many boulders are now perched on pedestals above the general level. The height of the pedestals (about 50cm) is a measure of the erosion since the Ice Age.

Below the erratics are Nappa Scars, with another example of unconformity, and the cliff-face of Robin Proctor's Scar, a name that demands an explanation. There are several but they have in common the legend that one Robin Proctor rode his horse over the precipice to their deaths – a small price to pay to become the only name in Loyne to be immortalised in full on Ordnance Survey maps.

These cliffs and those behind Wharfe, together with the various ridges and contortions in the fields of Crummackdale, tell us that this was a geologically active area long ago – long before the Norber erratics coincidentally added further geological interest. This is the line of the North Craven Fault that we met at Thornton Force above Ingleton. After the Silurian period the layers of sandstone were crumpled and subsequently eroded to leave steeply bedded, folded strata that are now exposed in places. After the Carboniferous period the area was raised above sea level with the greatest and most irregular movements along the Craven faults.

Austwick Beck passes the ancient village of Austwick, the old core of which is surrounded by modern houses, indicating that a legendary practice failed to achieve its purpose. According to tradition, the residents of Austwick used to pretend to be simpletons in order to discourage outsiders from moving in. Harry Speight's *Craven Highlands* (1895) gives several examples of Austwickian stupidity – but with no suggestion that this was feigned. Today, Austwick revels in its reputation as the 'Cuckoo Town'. It would do better to revel in the magnificent scenery with which it has been blessed.

There are man-made, as well as geological, features to be seen in the landscape. Across the beck from Austwick, Oxenber Wood is pockmarked with old quarries, and common rights still permit Austwick parishioners to gather stones there. Oxenber Wood and the adjacent Wharfe Wood are old wood pastures that are CRoW land. The dominant trees are ash and hazel, with some hawthorn and rowan, and, at the northern end, birch and holly. The ground flora includes various herbs such as wild thyme, salad burnet, dog's mercury and wood sorrel.

Also visible, especially in a low sun, to the west and east of Austwick are the stripes of ancient strip lynchets. These are terraces up to 10m wide that were created by Anglo-Saxons from the 7th century onwards as they ploughed along contours. These are the first lynchets we have met and indicate how far west the Anglo-Saxons colonised. Sometimes the characteristic stone walls of the Dales cross the lynchets, telling us that the former are younger. Originally, a farmer owned several strips of land but they were distributed about different fields in order to be fair to all. The need to improve efficiency led to the creation of individually owned enclosures, in a complex process that began informally in the 12th century and became enforced by parliamentary acts in the 18th century. The stone walls were built to delimit the enclosures.

Below Austwick, Austwick Beck passes the old and new Harden Bridge, a name that reminds us of Austwick's weaving industry that survived until the late 19th century, harden being a kind of coarse linen made from the hard parts of flax. By Harden Bridge is a campsite that uses buildings that until the 1980s formed an isolation hospital for people with infectious diseases.

The Top 10 dales in Loyne
1. Crummackdale
2. Dentdale
3. Kingsdale
4. Borrowdale
5. Roeburndale
6. Barbondale
7. Grisedale
8. Bretherdale
9. Littledale
10. Bowderdale

Walk 18: Crummackdale and the Norber Erratics

Map: OL2 (please read the general note about the walks in the Introduction).
Starting point: By Austwick Bridge (769683) or elsewhere in Austwick.

This walk takes in many of the visible geological features of Crummackdale and also provides fine views of limestone scenery.

Walk north through Austwick past a school to Town Head Lane on the left. 300m up the lane, before the last house on the right, take the footpath through its garden. Across three fields you meet up again with Crummack Lane, which you cross to head west for Nappa Scars. You can then stroll through the Norber erratics, heading for the stile in the northern corner (766703). From the stile make your way north 2km along the indistinct ridge of Thwaite, which provides a good view of Ingleborough, to the prominent cairn at Long Scar. From there take the clear path that runs to Sulber Gate, 1.5km northeast, with views of Pen-y-Ghent.

Follow the path south over Thieves Moss to the fine Beggar's Stile and then walk past ancient settlements and Crummack farm and, 1km on from the farm, turn left to the ford and clapper bridge (that is, a bridge using long slabs of local rock) over Austwick Beck at Wash Dub, where the sheep used to be cleansed. The unconformities on Studrigg Scar are visible from the track from Crummack farm but for a closer look detour briefly up the track north from Wash Dub.

From the bridge follow the track 1km southeast to Wharfe. Continue through Wharfe to the road and then after a few metres take the path right that leads over a footbridge and ford. Turn west, above the Wharfe Gill Sike waterfall, which deserves full marks for effort, producing a fine cascade from only a trickle, and then by Jop Ridding to Wood Lane and back to Austwick Bridge.

There is much to see on this walk and if you wish to take your time over it you might prefer to split the walk in two and do the western half one day and the eastern half (including Moughton) on another day.

Fen Beck

Fen Beck arises on the easternmost edges of Loyne, around Feizor and Lawkland. In this gently undulating land below limestone scars the watershed is uncertain. Some houses in Feizor used to be considered to be in the parishes of Clapham and Giggleswick (on the Ribble) in alternate years. Feizor itself is an out-of-the-way hamlet, nestled neatly under the cliffs of Pot Scar, a favourite with climbers. Southwest of Feizor, below limestone scars, is the Yorkshire Dales Falconry and Wildlife Conservation Centre, established in 1991 to help preserve birds of prey.

The parish of Lawkland is even more of a backwater. The main route from York to Lancaster used to pass by Lawkland Hall but the parish now lies anonymously between the busy A65 and the less busy Leeds-Lancaster railway line. The oldest part of the Grade 1 listed Lawkland Hall is 16th century, and much folklore surrounds the hall's peel tower and priest hole. From the 16th century until 1914 the renowned Ingleby family of Ripley, Yorkshire owned the hall. The first Ingleby described as 'of Lawkland Hall' was John, who died in 1648.

Somehow it seems appropriate that the central feature of Lawkland is the extensive peat land of Austwick and Lawkland Mosses, a Site of Special Scientific Interest. This now rare form of habitat was once much more common, as indicated by the many place names with "moss" in them. Lowland bogs are peat lands that have developed over thousands of years under waterlogged conditions. Over time, the surface of the peat, formed by plant debris, is raised above the groundwater level, resulting in a 'raised mire'. Typically, they are gently domed, but here peat cutting has obscured this impression.

From a distance Austwick Moss is seen as an island of ancient trees and scrub surrounded by pastures. It is also an island of CRoW land, inaccessible by public footpath, which is just as well because it is difficult, wet, tussocky walking. The conditions support many bog mosses and, in drier parts, birch woodland and fenland. Various wading birds, such as lapwing, redshank, reed bunting and snipe, and rare insects, such as the pearl-bordered fritillary butterfly, find a home there. It's good to know it's there, for the benefit of the birds and insects, but, in truth, it's a damp, desolate place of little appeal to most of us.

Kettles Beck

Kettles Beck is the first of many becks that we will meet that flow north off the Bowland Fells and that, because they flow over millstone grit, slate and sandstone covered with glacial till, have a different character to the becks of the mainly limestone Yorkshire Dales. At first, the marked contrast between the dry whiteness of the Dales and the muddy darkness of Bowland rather depresses the spirits.

Bowland valleys tend to be deeply eroded, with fast-flowing becks tumbling through rocky channels over small waterfalls. Trees have largely been cleared although patches of ancient woodland remain in some steep-sided valleys and there are a few conifer plantations, such as Brow Side Plantation by Kettles Beck. The valleys are rural, with verdant, rolling fields for cattle and sheep. Population is sparse, being scattered in small villages and isolated farmsteads, the latter being evenly but thinly distributed, although many are no longer actively farming. The buildings are usually of local gritstone, adding to the sombre greyness, particularly in winter. The farms are situated by flowing water and there is often evidence (in the form of old millraces, weirs, and so on) that it has been harnessed to power mills. There are few hamlets above the main rivers of the Wenning and Hindburn, and the lanes are narrow and winding, with only two venturing across the dark, bleak watershed to Slaidburn.

The valley farmsteads are sheltered compared to the windy, open higher fells. The fells are of heather and grass, generally boggy and with few walls. The high fells will be discussed further when we reach the highest points of Bowland, but Kettles Beck itself arises at the not very high but impressively knobbly peaks of Bowland Knotts (430m) and Knotteranum (405m), on the Lancashire – North Yorkshire border. The ridge is one of the finest gritstone outcrops in Bowland, with great jumbles of huge rocks, enabling a good scramble for those venturing a brief walk from the road at the watershed.

Kettles Beck runs 6km south from the boggy ground of Austwick Common through farmland that has not inspired the locals in their farm names: there's a High, East, New and Low Kettlesbeck (although Israel Farm is more intriguing). It doesn't inspire me much either although walking down beside Kettles Beck one can look wistfully across to Ingleborough.

Knotteranum

A Kettlesbeck welcome for visitors: a stile on the public footpath near East Kettlesbeck, with eye-level barbed wire

The Wenning from Kettles Beck ...

The Wenning runs east, being first joined by Crook Beck, which runs from Newby Moor on the southern slopes of Ingleborough through Newby Cote and Newby and across the rough ground of Newby Moss. This extensive area of common land is now a Site of Special Scientific Interest, noted for its purple moor-grass, mosses and fens. There are also breeding birds such as curlew, lapwing, redshank and snipe and a population of the pearl-bordered fritillary butterfly that perhaps flutters between here and Lawkland Moss.

The green hillocks that rise to 200m running west from Clapham towards Bentham and Ingleton are fields of drumlins created by glacial ice sheets flowing off the hills of the Yorkshire Dales. The oval-shaped contours on the map indicate the east to west trend of the glaciers. The gentle slopes of the drumlins and their rich boulder clay soil provided good sites for settlement and farming from prehistoric times, which is shown in the increasing occurrence of the Old English -ham, -ber and -ton in place names. The grazed pastures are divided into irregular

---

Walk 19: Ingleborough and Gaping Gill

Map: OL2 (please read the general note about the walks in the Introduction).
Starting point: At Newby Cote (732705), where there is space for one or two cars; otherwise by the green in Newby (727701).

None of the four well-worn routes up Ingleborough (from Ingleton, Clapham, Horton and Chapel-le-Dale) provides a satisfactory loop walk. I prefer to walk from Newby Cote on a grassy path from which we saw the new millennium dawn.

Follow the track north, through the gate and by the wall to the open fell. Bear slightly left. After ten minutes or so Little Ingleborough comes into view. Pick up the broad green path up it. From Little Ingleborough the beaten track to Ingleborough is obvious.

After a tour of the summit plateau, take the clear path east (part of the Three Peaks route). Note the Fell Beck spring (the source of the Wenning) close by the path. After 1km cross a stile but after a further 1km don't cross a second stile - instead, follow the wall south at the foot of The Allotment. A path just above the limestone terrace runs 10m or so west of the wall.

A fence will be seen partially enclosing Juniper Cave. Juniper Gulf, into which falls water that becomes Austwick Beck, is just above it. There's a series of potholes, dangerous and difficult to find – don't bother, as they do not compare with what's ahead. Keep near the wall. Eventually, a wall comes to it at right angles, leaving a gap. Don't go through the gap but follow the wall right and then left. A stile will be seen just ahead. Cross it and continue due west, which brings you to the unmistakable chasm of Gaping Gill.

Take the path south (which leads to Clapham) and when a stile comes into view after about 150m bear half right. There are many vague paths here but basically keep west of the wall, between the shakeholes, until, after 2km, as the wall swings south, you see ahead the gap between the green pastures by which you gained access to the moor. Cut across the dry Cote Gill and thence to Newby Cote.

---

patterns by stone walls and hedgerows, reflecting their origins as pre-medieval fields rather than the later, more systematic, enclosures of the higher fells.

The now well-established Wenning passes under Clapham Viaduct, which, unlike earlier viaducts, has no aesthetic merit. The viaduct carries the Leeds-Lancaster railway line. The original plan was to build the Lowgill-Clapham line via Ingleton first but work on this was suspended and instead the branch to Lancaster, completed in 1850, became the main line, with the Lowgill line eventually completed in 1861. The line to Wennington runs down the Wenning valley, naturally without all the meanders of the river, which it crosses seven times in all.

Beyond the new Skew Bridge, Keasden Beck joins the Wenning.

Keasden Beck

Our journey has taken us to many hidden and unknown becks but compared to Keasden Beck they are all gaudily extrovert. Nobody seems ever to have written a good or bad word about Keasden Beck. There are no postcards of Keasdendale (in fact, I may have just invented 'Keasdendale'). In the 4km from Gregson's Hill to Turnerford Bridge there are no footpaths in the valley or across it. There is no road in the valley: all

the farmsteads are reached by private tracks from the Clapham to Bowland Knotts road.

However, now that all of Burn Moor above the pastures has been made CRoW land we can at least gain a long distance view into this secretive valley. Burn Moor is tough going: all heather, grass tussocks and bog. When it was restricted to grouse shooting Burn Moor was called the 'forbidden moor': now, 'forbidding' would be a better word. There is a good path on springy peat (in summer) along the ridge from Bowland Knotts to Great Harlow (486m) and over Thistle Hill, but elsewhere walking is a struggle. Should your eye catch upon Ravens Castle and Raven's Castle on the map, be warned that there are no castles, although there are ravens. And yet there is compensation up here. The silence is complete, apart from birds such as skylark, curlew and merlin, and the view of the Three Peaks is much better than from the road, from where Whernside is rather obscured by Ingleborough.

The most striking feature on an aerial photograph of Burn Moor is the large stripes of different shades of green. At first glance they look like the fairways of golf courses. They are in fact the result of burning practices and remind us that the fells are far from natural, despite their familiar appearance.

After the last Ice Age the hills became covered with broadleaved woodland, which was cleared from about

3000 BC. Peat then formed from decaying vegetation on the gentle slopes and hilltops, so creating blanket bog. We use words like 'bog', 'heath' and 'marsh' informally but scientists need precise definitions. For them, 'blanket bog' is peat deeper than 50cm (even if it is dry). Less deep peat is 'heath' if there is at least 25% cover of small shrub heather-like plants; otherwise it is 'marsh' or 'marshy grassland'. It all gets more complicated, as there are different types of bog, heath and marsh, depending on altitude, slope, hydrology, geology, and so on. Although the vast areas of Bowland's bogs and heaths may seem ample, they are actually rare in global terms and, because of the **threat to the Bowland Fells**, are priority habitats in the UK's Biodiversity Action Plan.

Keasden Beck gathers all the water that flows east and north from the Burn Moor watershed, which here

Above: Bowland Knotts.
Right: the 'Standard on Burn Moor' boundary stone,
*   marked on OS maps.*

forms the county border. Like all Bowland becks, it cuts through hard millstone grit, occasionally exposing layers of underlying sandstone and shale.

After a hidden run through the valley, Keasden Beck emerges at Turnerford by Keasden Moor. This insignificant-looking moor is a Site of Special Scientific Interest, for being, according to its citation, "the only known site for the marsh gentian *Gentiana pneumonanthe* in the Yorkshire Dales" – which is quite something considering that it is not even in the Yorkshire Dales. The small pond in the middle of the moor is surrounded by common marsh-bedstraw, sneezewort and lesser skullcap (the names, at least, are fun).

By the moor are St Matthew's Church and a telephone box, which together constitute the hub of the scattered village of Keasden. The church has a fine view across to Ingleborough but, like most of Keasden, makes little attempt to compete with the beauty of the Dales hills. The peat brown Keasden Beck runs past various farmsteads, some converted, some not. Clapham Wood Hall is a rather sad cottage on the site of a much grander hall that was demolished in the 19th century. Until 1800 it was the home of the Faraday family, from which came the eminent scientist Michael Faraday (1791-1867), although Keasden cannot claim him, as he was born in London after his father had moved away from Keasden in 1780.

The **threat to the Bowland Fells** takes various forms: draining, pollution, burning, over-grazing and the presence of humans.

Land drainage for agricultural purposes is so damaging to the ecology of bogs and heaths that very few new hill drains have been allowed recently. Existing drains remain a problem, as they lower the water table and lead to shrinkage of the peat and increased fire risk.

As blanket bogs receive all their nutrients from the atmosphere, they are very sensitive to air pollution. The pollution provides too much nutrient and the increased growth threatens more sensitive species.

Perhaps the most important factor is the practice of rotational strip burning, which has been carried on for centuries. First, it must been conceded that the practice is necessary if the hills are to be conserved in something like their present state, because if left to nature they would revert to scrub and woodland. The controlled burning of strips of heather every few years produces areas of heather of different age and hence height and structure.

In recent years, the intention has been to provide suitable habitats for grouse, although farmers may also burn heather to produce young shoots for sheep to graze and so spread the sheep more evenly over the fells. Either way, there are benefits to many other species that depend upon healthy moorland. Overall, the management of grouse moors has helped retain the habitat but today the numbers of grouse are in decline.

We must also acknowledge the threat to this sensitive environment from increased human access, encouraged by the Countryside and Rights of Way Act. We can now wander where we will but the plants do not appreciate walkers' boots and neither do nesting birds. If horse-riders, mountain-bikes, motorbikes and off-road vehicles were allowed, would the fells survive?

The work of the Keasden mole-catcher

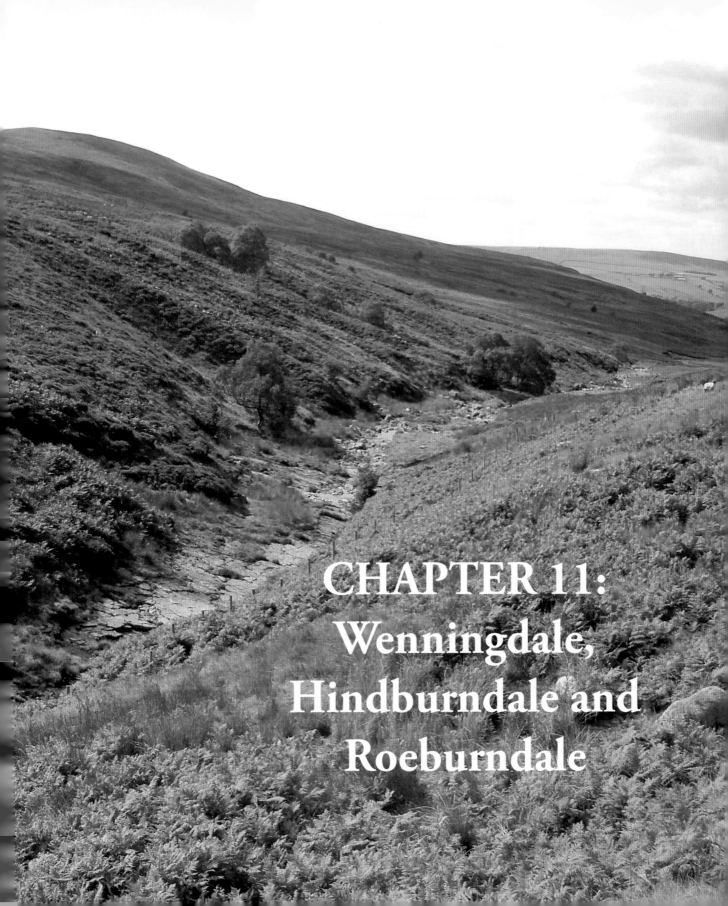

CHAPTER 11:
Wenningdale, Hindburndale and Roeburndale

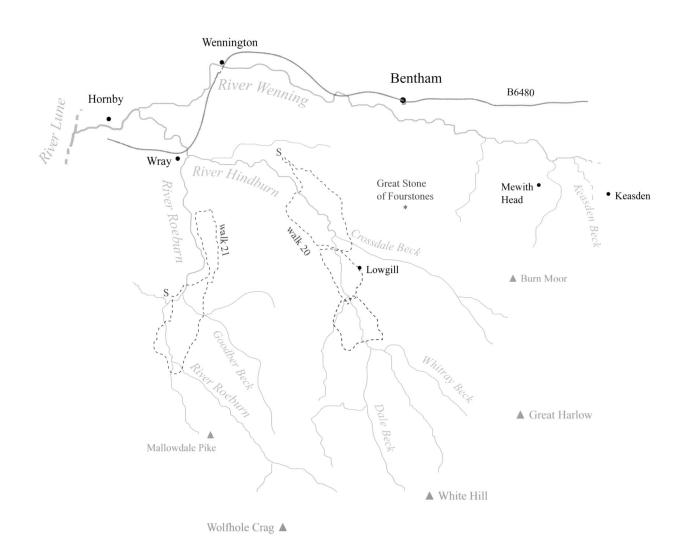

Scale: 1 cm to 1 km

0   5 kilometres

The Wenning from Keasden Beck ...

The Wenning runs by the Forest of Mewith, below the northern slopes of Burn Moor. Mewith is an area of undulating farmland, with scattered farmsteads, isolated woodlands, many paths and tracks, and no discernible pattern. It is crossed by many becks that flow off Burn Moor, where the county border runs northwest past the Queen of Fairies Chair and the Great Stone of Fourstones. The former is notable only for its name but the latter is a remarkable 4m-high monolith, from which there is a good view across to the Three Peaks.

The Wenning flows calmly between banks of alder, with birds such as common sandpiper, dipper and grey wagtail, although sadly there are few of the sea trout for which the river was once known, partly because so many alien rainbow trout have escaped from a trout farm. The river reaches High Bentham and, shortly after, Low Bentham, which is older but now smaller. High Bentham expanded north, south and east and Low Bentham expanded north, south, and west but recently they have taken tentative steps along the B6480 towards one another. I will consider this dumbbell shape to be Bentham.

Its leaflet for tourists begins with the sentence "Bentham is not a tourist centre", which must be welcome news for those staying at the large caravan park. Bentham was once more positive, for it had pioneered the idea of a holiday camp, long before Butlin and Pontin. From 1908 to 1925 a tented village was set up on the banks of the Wenning for holidaymakers: single men on the north bank, everyone else on the south bank, with a suspension bridge in between.

Bentham considers itself a market town and shopping centre with an industrial heritage. It appeared as Benetain in the Domesday Book and was granted a market charter in 1306. High Bentham Mill, using a millrace from the Wenning near Bentham Bridge, was established in 1750, possibly on the site of an old corn mill. It later worked in tandem with Low Mill (built 1785), mainly spinning flax. By 1795 the mills were importing Baltic flax to make sailcloths. The owner in 1814, Hornby Roughsedge, bought Bentham House, which no longer exists, and the manorial rights to Ingleton.

It was Mr Roughsedge who had funded the ill-fated hospice on Ingleborough (mentioned on page 112). His benefaction was more gratefully received in Bentham, where he paid for St Margaret's Church (Margaret coincidentally being Mrs Roughsedge's name), built in 1837 on a hill overlooking the unstylish Bentham Bridge, which replaced one washed away in 1964.

The mills were bought in 1877 by Benson Ford to manufacture silk. The Ford family were Quakers and their enlightened views on the treatment of employees enhanced the significant Quaker influence upon the region. Quakerism had been strong since the 1650s, with the Calf Cop meetinghouse being established in 1718. The Quakers have generally had a disproportionate influence on Loyne's society and commerce, to which they directed their energy and enterprise as their religious views barred them from professional and political careers.

The mills once employed up to 800 people and were the dominant factor in village life until they closed in 1970. One derivative company, Angus Fire (now called Kiddes), based on an invention to weave tubes to make fire hoses, still operates but now on a site across the railway line, the original mill site having been converted for small businesses and residences.

Before the 19th century, Bentham was unusual in having no wealthy gentry to build large mansions.

Previous page: upper Roeburndale.
Below: Great Stone of Fourstones.

There are some rows of 17th century cottages and Collingwood Terrace has an intriguing conception. In 1726 the will of William Collingwood of York provided for "the maintenance and support of six old decayed housekeepers in [Bentham], men and women, six of each sex". I don't know why he was so grateful to the housekeepers of Bentham. According to its plaque, we owe the continued existence of the terrace to a Mrs Titterington, who provided funds in 1900 to restore the houses as bungalows.

To the west of Bentham, the Wenning is joined by Eskew Beck, which begins life as County Beck near the Great Stone of Fourstones. Eskew Beck is important for its exposures of Carboniferous rocks with rare fossils. The county border is along County Beck and Eskew Beck and then continues west along the Wenning. The greater importance of county borders in earlier times, when, for example, fugitives could escape the law by crossing them, is reflected in the history of Robert Hall, just to the south. It was built in the 16th century for the Cansfield family, who, as recusant Catholics, needed hiding places and escape routes.

To the southwest of Robert Hall is a moor that has miraculously escaped the notice of man until recently, for it has never been ploughed or drained. Consequently, this is a Site of Special Scientific Interest for being "the only extensive example of species-rich undrained and unimproved base-flushed neutral grassland in Lancashire", including several rare plant communities. To the non-specialist, it gives an idea of what would be the natural state of this drumlin scenery.

In contrast, to the north at Clintsfield the signs of human activity are evident, with the only significant remains of the local coal mining industry. The old engine house, which operated until about 1840 and was later converted to a dwelling, and its adjoining square chimney still stand, more or less, and traces of the ten or more coal pits marked on old maps are still visible.

Just to the west, four pipes cross above the railway line. This is the continuation of the Haweswater Aqueduct, which we saw crossing the Lune near Kirkby Lonsdale. The pipes go under the Wenning and then up and over the railway. The aqueduct is gravity-fed (that is, there are no pumps) but it is clearly not downhill all the way. It is a single 2m pipe along most of its length but is split into four smaller cast-iron pipes to cross rivers and valleys.

Shortly after, the Wenning reaches its eponymous village, Wennington, a triangle of houses around a green bisected by the B6480. Its appearance has been improved by the restoration of the old Foster's Arms Hotel, empty for many years. Wennington Hall, now a school, lies to the north. It was re-designed in a Tudor-Gothic style by Edward Paley in 1855. A notice at the gate informs us of its history, including the fact that a motto of the Morley family (who owned the hall from 1330 to 1678) is inscribed in the headmaster's study: "S'ils te mordent, mord les" – 'if they bite you, bite them', which I trust hasn't been adopted as the school motto.

Left: Clintsfield.
Right (top): Wennington Hall.
Right (bottom): the Wenning at Wennington.

At Wennington, the dismantled railway line to Lancaster and the still-existing line to Carnforth separate, with the Wenning continuing beside the former. It passes under the large Tatham Bridge, which can be barely seen from the road. It has five arches, including one for the railway, which it therefore does not pre-date. The line opened in 1849 and for the first six months ran from Lancaster only as far as a temporary Tatham Station, just beyond the bridge. The bridge provides access to the neat St James the Less Church, on a site where a church is thought to have existed since Saxon times.

East of Tatham Hall on a small hill by Tatham Park Wood are various mounds and ditches that look like the remains of old settlements, although they are not marked as such on maps. According to old maps, there were many coal pits (Moorhead Pits) to the east. The nearby Netherwood Hall is much too trim to retain its old name of Bottom.

Below Hornby Park Wood the River Hindburn joins the Wenning.

The River Hindburn

By the time it reaches Botton Bridge the River Hindburn is already a considerable size, having gathered up all the becks that drain Greenbank Fell, Botton Head Fell and Whitray Fell below the semi-circular ridge that runs to the ancient Cross of Greet (which is no longer a cross but a large boulder with a socket in which the cross once stood). This is a vast area of peat bogs and heather, turning to grass tussocks lower down. It is CRoW land but walking here is more of a challenge than a pleasure. In winter, there are only grouse for company. There are broad views of Pendle and the southern Bowland Fells and to the north Whernside looks particularly noble (Ingleborough always does). The alignment of the ridges – Ingleborough, Whernside, Gragareth, and Barbon – shows clearly that they all belong to Loyne.

There is a rough path from the Cross of Greet to the highest point of the ridge, White Hill (544m), but it has

St James the Less Church, Tatham

few visitors, most of whom are puzzled by the tower that stands near the trig point. It's about 4m high, with a notch in the top. It is in fact the middle of three towers in a line, the other two being 500m north and south. The other two cannot be seen when standing at the middle one but if you walk to them you will see the notch of the middle one back on the horizon.

If you have followed the narrative carefully, you may suspect an answer to the puzzle. I think they are sighting pillars used for surveying the Haweswater Aqueduct. If we extrapolate the line of the towers on an OS map then we find "air vents" marked on the exact line 3kms in both directions. The towers seem to mark the line of the aqueduct below our feet as we stand on White Hill. It is a surprising thought, in the bleak emptiness of White Hill, but the aqueduct must cross the Bowland Fells somewhere and it certainly doesn't go over them.

Other than the towers, there is no trace of this engineering feat on the ground but if we plod over to Round Hill on Botton Head Fell we may visit a much older engineering construction that is (just about) visible.

Above: looking towards the Three Peaks from White Hill.
Below: the tower on White Hill.

We have passed many Roman roads on our journey but have always had to take the expert's word for it. Here we might be able to convince ourselves that the slightly raised ridge that runs between Goodman Syke and Dale Beck is the line of a Roman road. It is actually more convincing to view from a distance, for example, from the footpath between Botton Bridge and Botton Head. This is the Roman road that we have tracked from Over Burrow past Low Bentham and that is now heading for Ribchester.

Once off the open fell we are among the lush green pastures of the several farmsteads in the upper Hindburn valley. Apart from the intrusive conifer plantation at Higher Thrushgill, the map looks unchanged from a century or two ago, and moreover most of the farmsteads are still farmsteads, unlike most dales we have visited, where many are derelict or converted into residences and holiday cottages. There is an appealing timelessness here, with the farms going about their business, nestled below the rough fell and with open views across to Ingleborough and the Lake District.

In contrast to nearby Keasdendale, the Hindburn valley is crossed by many footpaths, which, to judge from the curiosity of the sheep, are not often used. The Hindburn passes below the quiet village of Lowgill, a gathering of a score or so cottages on the line of the Roman road. There's also a primary school for about forty pupils, some of whom must travel far to get here and understandably so for the school is known for the quality of education provided. The only other public building seems to be the Wesleyan Chapel of 1866. To the north, above Mill Bridge, is the older and more impressive Church of the Good Shepherd, a fitting name for this rural area.

To the south of Lowgill, at Ivah Great Hill, a new woodland of native trees was created in 2003 by the community group Treesponsibility's nifty scheme of engaging local people in tree-planting, to help slow global warming. We, or at least those who planted trees, are welcome to visit to see the trees growing.

Three kilometres below Lowgill, the Hindburn passes under Furnessford Bridge, which is carved with

Feathermire in Lowgill

Walk 20: Middle Hindburndale and Lowgill

Map: OL41 (please read the general note about the walks in the Introduction).
Starting point: A large lay-by east of Ridges on the Wray to Low Bentham back road (633679).

Walks in the upper Hindburn do not compare with other high-level walks I've suggested: it is better to stroll through the farmsteads of the middle Hindburn around Lowgill.

This walk uses four bridges over the Hindburn to make a route of three loops. There is some walking on roads but they are generally quiet. Careful use of the OS map is needed, to locate about fifty stiles or gates.

Take the path that starts on the drive to Ridges and skirts around Riggs Farm next to it, continuing on the path south and then southeast (diverted through a wood) to the Furnessford Road. Over Furnessford Bridge take the path past the barn and up a fine old track through the wood to Birks Farm, dated 1667. The four large manholes seen here and by Riggs Farm mark the line of the Haweswater Aqueduct. Follow the road southeast past Park House and take the track to Lower Houses. Turn left and after 0.5km drop down east by a wooded gully to a footbridge over the Hindburn.

Head south across an open field to the barn seen ahead. Then walk up through the wood behind it and across the fields, heading for Lowgill School. Walk south through Lowgill to High Ivah (along the line of the Roman road), and drop down southwest across the field to Stairend Bridge. Continue on the road past Botton Mill. After 1km turn left through Lower Thrushgill, continuing east to walk across a field and down to a footbridge. Continue for 0.5km to join the bridleway through Swans (0.5km north) and back to Stairend Bridge.

Walk 100m to the road corner again and this time take the path north, by the Hindburn. Follow this path for 2km past a few derelict barns back to the wooded gully, and drop to the footbridge again. Over it, this time turn left through a wood and up to the road near Mill Bridge, 1km east. Turn left and cross the bridge and, after an optional detour to the Church of the Good Shepherd, continue on the road north for 2.5km to Spen Lodge. Beware of traffic as you contemplate the views of distant hills.

Beyond Spen Lodge take the footpath through Little Plantation if it is not too overgrown – otherwise continue on the road and turn left onto Furnessford Road. Take the path west below Trimble Hall to rejoin the path from Ridges.

Clearly, using only three, two or one of the bridges will shorten the walk. However, parking in the valley is not easy although there is space on the corner near the track to Swans (655640).

that name, so telling us that it is newer than 1847, since the OS map of that date calls it Furnaceford Bridge. Below the bridge there are no footpaths by the Hindburn, which is a pity as it runs prettily by steep cliffs over minor waterfalls. I hardly need to say what Mill Houses used to be but I ought to mention the nearby meadow on the footpath from Clear Beck Bridge. This meadow is too small to have been affected by modern agriculture and as a result is a Site of Special Scientific Interest for being "one of the best examples of species-rich meadow grassland in Lancashire". It is so rich, in fact, that over 130 species have been recorded.

Clear Beck joins the Hindburn after Hindburn Bridge, running from Clearbeck House, which has a garden with follies, sculptures, a lake, and views of Ingleborough. The house is one of about twenty studios on the Lunesdale Studio Trail, in which local artists open their studios each summer to enable visitors to see their work in paintings, textiles, prints, sculptures, mosaics, jewellery, ceramics, drawings and photography.

Below Wray Bridge, the River Hindburn and the River Roeburn come together, as nature intends.

The River Roeburn

We were once accosted by a friendly couple in Roeburndale who felt that they had discovered the best place in England and often journeyed over from Blackpool to savour it. They were pleased, not disappointed, to find others who shared their secret. The view from the brow of the road after passing Thornbush is enchanting: to the alpine-like green pastures down by the woods up to the conical peak of Mallowdale Pike and beyond, with the Three Peaks arrayed on the left. And Roeburndale encompasses both the ancient and the new, as we'll see.

The River Roeburn rises at the old Yorkshire-Lancashire county border below Wolfhole Crag (527m) and Salter Fell. This is open fell country, far from any road and therefore likely to be deserted. It was not always so, for Hornby Road (or the Old Salt Road) was once an important route and in its southern part coincides with the Roman road that came up Round Hill from Lowgill.

It is possible that the CRoW policy will give a new lease of life to Hornby Road. The track, which is unusable

Wolfhole Crag

by cars, provides an excellent walking surface, although distances are long and any loop off-track involves strenuous going. Walking north, the view that opens up at Alderstone Bank is remarkable, with a long-distance 180° horizon from Black Combe to Ingleborough. The track marked on OS maps as going to a shooting cabin on Mallowdale Fell now continues over the ridge to join the track from Tarnbrook Fell. It may therefore be used to reach the ridge path to Ward's Stone but there will be awkward bogs around Brown Syke after wet weather.

If you venture up here you will become aware of the screeching gulls that nest on Mallowdale Fell and Tarnbrook Fell. These are a relatively new phenomenon, first being reported in 1936. There are now over 25,000 pairs nesting annually, forming England's largest inland colony of lesser black-backed gulls. Thousands more are culled to avoid possible bacterial contamination of the Lancaster water supply.

Hornby Road is a recommended route for mountain bikers, who are (at the moment) not allowed on the increasing numbers of tracks on the Bowland Fells proper. It is also part of the 45km North Lancashire Bridleway, opened in 2004. This runs from Denny Beck, Halton via Roeburndale to Chipping. Let us hope that the few residents in these remote areas benefit from, rather than resent, these new activities.

On Mallowdale Pike there is a memorial cairn to one Anthony Mason-Hornby (1931-1994). The cairn gives no explanation for its presence here. The area was out of bounds to the public until the CRoW Act took effect in 2004. Very few walkers will take advantage of the opportunity to venture here but even so it is a regrettably growing practice for private grief to impose upon special places, without good reason.

At Mallowdale the Roeburn leaves the open fell to run through woods past Lower Salter to be joined by Bladder Stone Beck (what a charming name) and Goodber Beck, which runs in a deep ravine from the empty grasslands of Goodber Common. Even the most desolate areas have their uses. Here the large heath butterfly, one of only two English butterflies that are on the European list of threatened species, survives at what is now the most southerly point of its range. Hare's tail cotton grass, its main larval food plant, flourishes on the Common.

Above the narrow Roeburn valley, the rolling fields are scattered with old farmsteads, notable amongst which is Stauvin, which was the home of Harry Huddleston (1910-2005). He was the first Englishman to represent his country abroad at sheepdog trialling. Sheepdog triallers do not rank high on the nation's sporting pantheon but for a section of the Loyne community the magnificent name of Harry Huddleston was one to be revered. He competed into his eighties and when no longer able to walk operated from his car, which he positioned next to the pen gate to help guide the sheep. Nobody objected.

The Roeburn runs through 5km of Roeburndale Woods, one of the most extensive deciduous woodlands in Lancashire, which is perhaps not saying much as it

The Top 10 body-parts in Loyne

1. Bladder Stone Beck, Roeburndale
2. Bosom Wood, Cautley
3. Backside Beck, east Howgills
4. High Stephen's Head, near Ward's Stone
5. Fleshbeck, below Old Town
6. Rotten Bottom, Dentdale
7. Heartside Plantation, Middleton Fell
8. Hand Lake, north Howgills
9. Long Tongue, Cockerham Sands
10. Bone Hill, near Pilling

one of the least wooded counties of England. These woods still provide an enclave for the red squirrel. A permitted path in Outhwaite Wood enables us to see as we walk north the gradations of tree types, reflecting the changes of soil, from lime, birch, hazel and alder to ash, elm and oak.

Hornby Road with the head of Roeburndale to the right

In a clearing opposite Outhwaite Wood is the Middle Wood environmental centre. This was established in 1984 to "advance, research and provide education for the public benefit in those techniques of farming, forestry, wildlife and countryside management, building, energy utilisation and human lifestyle, which are in tune with the natural cycle and which do not upset the long term ecological balance." Quite foresighted, then, and today a range of ecological buildings for sustainable development can be seen. The study centre uses solar panels and a wood-burning stove for heat and is powered by wind power. The community yurt (a Mongolian circular tent) is the main meeting place. Overall, though, it seems a forlorn site, with usually only a few wisps of smoke at most to indicate any human occupation.

As the Roeburn nears the village of Wray it is joined by Hunt's Gill Beck, which runs past Smeer Hall. Here the last coal pit in the region closed in 1896. On the Roeburn's right bank is a line of cottages associated with the old Wray Mill. Like many mills we have passed, it dates back centuries and went through many incarnations (cotton, wool, bobbins, silk, and so on) in a valiant attempt to survive, before finally succumbing in the 20th century.

Just after the mill cottages, the Roeburn passes under Kitten Bridge, the first of three bridges in Wray, the others being Wray Bridge over the Roeburn and Meal Bank Bridge over the Hindburn. The first and last were washed away in the notorious flood of August 1967 and have since been replaced. Wray Bridge survived but perhaps it would have been better if it hadn't, because the logs and debris piled up against the bridge, causing the torrent to back up and demolish a number of cottages. Luckily, there were no casualties but 37 people were made homeless. The event is commemorated in a garden close by Wray Bridge.

Some of the cottages washed away used to be the homes of various Wray artisans, because from about 1700 to 1850 Wray was a veritable hive of industry. Apart from the mill and local mining and quarrying, Wray was known for the production of hats, nails, clogs and baskets. It is unclear why Wray in particular became an industrial centre but no doubt once it began to build a reputation it was enhanced by other workers being attracted to the area for employment. The industries were relatively short-lived and Wray has since relaxed into a quiet, commuting community.

A walk up the Main Street from Wray Bridge reveals some of this history. First impressions suggest that Wray is different from other Loyne villages. The grey, stone buildings and converted farms and cottages are familiar but they are set back from the road, with cobbled areas

---

Walk 21: Roeburndale

Map: OL41 (please read the general note about the walks in the Introduction).
Starting point: Just north of the cattle grid north of Barkin Bridge (601638).

This walk gives a tour of middle Roeburndale, with views up to the wilderness of upper Roeburndale. It first makes use of a new permitted path to and through Outhwaite Wood. This path is not marked on OS maps but there are clear signs to follow, the first being by a stile a few metres northwest of the cattle grid. The footpath sign is a symbol of a deer: I hope that encouraging us to look for them doesn't scare them away.

The path crosses two fields and then drops down (rather muddily) to cross a new footbridge to the east bank. There are good views at times of the Roeburn below. The path continues just outside the wood, which it eventually enters. It then joins a loop walk within Outhwaite Wood. Take the lower path of the loop (it isn't necessary to cross the swing bridge to the camping barn, but it's fun to do so (twice)). After 1km the path emerges below the wood and joins the public footpath that has crossed the footbridge from Middle Wood. Continue north and then east up the path into fields.

Follow the footpath until it nearly reaches the road and then turn right, following the path for 3km above Outhwaite farm, past Wray Wood Moor, and all the way to Harterbeck, where Goodber Beck forms an impressive waterfall. Cut southwest across fields for 1km to reach High Salter, where Hornby Road ceases to be a road.

Drop down behind High Salter, cross Mallowdale Bridge, and after Mallowdale farm cross a footbridge to enter Melling Wood. This path climbs up to give good views down into secluded Mallow Gill. At Haylot Farm take the paved road down to the Irish bridge across the Roeburn. Pass Lower Salter, with its tiny Methodist church, and return to Barkin Bridge.

The map shows other footpaths that may be used to shorten (or lengthen) the walk but avoid the one shown crossing Goodber Beck in Park House Wood: a safe crossing point is hard to find and anyway slippage has made the path unusable. A stile linking Bowskill Wood and CRoW land (at 611646) enables many variations on our route.

Gragareth, Whernside, Ingleborough and Pen-y-Ghent from Roeburndale,
not forgetting the clouds

in front. By Loyne standards, Wray is a new village, as it is not listed in the Domesday Book. It was designed, if that is not too bold a term, by the then Lord of Hornby in the 13th century for his farm workers. The farm buildings were set out on the wide street, with a village green at the north end.

All except one of the farms have been converted into residences but the original forms can still be discerned. Overall, if Main Street were without its multitude of parked cars then it would have a picturesque quality of bygone times. The green, however, no longer exists, as the B6480 was built across it. With the original road, now called The Gars, it has made an island of Wray House and a few other houses.

Despite its youth, Wray seems proud of its age: almost every house bears a datestone, usually of the 17th century, even one built in the 20th century. One of the first houses met on the walk up Main Street from Wray Bridge is that of Richard Pooley, or Captain Richard Pooley as he insisted on being called. He flourished in the Civil War and returned to the family home in Wray to bequeath £200 a year to establish a primary school in 1684. A plaque on the school wall confirms this; a second asserts that "Bryan Holme (1776-1856) founder of the Law Society was at school here" (there should be an "a" before "founder", as he did not do so alone). The school is, unusually, not a church school, possibly because it pre-dates local churches: Holy Trinity Church was built in 1840 and the Methodist Chapel in 1867.

Anyone interested in rural architecture will enjoy a stroll along Main Street. But not on May Bank Holidays, for then the village and the roads around are jammed for the Wray Fair, featuring the celebrated Scarecrow Festival. The festival is part of an ancient springtime ritual, passed down through generations of Wray residents, dating all the way back to … 1996. The idea was copied from a village in the Pyrenees in an attempt to promote the Wray Fair. It succeeded beyond anyone's hopes and now tens of thousands visit, mainly to see the scarecrows. Rather ironically, if that is your intention then it is better to avoid the fair itself, as the scarecrows adorn the village in the days before the fair, to the distraction of unsuspecting passing motorists. Those industrious workers of the 18th century, striving to make a bare living, would be bemused by the feverish activity of today's villagers, as they strive to out-scarecrow one another.

Beyond Wray Bridge the Roeburn joins the Hindburn, which continues uneventfully for 2km to join the Wenning.

The Wenning from the Hindburn

The Wenning swings south below Hornby Castle, a prominent landmark of the lower Lune valley. The Earl of Montbegon was granted the Hornby estate after the Norman Conquest and was no doubt based at Castle Stede at first. At some time the village was relocated, with a castle being built on the present site in the 13th century. By the early 16th century the manor was in the hands of Sir Edward Stanley, or Lord Monteagle as he became after bravery at Flodden. It was the 4th Lord Monteagle who received the warning letter about the Gunpowder Plot of 1605. Actually, the letter advised him to stay away from Parliament, which may suggest that the plotters considered him to be a sympathetic friend.

As a Royalist stronghold the castle was besieged during the Civil War but for some reason was not demolished after capture as it was supposed to be. In time, however, all of the castle except the central tower

fell into ruin and has been replaced. Despite appearances, the present structure is mainly of the second half of the 19th century, when it was remodelled in the Gothic style, complete with battlements. The castle can be viewed from Tatham or from the Lune valley with Ingleborough behind or, at closer quarters, from Hornby Bridge, with the lawns sweeping down from the castle.

The castle's structures are echoed in the octagonal tower of St Margaret's Church, built by the 1st Lord Monteagle. It is probably on the site of an older church, as it houses several ancient stones and crosses, one, the 'loaves and fishes' cross, probably being pre-Norman. Opposite St Margaret's is the Catholic Church of St Mary, built in 1820, with the presbytery nearby, where the noted historian **John Lingard** lived. By the

Right: Hornby Castle and the Wenning.

John Lingard (1771-1851) is a rarity in Loyne – someone who achieved eminence through activities within the region. The plaque at the presbytery reads "Home of Dr John Lingard, Catholic priest and historian, 1811-1851", which needs careful interpretation. The dates are those for which the presbytery was Dr Lingard's home, not those of Dr Lingard himself. The *Catholic Encyclopedia* says that he "retired to Hornby" in 1811 and refers to the "fruits of his leisure there". It is a little unclear, therefore, how active he was as a Catholic priest in Hornby.

The ambiguity in "Catholic priest and historian" is probably deliberate, for a key question is whether Dr Lingard was a Catholic historian or a historian. He wrote his eight-volume *The History of England* whilst living in Hornby, the last volume appearing in 1830. The history was later re-published in ten and then thirteen volumes. This monumental work is important because, firstly, it provided a comprehensive account of English history that has been respected ever since it was first published and, secondly, his methodology of not relying upon general opinion but of going back to primary sources helped to change the nature of historical research.

Inevitably, that general opinion did not always agree with Lingard's interpretations but he was always able to refer back to his sources. Nowadays, we would not expect the dispassionate objectivity that Lingard sought. It is hardly surprising that his most controversial sections concerned the Reformation, for he was, after all, a Catholic. Nor that he was virtually ignored by academia but revered by Catholics, so much so that it is thought that he was made cardinal in petto (that is, in secret, to be announced later) by Pope Leo XII.

presbytery is indubitably the oldest bus stop in England, with a datestone of 1629.

The two Grade I listed buildings (the castle and church) set standards that the rest of Hornby does well to live up to, which it does via a further 26 Grade II listed structures. The main street has a number of fine sandstone buildings and the institute has recently been refurbished at a cost of £1.3m. The quiet residential tone reflects the fact that Hornby, despite the market charter granted in 1292, never developed any significant industrial activity, unlike nearby Wray. In fact, its market town status had lapsed by the 19th century.

The Wennington-Lancaster railway line ran to the south of Hornby, enabling a short-lived livestock market. Nearby is an interesting building built in 1872 by the Lunesdale Poor Law Union as a workhouse for the poor of 22 parishes. As with many other buildings, it has been redeveloped for residential use.

As the Wenning approaches the Lune it runs in a much straighter line than in earlier times, with old river channels visible on the south bank. Looking back from the Lune, the Wenning points directly to its source on the eastern flanks of Ingleborough.

Hornby Castle and Ingleborough

CHAPTER 12:
The Lune Floodplain
and the
Top of Bowland

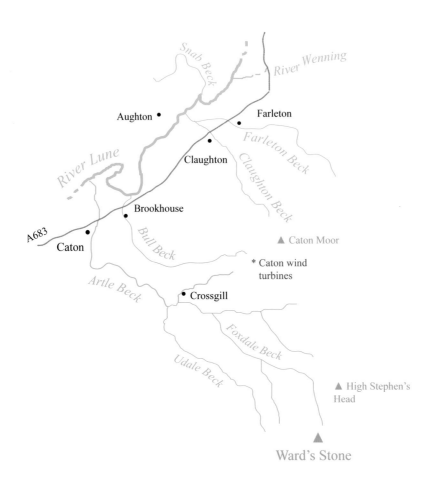

Scale: 1 cm to 1 km

0   5 kilometres

The Lune from the Wenning ...

The augmented Lune flows in the middle of its floodplain and there is naturally a sense of remoteness, with wide views back to Hornby and across to Claughton Moor. Birds of the river congregate here and noisily object to being disturbed. There are footpaths on both banks of the river, although walkers are rare in the middle section. On the east bank, a concessionary path from Hornby eventually joins the public footpath below Claughton and on the west bank the Lune Valley Ramble continues. The Ramble cuts across from the Lune to The Snab, leaving a long sweep of the Lune to the birdlife. The ponds that have formed here are well used by swan, coot, moorhen and heron. Above The Snab, on the footpath to Eskrigge, there are good views across to Hornby, with Ingleborough behind, and it's also possible to see the flat green centre of the ancient moat near Camp House.

Snab Beck makes its way to the Lune, running from Higher Snab through a deep, wooded gully. The beck used to be a fast-flowing tributary of the Lune until its banks were silted up from the trampling of cattle and sheep. The Lune Habitat Group has tried to restore the beck to its former state in the hope of attracting back wildlife that has been lost, such as otter and water vole. Otters are regularly recorded within Loyne, especially between Arkholme and Caton, but not so regularly that the event is not thought worth recording. The beck now runs below the footpath and then out to a large isolated pond, before following a route west back to the Lune, which is soon joined on the opposite bank by the combined forces of Farleton Beck and Claughton Beck.

Farleton Beck and Claughton Beck

Farleton Beck and Claughton Beck are usually small and sluggish but it is not always so. In 1967, on the day of the Wray flood, similar but not so extensive damage was caused in the villages of Farleton and Claughton, through which the becks flow.

Farleton is a cul-de-sac of mainly new houses lined up around the old farms of Bank House and Brades. Farleton's only claim to fame is that in 1920 the owner of the garage that used to exist next to the Old Toll House was the first to paint white lines on a road, in order to help motorists negotiate the dangerous corner. This fact is so often repeated that it has become a self-evident truth. However, it is my sad duty to report that many websites assert that Edward Hines, traffic engineer of Detroit, used white lines in 1912. Ah well, it wasn't such a glorious claim to fame, anyway.

Claughton Beck arises on Claughton Moor and runs through the clay pit of Claughton brickworks, now owned by Hanson Brick Ltd. This industry has survived, against the odds, since the late 19th century. One of the aerial ropeways installed in about 1900 is still used to bring down the clay and shale from the moor and is thought to be the last such ropeway still in use in England. The view into the pit, with the buckets swinging overhead, is a glimpse of a bygone industrial age. The pit, incidentally, is not as large as might be imagined for a centuries' worth of bricks but for those concerned that the whole

Previous page: the Lune at Lawson's Wood.
Below: the Claughton ropeway.

of Claughton Moor might eventually be carried away in these buckets it is reassuring that planning permission for mineral extraction ends in 2018. The pit is due to be returned to a natural state by 2020.

Halfway down the hill, Claughton Beck runs behind Claughton Hall, which has a magnificent view of Ingleborough and the Howgills. The hall, parts of which are said to be of the 13th century, looks grim and austere, with its front always in the shade. It is hard to get a close view of the hall because it is surrounded by fences, plantations and the bank of a large, new pond. There are two unequally large, stern towers, with oddly placed small windows and uneven roofs, and tall, narrow chimneys. It is difficult to believe that in the 1930s this hall was moved stone-by-stone from its position in Claughton and rebuilt to the original plan here, without the opportunity for more substantial change being taken. Perhaps the labourers reflected upon this while, as they hauled the stones up, the clay for new bricks was passing down over their heads.

Claughton Hall is owned by the Oyston family, which may explain its increasing reclusion. Owen Oyston, a media tycoon, was jailed for six years in 1996 after being controversially convicted of rape. After a groundbreaking legal battle to establish that it wasn't necessary to admit guilt first, he was released on parole in 1999. But his trademark sheepskin coat and large fedora have gone, and no longer do the bison roam extrovertly in the field in front of the hall as they used to.

Claughton Hall Farm, an old building of character, was left where it was, next to St Chad's Church, a medieval church re-built in 1815. One of the two bells is dated 1296, making it the oldest dated bell in England. As with Farleton's claim to fame, I am afraid that I have to pour some cold water. In 2002 St Chad's was declared redundant and permission granted for it to be converted to residential use. In 2005 there was a planning application to remove the bells to be displayed in St Margaret's Church, Hornby, although in 2007 they seemed to be still with St Chad's.

Sunset over a Lune-side lagoon

Bluebells in Burton Wood

The Lune from Farleton Beck and Claughton Beck ...

The Lune Valley Ramble passes Afton Barn Cottage, which is a kind attempt to help us with the pronunciation of the village above it, Aughton. I'm tempted to suggest an extra f is needed but it depends on how you say "good afternoon". Although most of Aughton's buildings have been adapted for Lancaster commuters, one or two barns managed to survive until the present ban on conversion came into force. The houses are arranged around a triangle, mainly on the two quiet sides (not that the third side is busy).

The village stirs itself every 21 years for the Aughton Pudding Festival, at which the 'world's largest pudding' is prepared. In the 18th century, Aughton, like other Lune villages, made baskets from osiers, which were made more supple by boiling. In 1782 someone had the bright idea to use the osier-boiler to make a large pudding, which became a tradition, which then lapsed and was revived in 1971. On the last occasion a concrete mixer was used. Why 21 years? I suppose it takes that long to forget what a jolly silly idea it is. Note it in your diary: the next great pudding is due in 2013.

Aughton Woods line the steep northern slopes above the floodplain. These woodlands have probably never been cleared and include many species, such as birch, oak, elm, ash and, notably, the small-leaved lime. The Wildlife Trust manages parts of the area, some of which are Biological Heritage Sites. There are concessionary footpaths in Burton Wood and Lawson's Wood, allowing extensive banks of bluebells to be viewed in spring.

Opposite Burton Wood the Lune turns on a huge meander. The lines of the parish boundaries and the public footpaths show that the course of the Lune has changed here. For some years the owner of the land on the south bank, eroded by the Lune, insisted that walkers must follow the official line of the footpath, that is, into the middle of the Lune. Happily, a concessionary path on the bank was eventually agreed. At the furthest point of the meander the Lune runs by the dismantled Wennington-Lancaster railway line, which at this point forms the beginning (or end) of the River Lune Millennium Park, a leisure area leading to Salt Ayre in Lancaster. Here also Bull Beck joins the Lune.

Bull Beck

Bull Beck rises as Tarn Brook – a name whose significance you may ponder for a minute – in the shadow of the **Caton wind turbines** and near the spoil heaps of the disused Claughton Quarries. Tarn Brook runs through a narrow wooded valley in a region of old farmsteads such as Annas Ghyll and Moorside Farm. The substantial Moorgarth was built in the 1820s as a workhouse for 150 paupers from parishes within about 15km. It was closed after an inspection in 1866 found it "wholly unsuitable" for the care of the poor and later, in 1902, it was converted into a residence for the architect Harry Paley, son of the Paley of Paley & Austin.

Tarn Brook becomes Bull Beck in honour of the Black Bull, the 16th century (or older) public house in the village of Brookhouse, a name that hints at the significance of Tarn Brook. Yes, it is the first 'brook', rather than 'beck', that we have met, a transition in nomenclature

The **Caton wind turbines** were the first modern windmills to be constructed in Loyne – and the second. Elsewhere in the Lune valley, wind turbine proposals have led to heated debates and campaigning in STILE, that is, in 'Stop Turbines In the Lunesdale Environment', seemingly oblivious of the fact that they are already here. Perhaps the second set of wind turbines, twice as high as the first, are more difficult to not notice.

Ten wind turbines were erected in 1994, even though the site is within the Forest of Bowland Area of Outstanding Natural Beauty. Its closeness to the pit being gouged out by Claughton brickworks made it hard to argue that the area was so outstanding that it must not be spoiled. These turbines had a maximum capacity of 3MW, enough to power about 1700 households.

In 2006 these were replaced by eight turbines, yielding 16MW. Actually, with the new turbines occupying four times the area, the yield per 'cubic metre of wind' is less. Maybe there is a plan to infill the area with more turbines, or, now that the turbines will be visible from all directions and not just from the north and west, to spread them across more of Caton Moor.

The aesthetic appeal of wind turbines is much debated but generally with the long-distance view in mind. What about the aesthetics on the spot? A position on Caton Moor above the semi-renovated Moorcock Hall gives the finest view there is of the middle stretches of the Lune, with the Lakeland hills behind. It also provides the longest possible view of the Lune valley, from the Lune Gorge to the estuary – but now the latter must be viewed through the blades of the wind turbines.

Left: the wind turbines on Caton Moor.

that is complete about 20km further south. This is not just a terminological curiosity but also an indication of the scope of Viking influence, consistent with the disappearance of 'fell' and 'thwaite' across the Forest of Bowland. Indeed, the name of Bowland is derived from the Norse 'bu' for cattle rather than from the bow and arrow.

Modern housing for Lancaster commuters has now engulfed the old core of Brookhouse. There are three halls within tottering distance of the Black Bull: the Hall, the Old Hall, and Old Hall Farm. The Old Hall was probably the ancient manor for the Caton estate, although the present building is of the 17th century. The church of St Paul's, where there has been a church since at least the 12th century, has helpfully retained something of its past in both major re-buildings. The 1537 re-building retained the 12th century arched doorway in the west wall, although it has been incongruously filled with a jumble of oddments, some of antiquity. In 1865 the church was again re-built (by the ubiquitous Paley) but this time retaining the 1537 tower.

Bull Beck continues past the A683 picnic site, which is a meeting point for bikers, to join the Lune.

Above: the Lune flowing towards Ingleborough.
Below: an alien black swan joins the Lune avifauna.

The Lune from Bull Beck ...

The steep banks of the Lune are pitted with holes. These are nests excavated by sand martins, which arrive back in England in April and can be seen in large numbers swirling and swooping over the river seeking flies before returning to their nest.

The Lune continues its long curve to face whence it came and then turns sharply under Lawson's Wood to head towards a bridge painted grey, with red roses. On the side it says "Manchester Corporation Water Works 1892". Within the bridge is an aqueduct carrying up to 250 million litres of water every day from Thirlmere to Manchester. The Victorian style contrasts with the 1950s austerity of the Haweswater Aqueduct passed near Kirkby Lonsdale. The two aqueducts are now part of a

The Thirlmere Aqueduct (or Waterworks Bridge)

more complex system, collecting water from Ullswater and Windermere as well, being joined near Shap, and providing water to Liverpool, Blackpool and Lancaster as well as Manchester.

The Thirlmere Aqueduct is 150km long, the longest in England to work by gravity alone. As can be seen, the four pipes across the bridge drop several metres to be taken underground on the south side of the Lune. This is the sharpest drop along the whole length of the aqueduct (the average drop is just 30cm/km, and the water flows at 6km/hour) and hence the point under the greatest hydrostatic pressure. The square buildings, south and on the hill north, have valves that can be closed to enable repairs. A £23m programme to inspect and repair the entire length of the aqueduct was begun in 2006, which is the first time that the aqueduct has been completely drained since it opened in 1894. A few years ago, the platform across the aqueduct was opened to walkers, who also appreciate the new bridge obviating the difficult ford across Artle Beck, 0.5km below the aqueduct.

Artle Beck

Artle Beck acquires its name somewhere between Crossgill and Potts Wood, by which point it has already absorbed innumerable becks flowing into the Littledale valley. From the north, Crossgill Beck runs from the Caton wind farm towards Roeburn Glade, built on the site of the old Brookhouse Brick Company, which closed down in the 1960s. Crossgill is probably named after the ancient cross, marked on old maps, that used to stand in the base that can be seen by a track (the old Littledale Road) to the north. It is an old farming hamlet: one building bears a date of 1681. In 1780 a corn mill was listed here – by 1850 it was a bobbin mill, and it closed in 1945 as a sawmill.

From the south, Foxdale Beck and Udale Beck drain Blanch Fell and Black Fell below Ward's Stone (561m), the highest point in the Forest of Bowland. Ward's Stone naturally affords a fine view of the extensive plateaux of southern Bowland, although the flat top prevents views into the valleys. On the top, erosion has exposed gritstone boulders, some with fanciful names, such as the Queen's

The trig point and Ward's Stone

Chair. A few raised islands of peat remain but generally the surface is stony. After dry weather, it is dusty and the gritstone sparkles in the sunlight but usually the sombre colours intensify the wild, windswept remoteness.

The upland moors provide a breeding habitat for birds such as curlew, snipe, redshank, ring ouzel, merlin, golden plover, peregrine falcon, and hen harrier. The last is the symbol of Bowland. The hen harrier is one of England's most threatened birds and Bowland is its most important breeding site in England. In 2005 fifteen pairs nested in Bowland, more than in the rest of England. Unsurprisingly, the Bowland Fells are a

Littledale, looking up Udale Beck to Blanch Fell, with Ward's Stone on the horizon

Autumn mists over Artle Beck

Special Protection Area under the European Union's Wild Birds Directive.

The Littledale region is also a good one for observing the lapwing, a bird that is distinctive in all three main identifying characteristics: appearance (with a long crest), flight (an acrobatic tumble) and call (a 'pee-wit'). The lapwing is declining drastically in other parts of the country but in higher areas of Loyne where the sheep numbers are not too high, such as Littledale, there has been an increase.

The Black Side of Ward's Stone is rough country that until recently was reserved for grouse and grouse shooting. The British record bag of 2929 grouse was recorded in Littledale and Abbeystead on August 12th 1915 (wasn't there a war on?). Today, it is CRoW land, with an access point from Littledale by Sweet Beck

above Belhill Farm and also by a concessionary path (not marked on OS maps) from near Deep Clough by Ragill Beck to Haylot Fell. Foxdale Beck below White Spout and Cocklett Scar is an attractive secluded spot. The best walking is to be found on the ridge that goes up to Gallows Hill, for this is mainly grass, in contrast to the heather, bogs and rocks found below Ward's Stone.

Foxdale Beck passes Littledale Hall, which is not as old as it looks. It was built in the Gothic Revival period for the Reverend John Dodson, who had been Vicar of Cockerham from 1835 to 1849. It became a Christian retreat in 1988 and a rehabilitation centre in 2006. Near the Hall is Littledale Chapel, also built by the Rev. Dodson but now used as a barn.

It is sometimes worthwhile to pause and ask: Why? Why did the Rev. Dodson leave his flock at Cockerham to build a hall and chapel in Littledale? It was because of the Gorham Judgement, a significant event in the history of tension between church and state. A Mr Gorham had been rejected as a vicar by the church because he did not believe in its teachings on baptism but, after an appeal to the Privy Council, the church had been overruled. Many clergy strongly objected to a secular court overriding spiritual authority, including our Rev. Dodson, who set out to build a 'free church', as it says above the doorway.

From Fostal Bridge Artle Beck runs through a deep valley shaded by woodland, which is important for its over 160 species of moss and liverwort, and past the sites of coal mines at Hollinhead and Hawkshead that were active until the early 19th century. The beck emerges at Gresgarth Hall, the country home of the internationally renowned garden designer Lady Arabella Lennox-Boyd (oh, and Sir Mark Lennox-Boyd, former MP for Morecambe). As we would expect, the gardens of Gresgarth Hall are impressive indeed, having been transformed since 1978 from a gloomy, dank, tree-shaded area, engulfed by rhododendron and laurel, into a light, open parkland with terraced gardens, herbaceous borders, a new lake, a water garden, an orchard, a nuttery, and so on, with Artle Beck running through them.

The gardens are open several times each summer, usually in aid of the Conservative party, but don't let that put you off. Apart from the gardens, you will be able to view the hall itself, which was largely rebuilt in the early 19th century. Perhaps you will be able to detect the rough external masonry of the little that remains of the older 14th century hall.

The Gresgarth estate came into the ownership of the historic Curwen family in 1330 when John Curwen married Agnes de Caton. The Curwens owned extensive land in Cumberland and Galloway when the England-Scotland border was more fluid. It is believed that after the First War of Scottish Independence, which ended in 1328, John Curwen was granted the Gresgarth estate (and dear Agnes, heiresses at that time being wards of the crown) in compensation for losing his land in Galloway.

John Curwen would have been well aware of the threat from the Scottish, since Robert the Bruce had ransacked Lancaster in 1322, and turned whatever building then existed (thought to have been a rest home for monks) into a tower house. The Curwens owned the hall until the 17th century, since when it has passed

The Top 10 halls in Loyne

1. Gresgarth Hall
2. Underley Hall
3. Whittington Hall
4. Middleton Hall
5. Leck Hall
6. Burrow Hall
7. Ingmire Hall
8. Killington Hall
9. Ashton Hall
10. Thurnham Hall

through many hands, including the Girlingtons, whom we met as owners of Thurland Castle.

Below Gresgarth, Artle Beck is more sedate. In the beck, opposite Bridge End, a Roman milestone was found in 1803. It is usually said to be six foot high but it is actually rather bigger, as can be checked in the Lancaster City Museum. Its carvings indicate that it marked a point four Roman miles from Lancaster, which is indeed the straight-line distance to the Lancaster fort. It is therefore an important indication of the path, now lost but probably straight along this section, of the presumed road between the forts at Lancaster and Over Burrow.

Artle Beck runs past Caton, which the afore-mentioned Thos Johnson considered "about the least interesting of all the villages in the vale of the Lune." Although Caton is a workaday place this characterisation is unfair because it doesn't distinguish between the parish and the village. Caton is old enough to be mentioned in the Domesday Book but until relatively recently Caton referred to four distinct communities: Littledale, Caton Green, Brookhouse and Town End. The seat of the manor, the original Caton Hall, was at Caton Green and the parish church was at Brookhouse, which was, if anywhere was, the centre of old Caton.

It was only from the late 18th century that Town End grew rapidly to become the industrial centre of Caton, after the building of five mills. Ball Lane Mill was burnt down in 1846; Rumble Row Mill and Forge Mill closed down in the 1930s; Willow Mill and Low Mill continued production until the 1970s. The last three survive after conversion to small business units and residences. Low Mill is reputed to have been the oldest cotton mill in England, built in 1783 on the site of an old corn mill that may have dated back to the 13th century. A millrace taken from Artle Beck at Gresgarth powered all the mills except Ball Lane. Its route across Artle Beck near Forge Mill and through Caton to Low Mill can still be traced. The millpond by Low Mill is now a fishery. As with all becks off the hills, the water supply was unreliable and Low Mill became one of the first to use steam power in 1819.

All this activity led the centre of gravity of Caton to move to Town End. This was confirmed by the building of the turnpike road, the present A683, in 1812, bypassing the old road through Brookhouse and Caton Green, and by the arrival in 1850 of the railway, with Caton Station.

This history explains the relative dearth of old buildings in Caton. The oldest church is the Wesleyan Methodist one of 1837. Many of the house names reflect Caton's practical past: the Rock m Jock cottages are said to refer to the noise from the nearby Willow Mill; Farrer House (which is an old building, dated 1680) is the old blacksmith's; the Ship Inn is supposed to refer to the sailcloths produced at Willow Mill. Even the Fish Stones are concerned with trade – the three semi-circular slabs are where fish were sold in the Middle Ages. By the Fish Stones is a very old oak tree, so decrepit that fears that it is disobeying its preservation order prompted the High Sheriff of Lancashire to plant a successor oak tree in 2007.

The Fish Stones and ye olde oake treee in Caton

CHAPTER 13:
The Lune to Lancaster

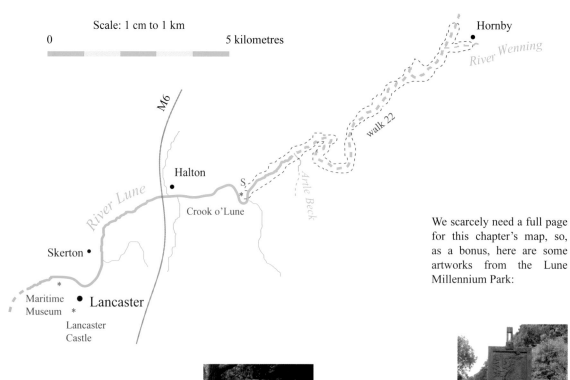

Scale: 1 cm to 1 km

We scarcely need a full page for this chapter's map, so, as a bonus, here are some artworks from the Lune Millennium Park:

*Heron's Head
(Marjan Wouda)*

*Gray's Seat bench
(Jim Partridge)*

*Maybe
(Colin Wilbourn)*

Captured Africans
(Kevin Dalton
Johnson)*

*When Traffic
Cones Take Root
(Mark Renn and
Mick Thacker)*

*River Rocks
(Colin Reid)*

**Strictly, this is not in the Millennium Park: it is a nearby
memorial to Lancaster's slave trade, unveiled in 2005*

The Lune from Artle Beck ...

After 1km the Lune reaches the Crook o'Lune, a popular picnic spot where the Lune meanders in a graceful curve under wooded banks. There are three bridges. The first and third, on opposite sides of the meander, were for the Wennington-Lancaster railway line. The second is Penny Bridge, which was built in 1883 after the 1806 bridge collapsed. This was a toll bridge but rather than pay the toll some people preferred to cross the Lune on foot, not always successfully.

At the Crook o'Lune a small beck, Escow Beck, slips into the Lune. This, with its tributary Deys Beck, originates 2km south in Flodden Hill Wood. This name is thought to be due to Richard Baines, who was given land in the area by Lord Monteagle of Hornby in reward for his bravery at the Battle of Flodden Field. He no doubt gave his own name to Baines Cragg, which provides a fine viewpoint over Lancaster and Morecambe Bay. Escow Beck flows through the pond at Escowbeck House, which John Greg, the then owner of Low Mill, built in 1842. He had the grounds landscaped so that a sight of what he owned did not spoil his view, and as a result it is difficult for us now to see the house.

Above the Crook o'Lune is Gray's Seat, a recently restored viewpoint that was eulogised by the poet Thomas Gray in 1769. He wrote that "every feature which constitutes a perfect landscape of the extensive sort is here not only boldly marked but in its best position". These words are carved at the viewpoint, beside a grand seat made by the renowned woodcarver Jim Partridge.

Gray's view seems intended to rival Ruskin's View at Kirkby Lonsdale, which, after all, it does pre-date. It was well known in the 19th century, as the effusive paraphrase of Gray's words in *A Pictorial History of the County of Lancashire* (1854) indicates: the view "leaves nothing to be desired in a landscape that pleases rather than surprises, and of which the prevailing character is more beauty than grandeur … we see nothing misplaced, and desire neither to add to nor take away [a] solitary object." Since then we have added eight wind turbines. Today, trees largely obscure the view and it is surprising that we are encouraged to dash across the dangerous A683 to see what's left of it. (Gray's Seat is probably not Gray's view at all: he stood to the north of the road, 400m below the "more advantageous station", according to the 1821 editor of Gray's *Guide to the Lakes*.)

Beyond the meander, the Lune curves west. Here, on a winter's afternoon, is a good place to spot the kingfisher, for in the absence of other colours the setting sun makes its iridescent blue and orange particularly

Previous page: the Lune Aqueduct.
Right: near the Crook o'Lune.

Walk 22: Crook o'Lune and Loyn Bridge

Map: OL41 (please read the general note about the walks in the Introduction).
Starting point: The Crook o'Lune (522647).

Guidance for this suggested walk is simplicity itself: walk from the Crook o'Lune on the east side of the Lune to Loyn Bridge and then back on the west side.

In a little more detail: Walk east over the old railway bridge and then immediately take the path right and then right again to go under the bridge you've just crossed to gain the footpath on the east bank of the Lune. At the Waterworks Bridge continue on the bank, as there is a good stretch of the Lune below Lawson's Wood, where salmon often leap. Follow the long loop round until you are again heading northeast. Don't take the public footpath to Claughton but continue on the river bank where there is a concessionary footpath not marked on OS maps. This continues to the Wenning, where it is necessary to walk east to Hornby Bridge and then back on the other side of the Wenning. Continue to Loyn Bridge where, if the footpath under the bridge is impassable because the river is too high, you should cut up through the wood to reach the road. Walk over the bridge and take the path south on the west bank of the Lune. As this is part of the Lune Valley Ramble there should be no difficulty in navigation. At the long meander near Burton Wood nobody will object if, through exhaustion, you need to walk straight across.

The walk can alternatively be started from Loyn Bridge, which would have the advantage of enabling a half-way cuppa at Woodies snack bar at the Crook o'Lune. Between the Crook o'Lune and Loyn Bridge there is only one way to cross the Lune - at Waterworks Bridge (the footpaths marked on the OS map as crossing the Lune are impossible for walkers). The bridge enables a 5km walk from the Crook o'Lune or a 15km walk from Loyn Bridge.

The Lune at Halton

vivid when seen from the south bank. According to the Lune Waterways Bird Survey there are at most half a dozen breeding pairs between Lancaster and Kirkby Lonsdale, so their frequency here seems surprising.

On the south bank, 100m before Forge Bank Weir, is the Lune Intake, the first sign of any significant **management of the Lune**. Up to this point the Lune and its tributaries have run largely unrestrained from their various fells. There used to be a millrace from the weir to power Halton Mills, a substantial industrial complex that survived for over two centuries, changing when necessary between cotton, flax, leather, oilcloths and coconut matting, until becoming derelict in the 1970s. A renovation of the site was begun in 2006 by a company with the motto "property touches emotion". How true! The residents of Halton's 1960s bungalows angrily objected to the scores of "rural townhouses" (a contradiction in terms?).

Between Forge Bank Weir and Lower Halton Weir the Lune's natural turbulence has been increased in order to provide rapids for canoeists. Stone banks protrude into the flow to create eddies and waves, suitable for novices at the lower end and experts at the higher, especially under spate conditions. On the south bank the Lune Millennium Park continues along the old railway line. Various artworks are passed, of which the most striking is that of Giles Kent, whose website says that he creates "in situ installations that enhance and elaborate on the natural properties of wood ... [the work] compliments the natural landscape by responding to lines and shapes found around each particular site". There are nine upside-down larch trunks with roots aloft.

The park reaches the old Halton railway station, which looks different from all the others we've passed because it was re-built in 1907 after a fire. By the station there's a temporary-looking bridge across the Lune that has stood since 1913. The crossing here has a chequered history. While the railway was being built there was no bridge across the Lune here and workers were ferried across from Halton. In 1849 eight of them died when washed away in a flood. Today such an event would be a national tragedy; then it seems to have been accepted as a price to be paid. A new bridge was opened in December 1849: it wouldn't do to have potential customers from Halton washed away. This was swept away in 1869 and replaced in the same year. This in turn was replaced in 1913 by using the remains of the old Greyhound Bridge then being demolished in Lancaster. The bridge operated

The **management of the Lune** is important to enable proper use of water resources, to make flood predictions, to assess the impact of discharges, and to support the use of the Lune for recreation.

There are four flow-measuring stations on the Lune (at Lune's Bridge, Tebay (3), Killington New Bridge (6), Caton (17) and Halton (16)) and a further four on the Conder, Hindburn, Rawthey and Wenning tributaries. The figures in brackets show the median flows in cubic metres per second. The Halton figure is lower than the Caton one because of water extraction, particularly at the Lune Intake.

Water is pumped from the Lune to help provide Langthwaite Reservoir with Lancaster's water supply and also to be transferred to the River Wyre along a 13km pipeline as part of Lancashire's 'conjunctive use scheme'. The Wyre catchment is heavily exploited for industrial and public water supply and may be supplemented from the Lune, provided that its flow is high enough.

There are over a hundred licences for water abstraction from the Lune and its tributaries and if all the allowed water were taken the Lune would be 'over licensed', that is, flows would fall below necessary levels. Thankfully, the actual level of abstraction is lower than licensed and has decreased recently because of changes in the region's industry.

The nature of the Lune catchment area makes this monitoring important. Flows in the floodplain are determined by rainfall on the fells, and these run-offs have different characteristics. Rain in the Howgills runs quickly off the hills but in the Dales water percolates into limestone until it is saturated, giving rise to flash flood conditions. The continued health of the Loyne riverside flora and fauna depends upon maintaining the required conditions of erosion and sedimentation, and this needs to be better understood.

as a toll bridge until the 1960s and since the railway line closed in 1966 it has been a matter of contention who is responsible for its upkeep.

North of the Lune is the village of Halton, the larger eastern part of which is mainly new housing for commuters but the older part of which is rich in heritage. This part is clustered around the small tributary of Cote Beck, which enters the Lune unobtrusively 200m below the bridge. Cote Beck arises south of Nether Kellet, rather tentatively, as is usual in limestone country, below the large quarries. It runs by the M6 and then past Furnace Cottage, where Cote Beck used to be called Foundry Beck.

Below Dale Wood, Cote Beck passes the site of Halton's motte and bailey castle, now marked by a flagpole. The site is relatively small but the motte, rising 3m above the bailey, can be clearly seen (although the present top is not original) and traces of the bailey are visible despite recent ploughing. The site is on private land.

On the other side of the beck is the church, dedicated to St Wilfrid, a 7th century Archbishop of York. Maybe there was a church here from that time, although the earliest remains are 12th century Norman stones built into the arch. As we have seen with other churches, the tower was retained when the church was rebuilt (by Paley & Austin again) in the 19th century.

A Roman altar was found in the churchyard in 1794 and is now in the Lancaster City Museum. It bears an inscription to the god Mars from Sabinus and his unit of boatmen, perhaps grateful for their safe passage up the Lune from Lancaster. There is no other evidence of any Roman settlement at Halton, although it is likely that there was a camp on what became the site of the castle and it is assumed that there was a Roman road on the north bank of the Lune up to Whittington and over a ford to Over Burrow. Still in the churchyard is a cross carved with Christian symbols and a version of the Sigurd the Volsung legend by Norse settlers who came to the region in the 10th century. It is 3.5m high, mounted on three steps, with the top parts having been rather inexpertly reassembled.

Halton, then, was an important centre before the Norman Conquest, when it was held, like many places we've visited, by Earl Tostig. At the time of the Domesday survey, Halton was regarded as the centre of lower Lune, with twenty-two villages, including Lancaster, considered to belong to the manor of Halton. When Roger of Poitou took over, he preferred to make Lancaster his centre and the importance of Halton waned. The Royal Foresters, responsible for managing the king's forests in Lancashire, had Halton for their

principal manor until the Gernet inheritance passed to the Dacre family in about 1290. The lords of the manor in 1715, the Carus family, perhaps still smarting from Halton's subordination to Lancaster, gave helpful information to the Jacobite Army on its way to occupy Lancaster. From the 18th century, the manor house, Halton Hall, passed through several hands, gradually being split up and demolished. Only one 19th century wing remains, the rest having gone by the 1930s, apart from the boathouse on the Lune.

The Lune is slow, deep and wide, and local rowing clubs make good use of this section, down towards

The Viking cross at St Wilfrid's, Halton

Skerton Weir. Rowers get the best view of the fine M6 bridge, whose single-span arch of 70m provides a frame for an attractive stretch of the Lune. In view of the on-going controversy about a proposed link road from the M6 just north of the Lune to Heysham, it is interesting that this was already part of the original plan in the 1950s. It was only when the Lancaster emergency services expressed concern at the difficulties of gaining access to the motorway that an interchange south of the Lune was built, to lower design standards than normal and only later, after public representation, that it was opened for general use.

After passing the Halton Training Camp for army cadets on the north bank and a hotel and industrial buildings on the south, the Lune reaches the Lune Aqueduct, one of the finest aqueducts in England. It is 200m long, with five semi-circular arches carrying the **Lancaster Canal** 18m above the Lune. It was one of the first bridges designed by John Rennie, who went on to design Waterloo Bridge and London Bridge, and was a great civil engineering feat for its time. The aqueduct was completed in 1797 and some indication of its impact and aesthetic appeal can be gained from the fact that Turner sketched it on his 1797 tour of northern England. This was the only time on his tour that he addressed a contemporary subject, although he could not resist framing a view of Lancaster Castle within one of the arches. However, the grandeur of the aqueduct's design was not without its critics. A committee set up in 1819 to review progress on the Lancaster Canal commented that resources had been wasted in "ornamenting the town of Lancaster, with a grand aqueduct over the Lune, upon which the water had lain stagnant for over twenty years."

After 1km the Lune reaches Skerton Weir, the normal tidal limit. A weir has existed here for centuries, to provide water for a millrace to power corn mills by the Lune, but the present structure was built in 1979 to prevent salt water entering intakes for the Lune-side industries upstream. It does, of course, have a fish pass for salmon and trout.

The weir is of disappointing design. It is dangerous for river users, who are regularly swept over it, sometimes with fatal consequences; it is unsightly; and it is not integrated into the so-called riverside parks to provide an appealing leisure amenity.

In the past the weir was renowned for its salmon fishing. Fishing is now regulated by the Environment

Lancaster Canal was intended to connect Kendal with Houghton, and hence the Leeds–Liverpool Canal, but has yet to achieve that goal. The Act approving its construction was passed in 1792 and the sections from Tewitfield to Preston and from Walton Summit (6km south of Preston) to Houghton were completed by 1803. The costs, however, were high: for example, the bill for the Lune Aqueduct (£48,000) was nearly three times the original estimate.

The Kendal to Tewitfield section took until 1819 but no canal link between Preston and Walton Summit was constructed – until 2003, when the Millennium Ribble Link was finally built. But by this time the Kendal to Tewitfield section, now cut off by the M6, had largely been filled in. The grandly named Association for the Restoration of the Lancaster Canal, formed in 1963 at the time of the M6-enforced separation, still hopes to re-open the Kendal to Tewitfield section for navigation.

The Lancaster Canal is misnamed because, although it was intended to help get goods to and from Lancaster avoiding the Lune, the main beneficiaries were Preston and Kendal and other villages en route. Preston, which had its own problems with navigation in the Ribble, was in 1792 smaller than Lancaster but its population trebled in thirty years as new markets opened up. The main effect within Lancaster, which had lacked water-powered mills, was the development of steam-powered mills alongside the canal, where coal could be delivered easily.

The eight-hour journey from Kendal to Preston could not compete with the railway when it arrived and the Lancaster Canal Company was duly dissolved in 1886, with the last freight being carried in 1947.

Today, the 66km from Tewitfield to Preston is for leisure only. As it follows the contour there are no locks, to the disappointment of today's canal travellers, who seem to revel in them. If that makes the canal too boring they could try counting the bridges (Lancaster City Museum asserts that there are 247 of them, including 22 aqueducts – which I assume includes those bridges still standing, mysteriously, in fields between Kendal and Tewitfield). Or they could tackle the Ribble Link, which has nine locks in 6km.

Agency, who own three beats on the Lune. Fishing directly below the weir is prohibited but further downstream fly-fishing is allowed. Above the weir, coarse fishing with a single rod is permitted, outside the close season, of course. The Agency's other two beats are upstream, at Halton Lower Beat and Halton Top Beat. The former is a game fishery, best fished at high water; the latter is slow, deep water and is said to be the most productive of all the Agency's salmon fisheries.

The M6 bridge

The Lune flows through the built-up areas on the outskirts of Lancaster and the becks, such as they are, run unobtrusively through culverts to the river. For example, Newton Beck joins on the east bank from the estates of Ridge and Newton. On the west bank is Skerton, which was mentioned as a separate village in the Domesday Book and remained apart from Lancaster until the late 19th century.

Skerton Bridge was designed by Thomas Harrison, who had studied in Italy, and is in a classical style similar to that of the old Roman bridge at Rimini. Its flat roadway and use of balustrades across the width were innovatory for English bridges. There are five elliptical arches, each spanning 20m. It was completed in 1788 and soon influenced other designers. We might, for example, detect an echo of Skerton Bridge in the Lune Aqueduct, for John Rennie came to see it and a flat design was exactly what was needed for the aqueduct.

A sixth, inferior arch was later added to Skerton Bridge on the east bank for the Wennington-Lancaster railway line. The station was just south of the bridge at Green Ayre, which is today a rare example of an industrial site that has been returned to a green field, quiet apart from the skate-boarders' ramp and the

traffic. The railway line continued from Green Ayre over Greyhound Bridge to Poulton-le-Sands, or Morecambe as it became called. The present Greyhound Bridge was built in 1911, replacing earlier bridges of 1849 and 1864, and converted for road traffic after the closure of the railway line in 1966.

Green Ayre has had a long and active past. Some experts believe that at the time of the Romans, Green Ayre was an island, with the main flow of the Lune being south of its present course, along the line of the present Damside Street. A millrace followed this line and powered what is believed to be the oldest recorded water mill in Lancashire, being referred to in the borough charter of 1193. Green Ayre then became a busy quay and from 1763 a shipyard. It doesn't seem an ideal spot for such activities because the old bridge, dating back to at least the 13th century, prevented large ships from reaching Green Ayre. Newly built ships were floated from the shipyard under the bridge in parts and assembled downstream.

When Skerton Bridge was built the old bridge became redundant. The shipyard bought the bridge in 1800 and removed one arch, which reduced its functionality somewhat but allowed tall ships to pass through. By 1845 the whole bridge had fallen down or been demolished.

The Millennium Bridge, opened in 2001 for cyclists and pedestrians only, is roughly where the old bridge stood. Opinions on this new bridge are mixed: some people don't like it much; others don't like it at all. Certainly, for cyclists and pedestrians it is a boon, because for them Skerton Bridge and Greyhound Bridge are inconvenient and dangerous. The bridge is a key part of the Lune Millennium Park, linking the cycleways along the old railway lines from Caton and Morecambe to form part of National Cycle Network route 6. It was designed by Whitby Bird, cost £1.8m, has a span of 64m and is suspended from 40m masts. Perhaps we will eventually come to admire the classic view of Lancaster's castle and priory now framed by the long blue fingers that are supposed to echo old sailing ships.

From Green Ayre, the castle and priory look as one, overseeing the city of Lancaster, dominating the strategically important lowest old fording point of the Lune, and providing extensive views over Morecambe Bay and up the Lune valley to Ingleborough. What is now called Castle Hill was settled long before the castle existed, with Neolithic and Bronze Age artefacts having been found here.

The Romans recognised its key position overlooking a main route between Scotland and western England. Of the Roman fort that was based on Castle Hill there is little to be seen but more than we saw at Low Borrowbridge and Over Burrow. Most of the site is under the present castle and priory but to the north in Vicarage Fields the remains of a 2nd century bathhouse, excavated and preserved in 1973, can be seen. The meagreness of the remains does not excuse the shabbiness of the site and the shamefully poor foreign language information board.

When Roger of Poitou moved his base from Halton to Lancaster he no doubt built a motte and bailey castle within the site of the old fort, although there is no trace of this castle today. The Domesday Book records a village called **Loncastre** here. The castle would have

Greyhound Bridge and the Millennium Bridge below the castle and priory

been rebuilt in stone and strengthened part by part. The 12th century keep is the oldest surviving part. Scottish raiders in 1322 and 1389 ruined much of Lancaster but spared the castle and, to a lesser extent, the priory. During the Civil War, Parliament ordered that the castle (apart from the courts and gaol) be demolished but in 1663 the king agreed to have it repaired. The gatehouse, the most impressive external feature, is 15th century, with the John of Gaunt statue added to it in 1822.

The grandeur of the long-distance view, with the battlements on the skyline, is not sustained at close quarters, where the bland, relatively modern, external wall dominates. If you prefer a castle to be in dramatic ruins redolent of historic battles then Lancaster Castle is a disappointment: it is still in good enough repair to continue as a working castle, functioning as court and prison. Even so, it is arguably Lancashire's greatest historical building.

Lancashire became a County Palatine in 1351, with John of Gaunt becoming Duke of Lancaster, a title that passed to his son, who became Henry IV in 1399. Since that date the monarch has continued to be Duke of Lancaster and has retained the Duchy and the castle as a separate estate to those of the Crown. As county town, Lancaster held the Assizes two or three times a year. They were held in the Crown Court from 1176 until 1971, when a Royal Commission on Assizes, chaired by Lord Beeching (a second, and less controversial, Beeching Report), recommended changes. Until 1835 it had been the only Assize Court in Lancashire. The regular influx of Lancastrian gentry helped to sustain Lancaster's relative importance and to preserve its status as county town even after the Industrial Revolution.

According to H.V. Morton's *In Search of England* (1927), "It is remarkable that Lancashire, which possesses Liverpool and Manchester, should own a delicious, sleepy, old county town like Lancaster, and this is itself symbolic of the fact that the great industrial new-rich cities of northern England – vast and mighty as they are – fall into perspective as mere black specks against the mighty background of history and the great green expanse of fine country which is the real North of England." Since then, the black specks

---

The name **Loncastre** may prompt some speculation on the origin of the name 'Lune'. Since the Domesday Book the name has appeared in many forms (Lon, Loin, Loon, Lonn, Lone, Lona, Loune, Loone, Loyne, Loine, Lan, and, of course, Lune) but clearly it has pre-Norman origins.

There is not yet agreement on what the Romans called their fort at Lancaster. The assignment of Alauna or Alone is now discredited. Possibly it was the Calunio or Caluvio of what's called the Ravenna Cosmography. The Artle Beck milestone's "I L M P IIII" suggests that the name began with 'L'. It seems probable, then, that a Lune-like name existed in Roman times.

So the origin is lost in pre-history and, in this case, we may as well adopt a suggestion that appeals. Eilert Ekwall concludes in *English River Names* (1928) that it comes from the old Irish (and probably old British) slán, meaning healthy, sound or safe, which is a fair enough description of the Lune.

Lancaster Castle gatehouse

of Liverpool and Manchester have been evicted from Lancashire.

Over the centuries, many famous and infamous trials have been held at the castle. In 1612 ten 'Pendle witches' were sentenced to death. Between 1584 and 1646 seventeen Roman Catholic priests were executed. From 1660, about 270 Quakers, including George Fox, were imprisoned. Innumerable felons were sentenced to death, to provide public spectacles that up to 1799 were held on the moor east of Lancaster and between 1799 and 1865 at what is now called Hanging Corner, outside the castle. This entertainment was more frequent than elsewhere, as the Lancaster court passed more death sentences than any other.

We do things differently nowadays, but less so than we might think. In 1975 the Birmingham Six, accused of the Birmingham pub-bombings, were tried in Lancaster, which with its high security prison next to the court was felt safest for Britain's biggest mass-murder trial. They were sentenced to life imprisonment mainly on the basis of confessions that were extracted under conditions that "if the defendants' stories were to be believed [implied that] many police officers had behaved in a manner that recalled the Star Chamber, the rack and the thumbscrews of four or five hundred years ago", as the judge said in his summing up. They had – and the convictions were eventually overturned in 1991.

The Shire Hall and Crown Court, which were designed by Thomas Harrison and completed in 1798, may be seen, along with Hanging Corner, in a tour of the castle. In the Shire Hall are the heraldic shields of all High Sheriffs of Lancashire since 1129. The High Sheriffs are appointed annually and the ceremony of Shield Hanging is deemed so important that it necessitated an adjournment of the Birmingham Six trial. Within the castle, the tour includes the ancient keep, the dungeons and the medieval Hadrian's Tower and Well Tower (or Witches' Tower).

Next to the castle stands Lancaster Priory. At least, that is what everyone calls it although there has not been a prior here since 1430. The church is said to date from 630, or earlier. There is a Saxon doorway in the west wall of the nave. The priory was founded in the 11th century and Roger of Poitou promptly gave it to the Benedictine Abbey of Saint Martin of Seez in Normandy. This arrangement, whereby income was sent to France, was strained by our war-like relationship with that country and duly ended in 1414 when Henry V gave

The 'HM Prison Service' flag on Lancaster Castle

The Top 10 historical sites in Loyne

By 'historical' I mean anything over a hundred years old:
1. Lancaster Castle
2. Norber erratics, near Austwick
3. Brigflatts, near Sedbergh
4. Castle Stede, Hornby
5. Middleton Hall
6. Sedgwick Trail, Garsdale
7. Leck Fell ancient mounds
8. Rayseat Long Cairn, near Sunbiggin
9. Claughton brickworks
10. Low Borrowbridge

---

the priory to the Convent of Syon in Middlesex. The priory then became the parish church of Lancaster and with the Dissolution of the Monasteries came under the see of Chester.

Unlike most other churches we have met, the tower (of the 18th century) is newer than the rest, which mainly dates from a 15th century restoration. In external appearance it retains the graceful serenity that we like to imagine for that period. Internally, there have been changes but not to the most outstanding feature, the carved choir stalls of about 1340, which some people consider the finest in England.

Despite its long history, Lancaster has few buildings older than 1750, other than the castle and priory. Most of its fine stone buildings in the Georgian style date from the 18th and 19th century. Usually unnoticed, perhaps because they are understandably not near the city centre, are some impressive buildings that possibly result from Lancaster's role as county town. The Royal Albert Asylum for "idiots and imbeciles of the seven northern counties" was built in 1870, its opening being declared a public holiday, suggesting that it was a matter of civic pride. It closed as a hospital in 1996 and is now the Jamea Al Kauthar Islamic College, catering for over four hundred girls from across the world. The 1816 County Lunatic Asylum at Lancaster Moor cared for three thousand people (and is now for sale) and the Ripley Orphanage (now a school) was built in 1864.

The Lune passes the most visible indication of Lancaster's period of prosperity, St George's Quay, built to inspire the 'golden age' of **Lancaster's shipping trade**, from 1750 to 1800. An Act was passed in 1749 "for improving the navigation of the River Loyne, otherwise called Lune, and for building a Quay or Wharf, etc." This was in spite of, or because of, the difficulties that the port faced. Daniel Defoe wrote in about 1730 that Lancaster had "little to recommend it but a decayed castle and a more decayed port" and Samuel Simpson considered in 1746 that "the port is so choaked up with sand, that it is incapable of receiving ships of any considerable burden, and consequently trade finds little encouragement here."

St George's Quay was duly built by 1755, with merchants buying blocks of land behind the new quay wall to build warehouses. The Custom House, for the payment of harbour dues, was built in 1764 with graceful Ionic columns, to the design of Richard Gillow, who had a particular interest in the success of the quay because his company (founded by his father, Robert) depended on the import of

mahogany from the West Indies. The Gillow company became world famous for the quality of its furniture, still widely admired today. Samples of its work can be seen in the Town Hall and in the Gillow Museum, which is housed in the Judges' Lodgings, Lancaster's finest town house. Later, Gillows fitted out royal yachts but, after merging with S.J. Waring in 1903, the company closed in 1961.

Today, most of the warehouses have been converted into flats. The Custom House ceased functioning in 1882 and passed through various roles, including that of theatre, before finding an eminently suitable one as the Maritime Museum in 1985. The museum provides an excellent picture of the lower Lune, including the port, the canal and Morecambe Bay.

The Jamea Al Kauthar Islamic College (née the Royal Albert)

Lancaster's shipping trade, in terms of ships arriving from or leaving for foreign ports, peaked in 1800 at 78 ships. It is a common, but mistaken, belief that Lancaster was once a much bigger port than Liverpool and that it was the rapid growth of the latter that ended Lancaster's trade. The figures show that both Lancaster and Liverpool were minor ports in the early 17th century, with Lancaster being the smaller, and that Lancaster grew slowly through the 18th century as Liverpool grew faster.

The main trade was with the West Indies, importing sugar, rum, mahogany and cotton and exporting hardware and woollen goods. Lancaster was the fourth largest port for the West Indies trade, with about 8% of the outward and 5% of the inward trade. The disparity in the two figures results from Lancaster taking less part in the triangular slave trade (whereby ships travelled to Africa, then America and back to England) than other ports. The register shows that the highest number of ships travelling from Lancaster to Africa in any one year was 6 in 1772 (Liverpool registered 107 such ships in 1771).

There was also considerable European trade, such as the import of timber from the Baltic, and much local shipping: in 1800, 273 ships registered for trade within Britain. After 1800, wars at sea harmed foreign trade generally and continued silting harmed the port of Lancaster in particular. Several local banks failed and merchants took their trade to Liverpool and elsewhere. Although the numbers of ships continued to rise until 1845, reaching a peak of 712, very few of these were from overseas and Lancaster's proportion of the increased national trade was much reduced. The quay was transferred from the Port Commission to Lancaster Corporation in 1901.

The Top 10 cultural sites in Loyne

1. Maritime Museum, Lancaster
2. Lancaster City Museum
3. Ruskin Library, Lancaster University
4. Farfield Mill, Sedbergh
5. Storey Gallery, Lancaster
6. Judges' Lodgings, Lancaster
7. Dent Village Heritage Centre
8. Cottage Museum, Lancaster
9. Bentham Pottery
10. Finestra Gallery, Kirkby Lonsdale

While we are on an aquatic theme, I'll mention the zenith of Loyne's sporting prowess. The region has no major sporting venues or events but in the suitably unsung sport of water polo Lancaster has won the British Championship for five years in a row, from 2003 to 2007.

The Lune passes under its 43rd and last bridge, Carlisle Bridge, for the west coast main line. Its construction in 1846 conceded defeat for St George's Quay, because larger ships could no longer reach it. The 1848 OS map marks Scale Ford 0.5km below the bridge, so presumably the Lune here was much too shallow for large boats anyway. The Port Commission did not give up entirely: it used the compensation received from the railway company to develop New Quay downriver of the bridge.

The Lune Shipbuilding Company was established beside New Quay in 1863, aiming to build iron clippers. Its first ship, the *Wennington* (the company chairman lived at Wennington Hall), took three sets of emigrants to New Zealand before disappearing in the Bali Straits in 1878. The Lune Shipbuilding Company had already disappeared by then, having gone bust in 1870, after building just fourteen ships.

The site was then bought to extend St George's Works, a factory built from 1854. Some say that this was "the biggest factory in the world owned by a single man". There is no way of verifying this but by the 1890s the company employed a quarter of Lancaster's workforce. The 'single man' was James Williamson the

Left: The Judges' Lodgings

The Priory and Custom House across the Lune
(savour the view while you can, before trees are re-planted and
a 1.4m high flood defence barrier is installed)

younger. His father, also James, had invented a type of oilcloth as a table baize and set up the company, which the son took over in 1875 and developed to manufacture linoleum, in particular. He eventually became Lord Ashton – the Lord Linoleum of Philip Gooderson's 1995 book, *Lord Linoleum: Lord Ashton, Lancaster and the Rise of the British Oilcloth and Linoleum Industry*.

In 2004 a £10m project for the Lancaster Economic Development Zone was launched to revitalise 'Luneside East'. The industrial eyesore will be cleared and sold to developers, who will build a "high quality, mixed-use urban neighbourhood" by 2009, it is hoped. In preparation, a 3km-long flood defence has been installed, designed to protect lower Lancaster against all except 1-in-500-year floods. It is a bold person who will predict the effect of climate change on sea levels in 500 years time.

CHAPTER 14:
The Salt Marshes

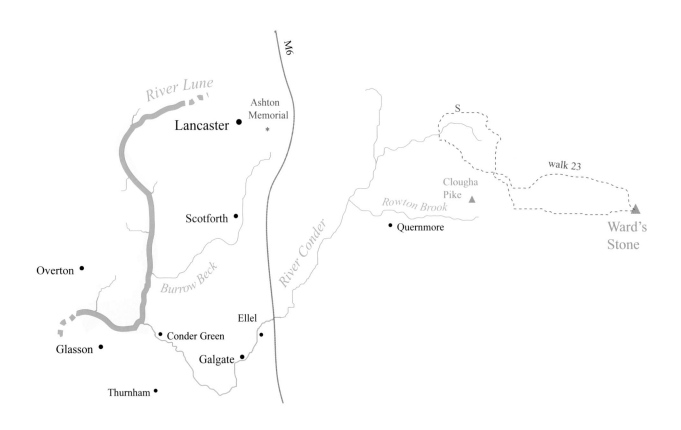

Scale: 1 cm to 1 km

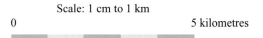

0   5 kilometres

The Lune from Lancaster ...

Beyond Carlisle Bridge the Lune swings south and takes on a different character - in fact, two characters and all shades in between. If the tide is out and there is little water flowing down the Lune, it is a gentle, low river, with sandy, or at least lightly muddy, beaches, providing long, flat views. If the tide is in and the Lune is flowing high, then it becomes a wide, raging river, threatening flood defences.

These conditions give rise to the characteristic coastal salt marshes of the lower Lune. The marshes form from marine alluvium deposited in sheltered areas that are covered only by occasional high tides. Aldcliffe Marsh, Heaton Marsh, Colloway Marsh, Lades Marsh and Glasson Marsh continue for 6km, on both banks of the Lune, down to Morecambe Bay. There's an esoteric appeal to these remote, simple, almost primeval, landscapes, often aglow under the setting sun. The land is naturally flat and open, heavily fissured with creeks, and littered with the debris of high tides and floods. If grazed the marshes are a close-cut, deep green; if not, they are in summer full of colourful flowers such as thrift and sea asters.

The Lune passes Salt Ayre, which, like Green Ayre upriver, used to be an island. It is now a sizable hill, of which the good citizens of Lancaster and Morecambe may be proud – it is created from their rubbish. Beyond Salt Ayre is the Golden Ball pub, facing the detritus left by tidal waters. It is known as 'Snatchems' because of the legend that passing ships short of crewmembers would grab inebriated drinkers from the pub, a tradition that has sadly lapsed. A similar custom would be welcome for the modern pest, the jet-skiers who are increasingly ruining the calm of the Lune estuary, now that they are no longer allowed on Windermere.

The salt marshes require peace – not for us, because the winding creeks and glutinous mud make this dangerous territory, but for the thousands of birds that gather here. There are no buildings on the marshes and the isolation and, ideally, tranquillity make this fine feeding and roosting ground for many wildfowl and wading birds, such as Bewick's swans, little egrets, ringed plovers and spotted redshanks.

Inland of the salt marshes are low coastal drumlins. They are oval-shaped, aligned north to south, indicating the direction of glacial flow. The scattered farmsteads are sited on the gentle slopes above the poorly drained pastures, with the few trees bent by the prevailing wind.

Previous page: Bazil Point, Overton.
Below: the Lune at the Golden Ball.

Aldcliffe Marsh, looking towards the Lakeland hills

The whole peninsula south of Morecambe reaches no higher than Colloway Hill (36m). Inland of the low Heaton-Colloway ridge is a wide, flat expanse, formerly of bogs and mosses but now reclaimed pasture, with many ditches lined with rushes. Seawaters have no doubt inundated the area in the past. Today, it is traversed by power lines from the nuclear power station and by the A683 to Heysham, for people travelling to the many caravan parks nestling by the power station and to the retirement village replacing the old holiday centre.

The highest point between the Lune and the A6 is Burrow Heights (59m), below which Burrow Beck runs to the Lune.

Burrow Beck

We followed the Roman road down the Lune valley, from the Fairmile Road near Tebay, past Over Burrow, by the assumed road that ran past the milestone found at Caton, and on to the fort at Lancaster. Fine place though it is, Lancaster is unlikely to have been the Romans' final destination. Common sense tells us that, in addition to the high road we met crossing the Bowland Fells above Lowgill, there would be a road heading south on the low coastal plains. And remembering Low Borrowbridge and Over Burrow, the name of Burrow Beck, flowing around Burrow Heights, will raise our suspicions.

Sure enough, aerial photographs indicate an old road to the east of the trig point on Burrow Heights, leading towards the Roman road known to pass east of Garstang, heading for Ribchester. More tangibly, four carved figures and two pillars were found near Burrow Heights in the late 18th and early 19th century. The pillars are usually described as milestones although they are half the height of the Caton milestone and their inscriptions only honour the emperor, without giving distances anywhere.

Other finds confirm that a road set off from Lancaster along the line of what is now Penny Street. Evidence is still being uncovered. In 2005 a memorial plaque or headstone, over 1m square, was found north of the canal by Aldcliffe Road. The inscription is to Insus, son of Vodullus, and the stone depicts a soldier on horseback above a kneeling, decapitated man.

Burrow Beck runs quietly for 7km from just east of the Ashton Memorial in Williamson Park through Bowerham and Scotforth, the southern suburbs of Lancaster, to Ashton Hall by the Lune. The memorial and the park were given to Lancaster by, and named after, the industrialist, James Williamson, later Lord Ashton (obviously, no shrinking violet). When ennobled in 1895, he named himself after the manor of Ashton, where he had bought the hall in 1884. He also gave to Lancaster the Town Hall and the Victoria Monument, with a mural of Victorian worthies, including his father.

Williamson Park was created in 1881 from the old Lancaster Moor quarry, stones from which had been used to build most of Lancaster's houses. The neo-classical Ashton Memorial of 1909 is often described as a folly, which my dictionary defines as "a building of strange or fanciful shape, that has no particular purpose." That seems a slander on the designer (John Belcher) and a slur to the wife of Lord Ashton, for whom it was intended as a memorial. If we called it the Jessy Ashton Memorial then we wouldn't mistake it for self-aggrandizement.

Today, it is the most prominent landmark in Lancaster, a proud symbol to all who pass on the M6. However, before it was restored in 1987, Lancaster residents seemed to disown it. According to the Lancaster City Museum exhibit, Lord Ashton left Lancaster in high dudgeon in 1911 to live at Lytham St Anne's. Writing to the local paper, he said that some of his workforce had become "disloyal and discontented" by joining trade unions and voting Labour. In return, the locals were content to let the memorial (which they called 'the structure') fall into decay, which it did.

Lord Ashton's main home was Ryelands House in Skerton rather than the grand Ashton Hall. The hall had been rebuilt in 1856 to retain a tower probably of the 14th century. The manor of Ashton was part of the lands of Roger of Poitou until taken over by the Lancaster family in 1102. Over the centuries, the estate passed through the hands of the Laurences, the Gerards, the Gilberts, the Hamiltons, and the Starkies, before reaching the Williamsons. The hall is now the headquarters of Lancaster Golf Club.

Burrow Beck runs across the golf course, through an ancient fishpond, into a lake, and under the old Lancaster-Glasson railway line, completed in 1883, before dribbling into the Lune. Lord Ashton had a private railway station (Waterloo) at which trains could be flagged down.

A further kilometre south the River Conder crosses salt marsh into the Lune.

The Jessy Ashton Memorial

The Lune after Burrow Beck joins, with a fisherman trying a variant of the traditional method of haaf netting

The River Conder

The River Conder arises at the Conder Head spring to the north of Clougha and flows west through Cragg Wood to the parish of Quernmore. The parish stretches 10km from Halton to Ellel and has long been settled. Two Roman kilns have been found, one below Lythe Brow Wood and the other near the village of Quernmore. In medieval times, Quernmore was a hunting forest, at one time in the charge of the Gernets of Halton and later passing into the hands of the Duchy of Lancaster. It was sold by the crown in 1630. The present Quernmore Park Hall was built in 1794 by Thomas Harrison for the Gibson family.

On Birk Bank there is a large three-arched bridge over Ottergear Clough and two sturdy towers. The function of these structures is unclear although they presumably have something to do with the Thirlmere Aqueduct. Below these slopes a few areas of reed bed, a rare habitat for Loyne, are being restored, perhaps to enable bearded tit and marsh harrier to breed.

The Conder merges with Mother Dyke, from near Quernmore Park Hall, and passes the isolated St Peter's Church, built in 1834. At Conder Mill, below the now ornamental pond, it is joined by Rowton Brook, which arises, properly enough, on Rowton Brook Fell on the south flank of Clougha Pike (413m). Clougha Pike is not really a peak, although it looks so from the southwest, but is merely the end of the westerly ridge from Ward's Stone. Its position offers an extensive panorama

---

The Top 10 viewpoints in Loyne

1. Clougha Pike
2. Great Knoutberry Hill
3. Wild Boar Fell
4. Orton Scar
5. Ingleborough
6. Combe Top, Middleton Fell
7. Caton Moor
8. Hornby Road, Roeburndale
9. Whinfell Beacon
10. Brownthwaite Pike

that includes, circling from the east: Ward's Stone, Hawthornthwaite Fell, Snowdon (on a very clear day), Blackpool Tower, Morecambe Bay, the Isle of Man (on a clear day), the Lakeland fells, the Howgills, Whernside and Ingleborough. At closer quarters is a view of the Lune valley, from its estuary up to the Lune Gorge in the Howgills.

In 1851 it was proposed to use the waters of Rowton Brook for a reservoir to supply water to Lancaster. However, the city architect Edmund Sharpe asked, "why … are we to drink the miserable storage of a dribbling brook, four miles off, when we have at our very feet the magnificent storage of the river Lune, through which a whole river runs daily to change and purify it?" In the end, it was decided, rather cheekily, to use the nearby Grizedale Brook, which drains to the Wyre, for the reservoir. The Lune was used much later.

To the north of Rowton Brook the jumbles of millstone grit provide evidence of the quarrying of querns that gave the region its name. In the fields you may well see sheepdogs at work and, if not, you will certainly hear them within Rooten Brook Farm, where a dozen dogs are housed. These are no ordinary dogs – they are the dogs of the champion sheepdog trialling family, the Longtons. Tim Longton senior won the English National in 1949 and his son, Tim junior, won it five times from 1965. So renowned was the latter that

the first programme of the BBC's *One Man and his Dog*, explaining the nature of sheepdog trialling, was filmed at Rooten Brook Farm. The fourth generation Longton, Michael, won the English National in 2004 at the young age of 24.

The village of Quernmore has only a Post Office, a converted barn or two, a row of new dwellings by Rowton Brook and a residence called Temperance House, dated 1826. The temperance movement was at that time becoming more powerful. Lancaster's Temperance

Two views at the head of the Conder - from Baines Cragg across Cragg Wood (above); Baines Cragg (below).

Walk 23: Ward's Stone

Map: OL41 (please read the general note about the walks in the Introduction).
Starting point: Near Little Cragg (546618).

There are three conditions for this walk: no closure of the access area for grouse shooting (this is allowed for up to 28 days a year: ring 0845 100 3298 if you want to check), no dogs and (preferably) good visibility. With few features marked on the map, I'll indicate the time to reach points en route, assuming a steady walk.

Ward's Stone is 5.5km southeast on the horizon but a direct route would involve much scrambling over heather and rocks. Set off west down the road, past Baines Cragg. After Bark Barn, climb a stile on your left, walk south across the infant Conder on a permitted footpath and enter CRoW land. Keep on the track. After cairns on the right (35 minutes), the track swings left and becomes less steep. With three cubic structures visible ahead (1 hour), note a small post just after a large rocky outcrop on the left (at 552596).

At a junction of tracks (1hr 12m), follow the sign pointing right. At the next side-track, not marked on OS maps (at about 562592), turn left (1hr 23m), ignoring the sign pointing ahead. Initially the track heads direct to Ward's Stone but it then curves left and then right. As you approach the shooters' hut (1hr 50m), note Ward's Stone to its right and imagine your route. Scramble up behind the hut, aiming for a cone-shaped stone on the horizon, and proceed to Ward's Stone.

At Ward's Stone (2hr 15m) the panorama is revealed, with the Three Peaks, the Lakeland fells, the Lune estuary, and your starting (and finishing) point. Ward's Stone (560m) is sadistic: after battling to the stone, you find that the official top, just 1m higher (the highest point of the Bowland Fells), is at a second trig point, visible 1km away. Climb the stone to get 1m above the first trig point and settle for that.

Head west on the ridge path and after 2km turn right at the track you meet (2hr 55m). Ignore the track off to the right (3hr 2m) – you went that way earlier. Ignore the second track to the right (3hr 13m), as you did earlier. The cubes, with enigmatic plinths, come into view to the left. Pass below the cubes (3hr 20m) and reach the rocky outcrop with the little post (3hr 25m). (If you miss the post, just continue back the way you came.) Turn right here on a path that heads towards the wind turbines. Small posts mark the way but they are difficult to see. Some kind souls are creating cairns.

The path continues towards the wind turbines and then curves left. A wall is seen 50m to your right (3hr 50m). Keep the wall to your right until (4hr) a stile is seen ahead. Climb the stile, turn right by Sweet Beck and walk past Skelbow Barn to Little Cragg.

Society was formed in 1833 and at one time Lancaster had twelve temperance hotels.

As you follow Rowton Brook west, you may be increasingly overcome by the nauseous stench from the mushroom farms near Nether Lodge. In 2002 thirty-three illegal immigrants were found working here and deported. The mushroom farms are an anomalous presence in the Quernmore valley, for it is a rich agricultural area that seems wasted on mushroom sheds.

Conder Mill Bridge is only wide enough for a stream 2m across. Something seems awry here. The Langthwaite ridge to the west rises 100m above the Conder and is 4km from Clougha Pike. The valley seems far too broad and deep for such a trickle. And indeed it is, for before the Ice Age the Lune ran through this valley, until glacial deposits blocked its path.

The engineers' attempt to defy this process of nature by laying a pipe through the Quernmore valley to take water from the Lune to the Wyre was sadly rebuffed by nature itself, when an explosion at the valve house in Abbeystead in 1984 killed sixteen people.

The investigation found that the explosion was caused by the ignition of methane but that "the likelihood of a flammable atmosphere arising there had not been envisaged" – which seems an oversight given the history of coal mining in the area.

The Langthwaite ridge from Knots Wood to Hazelrigg is formed from millstone grit overlain by boulder clay and supports mixed farming and woodland. It separates the coastal drumlin fields of Lancaster and its surroundings from the glacial sands and clay drift of Quernmore. As might be expected, communication masts are prominent.

Below the Forrest Hills fishery and golf course, the Conder crosses the Kit Brow stepping stones, where, as for all Loyne's becks, the 'trickle' is not always so. Lancaster University holds an annual race over the stepping stones, which one year were far under water, and I became so as well when I was washed away from the safety rope provided.

The Conder passes the small village of Ellel and the larger one of Galgate. Galgate has the misfortune to be bisected twice, by the A6 and the west coast main line railway. Perhaps that serves it right, for having a name proclaiming it to be the gate or road to Galloway. The only building of note is the old mill, which is said to be the first mechanical silk mill in England. It was bought as a corn mill in 1792, converted to spin silk, and operated until 1970. It now houses "the country's largest bathroom emporium" and various smaller units.

The marina on the Lancaster Canal is relatively peaceful although the public moorings are busy on summer weekends. Just south of here the canal begins a branch to Glasson, completed in 1826 with six locks. In the dry summer of 2006, the branch was closed for periods because the water levels were too low – which raises a question: where does canal water come from? Lancaster Canal itself is supplied by Killington Reservoir but for the Glasson branch most of its water is taken from the River Conder, small as it is and now even smaller than it should be.

The Conder runs slowly west, north of the canal, passing Thurnham Mill, now the Mill Inn. The mill operated using water from the canal, which is possible only through being next to a lock. To the south is Thurnham Hall, with an interesting history.

The usual pattern with the grand halls of Loyne is that for centuries they provided a home for the family at the apex of the local rural hierarchy; in the 18th or 19th century they may have been bought by a newly-rich industrialist; either way, the residents continued to lead the gentrified country life until the middle of the 20th century when societal changes meant that the halls had to be converted to some other use, such as offices, a school or flats. Thurnham Hall followed this pattern, with unhappy consequences.

Thurnham Hall was the manorial home from the 12th century and was bought by Robert Dalton in 1556. The Daltons continued to buy land around Lancaster, to become the largest landowner in the region. Dalton Square and nearby streets in Lancaster are named after members of the Dalton family. The Daltons were staunch Catholics and funded the nearby Church of St Thomas and St Elizabeth, built in 1745. After the Daltons left in the mid 20th century, the hall lapsed until it was restored in 1973, to be a classy restaurant for a while.

It was then bought to form the centrepiece of a timeshare operation, Thurnham Leisure Group,

with headquarters in Lancaster. Holiday courtyards and a swimming pool were built around the hall. However, amid rising complaints from customers, the Group crashed in 2004 leaving a £5m debt. The managing director, Fred Fogg, was given a two-year prison sentence for conspiring to defraud finance companies. Sunterra Europe, with a head office in Lancaster but part of the US-based Sunterra company, acquired the hall and other property, plus the irate customers, for £2m. Sunterra itself … treading carefully here … has experienced some turbulence (Sunterra Europe was put up for sale in 2006). Today it is an unnerving experience to walk on the public footpath amongst the possibly disgruntled holidaymakers of Thurnham Hall Country Club. Perhaps the renowned ghosts of Thurnham Hall are restless.

For its last kilometre the Conder is tidal, with the nearby roads occasionally under water, especially the one to Glasson, which was badly flooded in 2002. In the tranquil meanders derelict craft fall and rise but seem never to be resurrected. Above the flood level is the Stork, a 17th century inn that has retained something of its old character. By the viaduct for the old Lancaster-Glasson railway line is the Conder Green picnic site, which is on the route of the 220km Lancashire Coastal Way. The Conder Green salt marshes are not grazed and as a result have a great variety of plants, including the rare lax-flowered sea-lavender.

Lax-flowered sea-lavender

The Conder (three times) at the Stork, Conder Green

Glasson marina

The Lune from the Conder ...

East of the Conder the Lune passes Glasson, which is part port, part resort, but not much of either. On a fine day, with a sea breeze gently fluttering the mastheads in the marina, it makes a pleasant outing, although there is not much to do or to see, apart from leisurely activity about the boats. There is no beach or seaside promenade, and only a few old-style catering establishments, with two pubs.

A large barrier separates the Lune, and hence the sea, from a dock that was completed in 1787 after the Lancaster Port Commission resolved to build it for ships unable to navigate the Lune to reach the new St George's Quay. Before then, the area was a marsh, with the farms of Brows, Crook and Old Glasson to the south.

The dock did not flourish for long, against competition from better docks at Preston and Fleetwood, although the Glasson Group of companies is still an active importer, especially of animal feedstuffs. Still standing are the Custom House (which functioned from 1835 to 1924) and the Watch House (built 1836), which with typical Loyne immodesty is claimed to be the smallest lighthouse in England. A nearby dry dock for ship repair

Glasson Watch House

functioned from 1841 to 1968, when it was filled in to become an area for light industry. The Port of Lancaster Smoke House, winner of the 2007 North West Fine Food Producer of the Year award, is on the West Quay.

A further barrier separates the dock from the large marina on the Glasson branch of the Lancaster Canal. Commercial traffic ended long ago but canal-based tourism is now Glasson's main occupation. This it supplements with other unassuming activities: an annual folk-music festival; the racing of radio-controlled laser boats in the marina; a weekend gathering point for bikers; the Maritime Festival, moved from Lancaster in 2007.

The railway, arriving late (1883) and departing early (1930 for passengers, 1964 for freight), left little trace in Glasson, apart from Railway Place, a group of cottages that pre-date the railway. The line of the track now forms part of the Lancashire Coastal Way, which continues over the barrier separating dock and marina, through Glasson, and up Tithe Barn Hill, which at a magnificent height of 20m provides a fine view, often with excellent sunsets, across the estuary to Overton and Sunderland, with the Lakeland hills beyond. There's a 360° view-indicator and five benches, all facing Heysham power station.

Overton, across the Lune, is an ancient village, appearing as Oureton in the Domesday Book. Modern building for commuters surrounds the old core of the village, leaving little trace of the traditional activities of shipbuilding and fishing. Even so, the aroma of the fields and the sea remains. Farms are still active in and around the village, and twice a day the tide laps on its shores. A walk around Bazil Point, from where there used to be a ferry to Glasson, involves stepping through tidal debris but provides open views across the marshes and the Lune estuary.

The most notable feature of Overton is St Helen's Church, which is said to be the oldest church in Lancashire. The church itself is more reticent, claiming only, on a notice board inside, that the west wall is "11th century or earlier" and that other parts, such as the doorway arches, are "of about 1140". Whatever its age, it must have been one of the most isolated of early churches. In outward appearance, the church is rather colourless, with uninspired windows. Inside, however, the small church is transformed, with the windows now enlivened. The arrangement is novel, with a gallery to the west, the pulpit by the south wall, and the 1830 extension on the north side having no view of the altar to the east.

The Top 10 churches in Loyne

(for the nonreligious)
1. St Helen's, Overton
2. St John the Baptist, Tunstall
3. St Mary's, Lancaster Priory
4. St Mary the Virgin, Kirkby Lonsdale
5. St Andrew's, Sedbergh
6. St Wilfrid's, Halton
7. St Margaret's, Hornby
8. St Wilfrid's, Melling
9. St Mary's, Ingleton
10. St Andrew's, Dent

Right: St Helen's Church, Overton.

Sunderland across Lades Marsh

DANGER
Beware of fast tides
hidden channels and
quick sands

CHAPTER 15:
Into Morecambe Bay

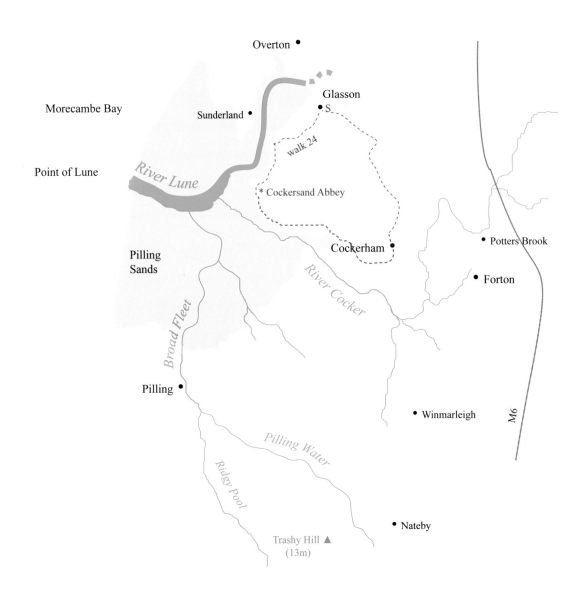

Overton •

Glasson
• S

Morecambe Bay

Sunderland •

walk 24

Point of Lune

River Lune

* Cockersand Abbey

Pilling
Sands

Cockerham •

River Cocker

Broad Fleet

• Potters Brook

• Forton

Pilling •

• Winmarleigh

Pilling Water

M6

Ridgy Pool

Trashy Hill ▲
(13m)

• Nateby

Scale: 1 cm to 1 km

0   5 kilometres

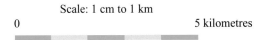

The Lune from the Conder
(continued) ...

The road south from Overton across Lades Marsh leads to Sunderland, the end of the west bank of the Lune. Unlike Overton, Sunderland has had no new building for nearly a century. It looks like the set for a film based in a 19th century fishing village, as indeed it became in 2006 when used to film *The Ruby in the Smoke*. With the tidal waters covering the road, it is detached, both physically and mentally, from the modern world.

It consists of two terraces, First Terrace and Second Terrace, reasonably enough, and, a little apart, the Old Hall of 1715. All have their backs to the prevailing westerly winds and hence have views across the estuary to the masts of Glasson Dock and the Bowland Fells beyond. There is even a glimpse of our old friend, Ingleborough.

The terraced cottages are mainly 18th century, some converted from old warehouses. They have charm but are not pretty as this is too tough a place for adornment. A few cottages are named after the 'cotton tree', once a feature of Sunderland but a victim of a gale in 1998, after surviving for nearly 300 years. There is still debate over exactly what kind of tree it really was but it is literally academic now, unless the stump revives.

In front of the cottages a dozen boats rest at anchor or doze on the mud, depending on the state of the tide. A couple of them look like active fishing boats, a remnant

Previous page: the road from Sunderland to Overton
Below: Second Terrace, from First Terrace

of the traditional occupation of Sunderland residents. The heyday (such as it was, for Sunderland can never have been much larger than it is now) was the period from 1680, when it was recognised as a 'legal quay', which meant that ships were allowed to unload goods there, until about 1750, when St George's Quay became active. During that period, many ships avoided the difficult journey up the Lune by having goods taken ashore at Sunderland for transport across land or by ferryboat to Lancaster. There was also a good trade in towing or guiding boats up the estuary to Lancaster but Sunderland's business evaporated as fast as it had begun, with the development of better docking facilities in Lancaster, Fleetwood and especially Glasson.

The most remarked upon feature of Sunderland is that it is one of only two places in England (the other being Lindisfarne) that is cut off twice a day by the tide. However, this is only the case if lack of vehicular access constitutes being cut off: Sunderland can always be reached on foot from the west. It would seem easy to provide a road on the landward side of the flood embankment, but no doubt the residents of Sunderland want no more than the few visitors prepared to make a committed effort to get there.

The best way to visit Sunderland, where there is not really anywhere to park a car anyway, is to park at or cycle to Potts Corner on the Morecambe Bay shore and then walk south along the coast. There are magnificent views across the bay, with the Fylde coast to Fleetwood to the south, the south Lakes coast to the Isle of Walney to the north, and on the horizon the glinting blades of the offshore wind turbines.

The mud and sea stretch for miles, glittering in the sunlight and providing spectacular sunsets. There is the odd abandoned craft and the perhaps odder individual who feels confident enough about the tides and the mud to venture far off shore but it is the enormous numbers of wading birds that catch the eye. In winter Morecambe Bay has more birds than anywhere else in Britain, save perhaps the Wash – greylag geese, mallard, red-breasted merganser, pintail, pochard, shelduck, shoveler, wigeon, and so on. Over 160 species have been recorded. They are attracted, of course, by the food in the mud, which may look unappetising to us but contains, for example,

Pebbles and old fish baulks at Sunderland Point

Hang glider over Sunderland

about 5000 Baltic tellins, which are small shellfish, per square metre (I have taken the experts' word for this).

If you keep your eyes to the west, as you should, you will miss Sambo's Grave, which is to be recommended. This is apparently a tourist attraction but it is a tawdry and maudlin site, a poignant but pathetic memorial to our own inglorious past as much as to Sambo, a slave who died at Sunderland in 1736: "here lies poor Sambo: a faithful Negro", isolated as a heathen unfit for consecrated ground.

If you must look landward, look instead for the Belted Beauty moth. This endangered moth has colonies at only three sites in England and Wales and, until the colony at Sunderland was confirmed in 2004, it was thought to live only on coastal sand dunes. Here its habitat is salt marsh, with sea rush and autumn hawkbit. The males fly at night, as moths tend to do, but can be seen resting during the day; the poor females are wingless and can be spotted crawling about.

Searching for moths in salt marsh is not to everyone's taste but the moths' existence here is an indication of the special nature of this vulnerable promontory. If you continue the walk south to Sunderland Point (there is no public footpath but I don't think anyone will object), you'll see that the fields, some 2m above beach level, are virtually unprotected and appear to be crumbling fast under the western gales.

From the end of the promontory, we can see across to the Plover Scar lighthouse and may fear that our journey down the Lune and its tributaries has come to an end. But if the beginning of a river is always a matter of

debate, so is its end. At high tide the Lune is 1km wide from Sunderland Point and disappears into the wide expanses of Morecambe Bay, but at low tide the Lune can be considered to continue for a further 7km or so between Cockerham Sands and Middleton Sands before finally joining the waters of Morecambe Bay at the Point of Lune. According to the Environment Agency by-laws, the Lune estuary lies landward of a line from Knott End jetty to Heysham No. 2 buoy and thence to Heysham lighthouse. For the sake of completeness, then, we will take the Point of Lune as the end of our story, which will enable us to include the gentle tributaries of the River Cocker and Broad Fleet.

The River Cocker

The Cocker is barely large enough to be a river but is not sprightly enough to be a beck. It arises north of Cocker Clough Wood on a ridge between the Conder and the Wyre, carefully avoiding both. It runs past Hampson Green, under the M6 and railway line, past Bay Horse, and is joined by Potters Brook just before crossing the Lancaster Canal.

Potters Brook flows from Forton, known to many through the distinctive Forton (recently renamed Lancaster) Service Station, with its tower no longer a restaurant-cum-viewpoint. For travellers from the south the tower marks a gateway to the dramatic northern landscapes. Forton has long been on travellers' routes: before the railway and canal, the Roman road from Lancaster passed here, probably by Forton Hall Farm

Plover Scar lighthouse

and Windy Arbour. Today, Forton consists mainly of new bungalows, plus the 1707 United Reformed (formerly Independent) Church, with bright yellow door to enable it to be located in the overgrown churchyard.

The Cocker swings north towards Ellel Grange. This Italianate villa, as it's always described, was built in 1859 for William Preston, who became High Sheriff of Lancashire in 1865. It is said to be modelled on Queen Victoria's Osborne House (completed in 1851), but then so are innumerable contemporary British villas. The grange is now the international headquarters and Special Ministries Unit of the **Ellel Ministries**.

The Cocker continues south past Cockerham, flowing under Cocker House Bridge, where there is an old boundary stone. Cockerham is an old village, appearing in the Domesday Book as Cocreham. Its ancient church, most recently rebuilt in 1911, now stands apart but originally the village houses were clustered around it. A fire in the 17th century moved the village east.

At the north end of Cockerham is the vicarage built in 1843 for the Rev. Dodson, whom we met in Littledale. The earnestness we saw there is seen also in his determination to rid Cockerham of all sinful activities, such as cock fighting, hare coursing, horse racing and even bowling. After the Rev. Dodson left, a public house

was built in 1871 without, it seems, unduly disturbing the peace of the village.

The Cocker dawdles through flat land drained by many ditches in Winmarleigh Moss. This is Lancashire's largest remaining uncultivated peat mossland, supporting

Ellel Grange

The **Ellel Ministries** make the name of Ellel known worldwide but few people are aware that the name refers to a tiny village near Lancaster. The story of the Ellel Ministries begins in 1970 when Peter Horrobin was repairing a sports car and – here I must quote from their website so that you don't think me lacking in due seriousness – "God spoke to him about how he could straighten the chassis and rebuild the car, but much more importantly, God could rebuild broken lives." And if He whispered 'Ellel' that was fortunate because apparently in old English it means 'all hail'.

When Ellel Grange came up for sale in 1985 Horrobin raised nearly £0.5m from supporters to convert the grange into a ministry. The Ellel Ministries are now an international brand with branches in Australia, Canada, Germany, India, Norway, Scotland, Singapore, South Africa and the United States.

What do the Ellel Ministries do? This may be as treacherous as the sands of Morecambe Bay, but I will venture in. The mission is "to proclaim the Kingdom of God by preaching the good news, healing the broken-hearted and setting the captives free." In practice, this means "discipleship, healing and deliverance training".

The theology, however, is controversial. According to others, the Ellel Ministries have "extreme doctrinal positions on deliverance and demonology" that "are void of biblical foundations". A review of Horrobin's book *Healing through Deliverance* concluded that it argued that "those who did not believe that Christians can be demonized … are themselves demonized." Verily, I should steer clear, at least until my broken heart needs healing.

rare insect species such as the large heath butterfly and bush cricket. Winmarleigh itself is a scattered village. Winmarleigh Hall was built on the site of Old Hall in 1871 for John Wilson-Patten, MP for Lancashire North for 42 years. He became Baron Winmarleigh, the first and last, as he outlived his two sons and grandson. The hall is now owned by NST Travel Group, which claims to be "Europe's largest educational and group travel company".

Beyond Cocker Bridge, the Cocker runs between sea defence embankments built in 1981. In 1969 the only colony of natterjack toads in Lancashire had been found on Cockerham Moss. Natterjack toads are the rarest of six British amphibians and are protected by law. The site was washed over by the highest tides but not after the wall was built. Perhaps coincidentally, the colony became extinct after 1981. The Herpetological Conservation Trust is now trying to restore the habitat and reintroduce the natterjack toad.

Part of Cockerham Moss was enclosed only after draining in the 19th century. The few buildings are modern and of brick. The terrain is flat and featureless, given over to sheep and cattle, with some arable farming if dry enough.

Similarly, north of the Cocker Channel, lies the flat drained land of Thurnham Moss. At the seaward extremity of this bleak landscape are the remains of **Cockersand Abbey**. The meagre remains today do not indicate the extent and importance of the abbey.

Walk 24: Glasson, Cockersand Abbey and Cockerham

Map: 296 (please read the general note about the walks in the Introduction).
Starting point: Near Glasson marina (446561).
This is a walk best done on a grey, rainy day with a strong westerly wind and a high tide – to better get into the spirit of the place. (Only joking.)
Walk southwest through Glasson to Tithe Barn Hill, and then turn right along Marsh Lane to Crook Farm. Follow the sea wall south to the Abbey Lighthouse Cottage, Plover Hill (7m high) and Cockersand Abbey, to which make a short detour. Across the shimmering waters of Morecambe Bay, Fleetwood and the Isle of Walney may be seen.
Continue past Bank Houses and the Cockerham Sands caravan park, and along the 1km embankment. Turn right towards the Patty's Farm holiday cottages, before which you cut southeast through the Black Knights Parachute Centre, which may be busy with planes and parachutists (but not if you've chosen a windy day).
Across the fields, turn left on the A588 for 200m, and then walk to St Michael's Church. From the church take the path northeast to the Main Street of Cockerham.
Walk north through Cockerham and take the path northeast to Batty Hill. Continue north along a muddy track and then walk northeast to Cock Hall Farm (the high point of the walk, at 27m). Turn northwest past Thurnham Church and walk through the Thurnham Hall Country Club and across a field to Bailey Bridge. Cross the bridge and stroll along the canal towpath back to Glasson.

The remains of Cockersand Abbey

Originally, the abbey stood up to where the sea wall is now. Today, there are just a few stones scattered about with only the chapter house still standing, partly because it was used as a burial place after being adopted by the Daltons. The red sandstone masonry of the old abbey was re-used in nearby farm buildings and in the sea wall, a somewhat ironic use of the stones since the abbots lived in fear of being submerged by the sea.

Beyond the sea wall and embankment the Cocker disappears into the mudflats of the Lune estuary and Morecambe Bay, forming part of the Wyre and Lune Sanctuary Nature Reserve, established as a national wildfowl refuge in 1963. This affords protection for internationally important numbers of wintering knot, grey plover, oystercatcher, pink-footed geese and turnstone. It also provides an important staging post for birds such as sanderling. The embankment runs 8km west, past the village of Pilling, and is crossed through flood gates by Wrampool Brook and Broad Fleet.

Broad Fleet

Broad Fleet slides into the Lune estuary from Pilling Moss, especially via Pilling Water from Nateby. In the Lake District a 'water' is a lake; Pilling Water is not a lake but it flows almost as slowly as one. Nateby is 10m above sea level and it takes Pilling Water 10km to reach the Lune.

Obviously, the region is flat. There are long, wide views over large, rectangular fields for cows, sheep and intensive crop production. Given the monotonous terrain perhaps I should argue that Broad Fleet is not really a tributary of the Lune and not bother with this section. However, there is nowhere that some expert in something doesn't find engrossing. Unfortunately for the visitor, the main interest here is underground, where recent studies have revealed unexpected insights into the past, present and possibly future of Pilling Moss.

The story begins with the Ice Age, when boulder clay was dumped over the Fylde region, leaving occasional

Cockersand Abbey was established as a monastic cell in the 12th century by Hugh the Hermit, as he would need to have been to choose this bleak, exposed, otherwise godforsaken spot, cut off from the mainland by Thurnham Moss. By 1190 this St Mary's of the Marsh had become a Premonstratensian abbey.

The abbey became very rich during the 13th century, through being granted much land in the northwest of England. At that time people were desperate to go to heaven and believed that a prayer on their behalf from monks would help. A gift to the abbey proved your piety.

The monk's life was not entirely one of cloistered contemplation. According to *British History Online*: in 1316, the abbey suffered badly from Scottish raids; in 1327, a canon was pardoned for the death of a brother; in 1347, the abbot and four canons were accused of using violence; in 1363, the abbey was ravaged by plague; in 1378, the king was begged for special compensation because "each day they are in danger of being drowned and destroyed by the sea"; in 1402, there was fear of violence from parties with whom they were in litigation; in 1488, two apostate canons were excommunicated, the brethren were forbidden to reveal the secrets of the order, and two other canons were accused of breaking their vow of chastity; in 1497, the canons were forbidden to "exchange opprobrious charges" and to draw knives upon one other; in 1500, various diseases were attributed to "inordinate potations" and there were minor disorders, such as disobedience to the abbot, lingering in bed and neglecting services on pretext of illness.

It all gives new meaning to the Dissolution of the Monasteries. At that time (1539) Cockersand was the third richest abbey in Lancashire. Its annual income was estimated at £157, revised (to no avail) to £282 after it was decreed that monasteries with an income less than £200 would be taken over by the king. Its lands, valued at £798, were bought by John Kechyn of Hatfield in 1544 and then passed to Robert Dalton of Thurnham Hall.

The rather serious Nateby church

small drumlins. By 4000 BC, the region had become a forest, as shown by the large number of 'moss stocks', that is, old tree trunks uncovered in the fields and dated to that period. The roots were upright and the trunks had been hacked off, showing that the trees were felled and that there was a large local community to carry out this arduous work.

This is supported by extensive finds of Neolithic implements and the discovery of ancient earthworks around Nateby. Today, the gentle undulations in the fields appear unremarkable but aerial photographs reveal various regular shapes, such as a 200m-diameter henge dated to about 2500 BC. Many Bronze Age remains have been found north of Nateby.

With the forest removed, the region became heathland but after the climate became damper in about 1400 BC it slowly became a bog, a process thought to have been complete by 800 BC. Old tracks, formed by laying down tree trunks to cross the bog, have been dated to that time. Over the centuries, layers of peat were formed, the first 1m or so being of rough peat, from the heathland vegetation, and then up to 4m of softer peat, mainly from sphagnum moss. The extent of the bog can be judged by the place names on today's map: I counted eight Moss Sides and three Moss Edges surrounding an area of about 25 sq km. (One of the former, Moss Side Stables, made the news in 2006 when the racehorse trainer there, Alan Berry, was charged with race-fixing.)

During the investigations of the Nateby earthworks a Roman road (or by-road) was discovered. It has been traced to join the Roman road that we've followed south from Lancaster and is believed to have continued west, south of Pilling Moss, to meet a port on the River Wyre. In the following centuries, habitation was limited to the drumlins raised a metre or two above the bog. Many farmsteads were drolly given a name with 'hill' in it. Unsurprisingly, there are few old buildings of architectural merit. For example, the village of Nateby, mainly a row of semi-detached houses today, was little more than a church a century ago. The new buildings in the region are mostly of red brick.

Pilling, however, is an old village, being owned by Cockersand Abbey in the 12th century and passing to the Dalton family in the 16th century. It was very isolated, having the sea to the north and Pilling Moss to the south. There are only two buildings that interrupt the flat horizons: Damside mill and the church steeple.

The windmill was built in 1808 to a height of 22m, the tallest in Fylde. By the 1940s it had become derelict but, rather miraculously, it has been restored as a residence, complete with a traditional 'boat top', installed in 2007.

The steeple belongs to the St John the Baptist Church built in 1887 by Paley and Austin again. Here, they not only tackled the novelty (for Loyne) of a steeple but enlivened it by using different coloured stones, such as pink ones for the parapet. The church replaced one that

still stands in the field behind, with a date of 1717 over the door and a sundial commemorating George Holden, who in Pilling literature is described as the inventor of tide tables.

On this journey I have learned to be wary of repeating such claims. The facts seem to be these: George Holden (died 1793) was a master at Bentham Grammar School; George Holden (died 1820) was vicar of Pilling Church from 1758 to 1767 before moving to Horton-in-Ribblesdale; George Holden (died 1865) of Maghull compiled the Liverpool tide tables. The prediction of tides has been of practical importance for millennia and the history of tide tables is complex, but the name of Holden does not feature strongly in neutral accounts of that history. The three Georges are probably grandfather, father and son, and the Pilling George no doubt had a close interest in tides, since the parsonage was right beside the tidal floodgates.

Today, Pilling Moss is dry farming land, with many ditches. It was drained in the 19th century, after which it was possible to lay a railway line across it in 1870. The single-line track ran, rather informally, from Garstang to Pilling. The 'Pilling Pig', named from the sound of the engine or whistle, became a familiar feature, and today stands at Fold House as one of the few things for tourists to look at. The line closed for passengers in 1930 and for freight in the 1950s.

Once the bog had been drained, the peat began to shrink and much of it was cut for fuel, an activity that ended in the 1960s. The land is now lower, the rich soil is disappearing, and, who knows, the area is ready for its second flooding. This is precisely what the Pilling Embankment built in 1981 is intended to prevent. In the meantime, the embankment provides (from the section open to the public between Lane Ends and Fluke Hall) a view of Broad Fleet seeping into Morecambe Bay, with, suitably enough, a view of the Howgills far behind the Ashton Memorial. And to show that I am not alone in considering this still to be within Loyne, the last house as the road peters out beyond Fluke Hall is called Lune View Cottage.

Here's a fascinating fact that I've kept up my sleeve in order to finish this flat Fylde section with a flourish: when it's in the mood, the River Lune can bring 700,000,000,000 litres of water into Morecambe Bay in one day. We now know where they all come from.

Damside mill, Pilling

Broad Fleet at low tide, entering Morecambe Bay

Reflections from the Point of Lune

And so, at the Point of Lune, the waters of the Lune and all its tributaries finally merge into Morecambe Bay and the Irish Sea. The final sentence of *Return to the Lune Valley* (2002) concludes that a tour down the Lune valley is "an interesting journey and a pleasant one". 'Pleasant' is perhaps as positive as one can be about the Lune valley itself but it is possible to support a claim that the wider area within the Lune watershed is the most varied of any river in England.

English Nature and the Countryside Agency have produced an analysis of England in terms of 159 'Character Areas', that is, areas that are "distinctive with a unique 'sense of place'". Loyne includes parts of ten of these Character Areas. No other English river of the size of the Lune and its tributaries, if any at all, passes through so many Character Areas. In the following review of our journey, the Character Areas are indicated in italics.

The River Lune rises in the *Howgills*, which are composed of ancient sedimentary rocks that have been eroded into steep, rounded, grassy hills, incised by swift-flowing becks and grazed by sheep, but largely devoid of people. As the Lune swings west, on its northern side are the *Orton Fells*, composed of limestone. Below dramatic limestone pavements, there is fertile soil supporting improved pasture.

At Tebay, the Lune turns south and is joined by becks from the western Howgills and, from the west, from the Birkbeck and Shap Fells, part of the *Cumbria High Fells*. Below Sedbergh, the Lune forms the western boundary of the *Yorkshire Dales* Character Area, which is not the same as the National Park. From the Yorkshire Dales the major tributaries of the Rawthey, Dee, Greta and Wenning flow. This part of the Yorkshire Dales is mainly of limestone, overlain with sandstone and siltstones, capped by millstone grit on the highest tops. It includes some of the best limestone scenery in England, with impressive pavements, gorges, potholes and cave systems.

As the Lune continues south of Sedbergh, its western watershed is much closer than that to the east. The rolling semi-improved, upland pastures from Firbank Fell down to Kirkby Lonsdale form part of the *South Cumbria Low Fells*, which stretch west towards Windermere and Coniston. From Kirkby Lonsdale the west bank of the Lune forms the eastern fringe of the *Morecambe Bay Limestones* Character Area, which extends to Kendal and Ulverston.

To the east of the Lune south of Kirkby Lonsdale is the *Bowland Fringe*, an area of lush pasture, hay meadows, woodlands, marshes and becks, in which there are many isolated stone farmsteads and small villages. The pace of change is slow and many prehistoric features survive, including traces of Roman roads. The Lune and its tributaries are notable for the number of medieval and later halls and manor houses, later adapted for a variety of contemporary uses.

As the Lune flows on in its widening floodplain, it is joined by becks from the *Bowland Fells*, an area of millstone grit forming a wild, windswept, upland plateau of bog and heath. Just north of Lancaster, the Lune becomes tidal and enters the *Morecambe Coast and Lune Estuary* Character Area. Here the low-lying land is covered with glacial and alluvial deposits and was once an area of fens, marshes and bogs. Today, it has been largely drained to provide pasture but there are still extensive areas of inter-tidal marshes. Finally, joining the Lune estuary, are rivers and drainage channels from the flat lands of the northern Fylde, part of the *Lancashire and Amounderness Plain*.

From this great variety of landscape types derives a range of human activities, although the Lune and its tributaries remain relatively undeveloped. It also provides such varied scenery and specific habitats for wildlife that much of the area has been recognised nationally and internationally, through designations as parts of National Parks, Areas of Outstanding Natural Beauty and Sites of Special Scientific Interest. Most of the region is farmed but even the areas that seem most like wilderness require a delicate balance between conservation and development, between the past and the future.

Even within such an apparently timeless region as Loyne, the threat of the future looms. On many mornings I set off to investigate a part of Loyne without a cloud in the sky. As the day progressed and the boots became muddier and the legs became wearier, so the sky often became hazier. But this was usually not a natural haze. It was caused by the vapour trails of the jets crossing the Loyne skies. The Loyne is on a busy flight path: often I could count a dozen or more jets in the sky at one moment.

As I wander on the green hills and among the grey villages of Loyne, many thousand people a day cross the skies above me. Clearly, I am misguided. I am envious of people who have acquired a sufficiently deep appreciation of their local surroundings and can, in a week or two, similarly appreciate wherever they are off to. Perhaps I should join them, but I suspect that I will look forward most to seeing those green hills and grey villages out of the jet's windows as I return.

The last view of the Lune, at high tide from the embankment beyond Fluke Hall, with the Bowland Fells in the distance.

Bibliography and References

Abram, Chris (2006), *The Lune Valley: Our Heritage* (DVD).

Alston, Robert (2003), *Images of England: Lancaster and the Lune Valley*, Stroud: Tempus Publishing Ltd.

Ashworth, Susan and Dalziel, Nigel (1999), *Britain in Old Photographs: Lancaster & District*, Stroud: Budding Books.

Baines, Edward (1824), *History, Directory and Gazetteer of the County Palatine of Lancaster.*

Bentley, John and Bentley, Carol (2005), *Ingleton History Trail.*

Bibby, Andrew (2005), *Forest of Bowland (Freedom to Roam Guide)*, London: Francis Lincoln Ltd.

Birkett, Bill (1994), *Complete Lakeland Fells*, London: Collins Willow.

Boulton, David (1988), *Discovering Upper Dentdale*, Dent: Dales Historical Monographs.

British Geological Survey (2002), *British Regional Geology: The Pennines and Adjacent Areas*, Nottingham: British Geological Survey.

Camden, William (1610), *Britannia.*

Carr, Joseph (1871-1897), *Bygone Bentham*, Blackpool: Landy.

Champness, John (1993), *Lancaster Castle: a Brief History*, Preston: Lancashire County Books.

Cockcroft, Barry (1975), *The Dale that Died*, London: Dent.

Copeland, B.M. (1981), *Whittington: the Story of a Country Estate*, Leeds: W.S. Maney & Son Ltd.

Dalziel, Nigel and Dalziel, Phillip (2001), *Britain in Old Photographs: Kirkby Lonsdale & District*, Stroud: Sutton Publishing Ltd.

Denbigh, Paul (1996), *Views around Ingleton*, Ingleton and District Tradespeople's Association.

Dugdale, Graham (2006), *Curious Lancashire Walks*, Lancaster: Palatine Books.

Garnett, Emmeline and Ogden, Bert (1997), *Illustrated Wray Walk*, Lancaster: Pagefast Ltd.

Gibson, Leslie Irving (1977), *Lancashire Castles and Towers*, Skipton: Dalesman Books.

Gooderson, Philip (1995), *Lord Linoleum: Lord Ashton, Lancaster and the Rise of the British Oilcloth and Linoleum Industry*, Keele: Keele University Press.

Gray, Thomas (1769), *A Guide to the Lakes, in Cumberland, Westmorland, and Lancashire*, Kendal: Pennington.

Halton Rectory (1900), *Annals of the Parish of Halton.*

Harding, Mike (1988), *Walking the Dales*, London: Michael Joseph.

Hayes, Gareth (2004), *Odd Corners around the Howgills*, Kirkby Stephen: Hayloft.

Hayhurst, John (1995), *Glasson Dock - the survival of a village*, Lancaster: Centre for North-West Regional Studies.

Hindle, Brian Paul (1984), *Roads and Trackways of the Lake District*, Ashbourne: Moorland Publishing.

Hindle, David and Wilson, John (2005), *Birdwatching Walks in Bowland*, Lancaster: Palatine Books.

Hudson, Phil (1998), *Coal Mining in Lunesdale*, Settle: Hudson History.

Hudson, Phil (2000), *Take a Closer Look at Wenningdale Mills*, Settle: Hudson History.

Humphries, Muriel (1985), *A History of the Ingleton Waterfalls Walk*, Ingleton Scenery Company.

Hutton, Rev. John (1780), *A Tour to the Caves, in the Environs of Ingleborough and Settle, in the West-Riding of Yorkshire. With some Philosophical Conjectures on the Deluge, Remarks on the Origin of Fountains, and Observations on the Ascent and Descent of Vapours, occasioned by Facts peculiar to the Places visited*, Kendal: Pennington.

Johnson, Lou, ed. (2005), *Walking Britain* (on-line guide).

Johnson, Thos (1872), *A Pictorial Handbook to the Valley of the Lune and Gossiping Guide to Morecambe and District.*

Jones, Clement (1948), *A Tour in Westmorland*, Kendal: Titus Wilson & Son.

Lancashire County Council (2006), *Lancaster: Historic Town Assessment Report*, Preston, Lancashire County Council.

Lancaster Group of the Ramblers' Association (2005), *Walks in the Lune Valley.*

Lord, A.A. (1983), *Wandering in Bowland*, Kendal: Westmorland Gazette.

Marshall, Brian (2001), *Cockersand Abbey*, Blackpool: Landy.

Mason, Sara (1994), *The Church and Parish of Tunstall.*

Mitchell, W.R. (2004), *Bowland and Pendle Hill*, Chichester: Phillimore & Co. Ltd.

Mitchell, W.R. (2005), *Around Morecambe Bay*, Chichester: Phillimore & Co. Ltd.

Moorhouse, Sydney (1976), *Twenty Miles around Morecambe Bay*, Morecambe: Trelawney Press.

Morton, H.V. (1927), *In Search of England*, London: Methuen.

Penney, Stephen (1983), *Lancaster in Old Picture Postcards*, Zaltbommel: European Library.

Raistrick, Arthur, Forder, John and Forder, Eliza (1985), *Open Fell Hidden Dale*, Kendal: Frank Peters.

Roskell, Ruth Z. (2005), *Glimpses of Glasson Dock and Vicinity*, Blackpool: Landy.

Routledge, George (1854), *A Pictorial History of the County of Lancaster.*
Salisbury, John (2004), *Nateby and Pilling Moss: the Pre-Historic Legacy*, Pilling: Sue White.
Sellers, Gladys (1986), *The Yorkshire Dales: a Walker's Guide to the National Park*, Milnthorpe: Cicerone Press.
Sharp, Jack (1989), *New Walks in the Yorkshire Dales*, London: Robert Hale.
Shotter, David and White, Andrew (1995), *The Romans in Lunesdale*, Lancaster: Centre for North-West Regional Studies.
Slater, David et al (1989), *The Complete Guide to the Lancaster Canal*, Lancaster Canal Trust.
Speight, Harry (1895), *Craven and the North West Yorkshire Highlands*, London: Elliot Stock.
Stansfield, Andy (2006), *The Forest of Bowland and Pendle Hill*, Tiverton: Halsgrove.
Swain, Robert (1992), *Walking down the Lune*, Milnthorpe: Cicerone Press.
Trott, Freda (1991), *Sedbergh*, Sedbergh: T.W. Douglas & Son.
Trott, Stan and Trott, Freda (2002), *Return to the Lune Valley*, Kendal: Stramongate Press.
Wainwright, Alfred (1970), *Walks in Limestone Country*, Kendal: Westmorland Gazette.
Wainwright, Alfred (1972), *Walks on the Howgill Fells*, Kendal: Westmorland Gazette.
Wainwright, Alfred (1974), *The Outlying Fells of Lakeland*, Kendal: Westmorland Gazette.
Wainwright, Martin, ed. (2005), *A Lifetime of Mountains: the Best of A. Harry Griffin's Country Diary*, London: Aurum Press Ltd.
Wellburn, Alan R. (1997), *Leck, Cowan Bridge and the Brontës.*
White, Andrew (1990), *Lancaster: a Pictorial History*, Chichester: Phillimore & Co. Ltd.
White, Andrew, ed. (1993), *A History of Lancaster*, Keele: Ryburn Publishing.
Wildman, Dorothy (2004), *Caton as it was.*
Williamson, Peter (2001), *From Source to Sea: a Brief History of the Lune Valley.*
Wilson, Sue, ed. (2002), *Aspects of Lancaster*, Barnsley: Wharncliffe Books.
Winstanley, Michael, ed. (2000), *Rural Industries of the Lune Valley*, Lancaster: Centre for North-West Regional Studies.

Contact Details for Further Information

The entries under each heading are in the order they would be met on our journey.

Place	Name	Tel:	www.
Cafés			
Newbiggin-on-Lune	Lune Spring Garden Centre	015396 23318	
Dent	Meadowside Café	" 25329	dentdale.com/meadowside.htm
	Rise Hill Kitchen	" 25209	dentdale.com/risehillkitchen.htm
	Stone Close Tea Room	" 25231	dentdale.com/stoneclose.htm
Kirkby Lonsdale	Bay Tree Café	015242 72160	
	Mews Coffee House	" 71007	
Ingleton	Bernie's Café (The Cavers' Café)	" 41802	berniescafe.co.uk
	Copper Kettle	" 41020	
	The Falls Café	" 41617	thefallscafe.co.uk
Bentham	Nose Bag	" 63150	
Wray	Bridge House Farm Tearooms	" 22496	bridgehousefarm.co.uk
Lancaster	Amy's Tea Shop	01524 841510	
	Old Bell Café	" 36561	
	Sun Café	" 845599	
	Whale Tail Vegetarian Café	" 845133	10000things.org.uk/whale_tail_cafe.htm
Galgate	Canalside Craft Centre	" 752223	
	Silk Mill Café	" 752450	
Glasson	Lantern o'er Lune	" 752323	
Caravan & Camping Sites			
Cautley	Cross Hall Caravan Park	015396 20668	
Sedbergh	Pinfold Caravan Park	" 20576	hanleycaravans.co.uk/ pinfold-caravan-park.php
Dent	Conder Farm	" 25277	
	Ewegales	" 25440	
	High Laning Caravan Park	" 25239	highlaning.co.uk
	Mill Beck	" 25275	dentdale.com/millbeckcaravan.htm
Casterton	Woodclose Caravan Park	015242 71597	woodclosepark.com
Cowan Bridge	New House Caravan Park	" 71590	
Ingleton	Broadwood Caravan Park	" 41253	ukparks.co.uk/broadwood
	Greenwood Leghe Holiday Park	" 41511	greenwoodleghe.co.uk
	Holme Head Caravan Park	" 41874	holme-head.bizhosting.com
	Moorgarth Farm	" 41428	
	Parkfoot Caravan Park	" 61833	parkfoot.co.uk
	Stackstead Farm Caravan Park	" 41386	
Burton-in-Lonsdale	Gallaber Farm Caravan Park	" 61361	gallaber.btinternet.co.uk
Clapham	Flying Horseshoe Caravan Site	" 51532	laughing-gravy.co.uk
Austwick	Dalesbridge	" 51021	dalesbridge.co.uk
	Wood End Farm	" 51296	
Ireby	Ireby Green Caravan Park	" 41203	
Bentham	Goodenbergh Caravan Park	" 62022	
	Lowther Hill Caravan Park	" 61657	
	Riverside Caravan Park	" 61272	riversidecaravanpark.co.uk
Caton	Crook o'Lune Caravan Park	01524 770216	ukparks.co.uk/crookolune
	New Parkside Farm Caravan Park	" 770723	
Glasson	Marina Caravan Park	" 751787	
Cockerham	Cockerham Sands Country Park	" 751387	cockerhamsandscountrypark.co.uk
	Mosswood Caravan Park	" 791041	mosswood.co.uk
Pilling	Fold House Park	01253 790267	foldhouse.co.uk
Events			
Orton	Farmers Market (2nd Sat of each month)		ortonfarmers.co.uk
Greenholme	Greenholme Show (2nd Sat of June)		

Sedbergh	Festival of Books & Drama (Aug/Sep)		
	Sedbergh Gala (mid-May)		
Dent	Dentdale Festival (Aug Bank Holiday)		
Barbon	Barbon Show & Sheepdog Trials (3rd Sat in Aug)		
Underley	Lunesdale Agricultural Show (2nd Tues in Aug)		
Kirkby Lonsdale	Victorian Fair (early Sep)		
Chapel-le-Dale	Three Peaks Race (late April)		threepeaksrace.org.uk
Ingleton	Ingleton Gala (3rd Sat in July)		
Austwick	Cuckoo Festival (late May)		
Bentham	Agricultural Show (Sep)		
Wray	Wray (Scarecrow) Festival (Apr/May)		wrayvillage.co.uk/scarecrows.htm
Lancaster	Outdoor Theatre, Williamson Park (July/Aug)		
	Jazz Festival (Sept)		
	Fireworks Spectacular (early Nov)		
Glasson	Maritime Festival (Easter)		
	Glasson Dock Festival (early July)		glassonfestival.org.uk
general	Bowland Festival (early June)	01484 861148	
	Lunesdale Open Studio Trail (June)	015242 61718	lunesdalearts.co.uk

Fisheries

Newbiggin-on-Lune	Bessy Beck Trout Fishery	015396 23303	bessybecktrout.co.uk
Arkholme	Redwell Fisheries	015242 21979	redwellfisheries.co.uk
Caton	Bank House Fly Fishery	01524 770412	
Quernmore	Forrest Hills Fly Fishery	" 752566	forresthills.net
Thurnham	Thursland Hill Fishery	" 751076	thurslandhillfishery.co.uk

Galleries

Kirkby Lonsdale	Finestra Gallery	015242 73747	finestragallery.co.uk
Ingleton	Peter Bolton Gallery	" 41703	visitingleton.co.uk/peterbolton.html
Bentham	Bentham Gallery	" 63366	
Lancaster	Arteria Ltd	01524 61111	
	Paper Gallery	" 36636	
	Peter Scott Gallery	" 593057	peterscottgallery.com
	Storey Gallery	" 844133	storeygallery.org.uk
	Town House Gallery	" 63436	townhousegallery.co.uk

Golf Courses

Sedbergh	Sedbergh Golf Club	015396 21551	sedberghgolfclub.co.uk
Casterton	Casterton Golf Course	015242 71592	castertongolf.co.uk
Kirkby Lonsdale	Kirkby Lonsdale Golf Club	" 76365	klgolf.dial.pipex.com
Bentham	Bentham Golf Club	" 62455	benthamgolfclub.co.uk
Lancaster	Lancaster Golf Club	01524 751247	lancastergc.co.uk
Quernmore	Forrest Hills	" 752566	forresthills.net

Groups &Societies

	Cave Rescue Organisation		cro.org.uk
	Craven Pothole Club		cravenpotholeclub.org
	Friends of the Lake District	01539 720788	fld.org.uk
	Lancaster Civic Society	01524 845301	lancastercivicsociety.org.uk
	Limestone Pavement Action Group	01539 816300	limestone-pavements.org.uk
	Lune Habitat Group	015242 22174	
	Middlewood Trust	" 22214	middlewood.org.uk
	Yorkshire Dales Society	01943 461938	yds.org.uk

Guest Houses and B&B (see also Hotels and Inns)

Tebay	High Bank House	015396 24651	
	Primrose Cottage	" 24791	primrosecottagecumbria.co.uk
	The Old School	" 24286	cottageguide.co.uk/oldschool-tebay
Sedbergh	Brantrigg	" 21455	brantrigg.co.uk
	Holmecroft	" 20754	holmecroftbandb.co.uk
	Number Ten	" 21808	
	Summerhill	" 20360	summerhillsedbergh.com

Cowgill	River View	" 25592	dedicate.co.uk/river-view
Dent	Garda View	" 25209	dentdale.com/gardaview.htm
	Low Hall Farm	" 25232	dentdale.com/lowhallfarm.htm
	Slack Cottage	" 25439	dentdale.com/slack.htm
	Smithy Fold	" 25368	smithyfold.co.uk
	Stone Close	" 25231	dentdale.com/stoneclose.htm
	Whernside Manor	" 25213	whernsidemanor.com
Barbon	Kemps Hill B&B	015242 76322	kempshill.co.uk
Ingleton	Bridge End	" 41413	
	Dales Guest House	" 41401	dalesgh.co.uk
	Gatehouse Farm	" 41458	gatehouseingleton.co.uk
	Ingleborough View	" 41523	ingleboroughview.com
	Inglenook Guest House	" 41270	inglenookguesthouse.com
	Nutstile	" 41752	nutstile.co.uk
	Riverside Lodge	" 41359	riversideingleton.co.uk
	Seed Hill Guest House	" 41799	come2ingleton.com
	Springfield Country	" 41280	yorkshirenet.co.uk/stayat/springfieldhotel
	Thorngarth Country	" 41295	thorngarth.co.uk
Burton-in-Lonsdale	River Cottage	" 64988	
Tunstall	Barnfield Farm B&B	" 74284	a1tourism.com/uk/barnfield.html
Clapham	Arbutus	" 51240	arbutus.co.uk
	Brookhouse	" 51580	brookhouseclapham.co.uk
Austwick	Wood View	" 51190	woodviewbandb.com
Bentham	Fowgill Park	" 61630	fowgillpark.co.uk
	Halsteads Barn	" 62641	halsteadsbarn.co.uk
	New Butts Farm	" 41238	
Claughton	Low House Farm B&B	" 21260	lowhousefarm.co.uk
Lancaster	Greaves House B&B	01524 39344	
	The Old Station House	" 381060	
	The Shakespeare B&B	" 841041	
Bay Horse	Salt Oke South B&B	" 752313	
Forton	Middle Holly Cottage	" 792399	

Holiday Cottages

Bentham	Oysterber Farm	015242 61567	oysterberfarm.co.uk
	Fourstones	" 64876	fourstoneshouse.co.uk
Tatham	Hill Farm	" 62424	

Hotels (see also Inns)

Newbiggin-on-Lune	Brownber Hall Country House	015396 23208	brownberhall.co.uk
Orton	George Hotel	" 24229	georgehotel.net
Salterwath	Shap Wells Hotel	01931 716628	shapwells.com
Sedbergh	Bull Hotel	015396 20264	bullhotelsedbergh.co.uk
Dent	George & Dragon Hotel	" 25256	thegeorgeanddragondent.co.uk
Middleton	Head at Middleton	" 20258	middleton-head.co.uk
Kirkby Lonsdale	Kings Arms Hotel	015242 71220	thekingsarms.net
	Orange Tree Hotel	" 71716	theorangetreehotel.com
	Snooty Fox Tavern	" 71308	a1tourism.com/uk/snootyfoxinn.html
Cowan Bridge	Hipping Hall	" 71187	hippinghall.com
Thornton-in-Lonsdale	Marton Arms Hotel	" 41281	martonarms.co.uk
Whittington	Dragons Head Hotel	" 72383	
Arkholme	Bay Horse Hotel	" 21425	
Clapham	New Inn Hotel	" 51203	newinn-clapham.co.uk
Austwick	Traddock Hotel	" 51224	austwicktraddock.co.uk
Bentham	Black Bull Hotel	" 61213	
	Punch Bowl Hotel	" 61344	
Caton	Scarthwaite Country House Hotel	01524 770267	thescarthwaite.co.uk
	Station Hotel	" 770323	
Halton	Greyhound Hotel	" 811356	
Skerton	Skerton Hotel	" 37580	
Lancaster	Bowerham Hotel	" 65050	

	Fox & Goose Hotel	" 66899	
	Golden Lion Hotel	" 842198	
	Greaves Hotel	" 63943	mitchellshotels.co.uk/greaves-hotel.shtml
	Horse & Farrier Hotel	" 63491	
	Lancaster House Hotel	" 844822	elh.co.uk/hotels/lancaster
	Moorlands Hotel	" 33792	
	Park Hotel	" 64886	
	Railton Hotel	" 388364	
	Ring O'Bells Hotel	" 64747	
	Royal Kings Arms Hotel	" 32451	
	The Sun	" 66006	thewaterwitch.co.uk/Sun/
Galgate	Green Dragon Hotel	" 751062	
Conder Green	Stork Hotel	" 751234	tp-inns.co.uk/stork/stork_index.htm
Overton	Globe Hotel	" 858228	
	Ship Hotel	" 858231	
Pilling	Springfield House Hotel	01253 790301	springfieldhousehotel.co.uk

Inns (see also Hotels & Pubs)

Tebay	Cross Keys Inn	015396 24240	
Cautley	Cross Keys Temperance Inn	" 20284	cautleyspout.co.uk
Sedbergh	Dalesman Country Inn	" 21183	thedalesman.co.uk
Cowgill	Sportsman's Inn	" 25282	thesportsmansinn.com
Dent	Sun Inn	" 25208	
Middleton	Swan Inn	015242 76223	
Barbon	Barbon Inn	" 76233	barboninn.co.uk
Casterton	Pheasant Inn	" 71230	pheasantinn.co.uk
Kirkby Lonsdale	Red Dragon Inn	" 71205	
	Sun Inn	" 71965	sun-inn.info
	Whoop Hall Inn	" 71284	whoophall.co.uk
Ribblehead	Station Inn	" 41274	thestationinn.net
Chapel-le-Dale	Old Hill Inn	" 41256	
Ingleton	Craven Heifer Inn	" 41515	cravenheiferingleton.co.uk
	Three Horseshoes Inn	" 41247	
	Wheatsheaf Inn	" 41275	wheatsheaf-ingleton.co.uk
Arkholme	Redwell Inn	" 21240	
Austwick	Game Cock Inn	" 51226	gamecockinnaustwick.co.uk
Bentham	Coach House	" 62305	coachhousebentham.co.uk
	Horse & Farrier Inn	" 61381	horseandfarrier.org.uk
	Sun Dial Inn	" 61532	sundialinn.co.uk
Wennington	Bridge Inn	" 21326	
Wray	New Inn	" 21722	
Caton	Ship Inn	01524 770265	theshipatcaton.co.uk
Lancaster	Holiday Inn	0870 4009047	
Galgate	New Inn	01524 751643	
	Plough Inn	" 751337	the-plough.co.uk
Glasson	Victoria Inn	" 751423	
Bay Horse	Bay Horse Inn	" 791204	bayhorseinn.com
	Fleece Inn	" 791233	
Cockerham	Manor Inn	" 791252	

Market Days

Sedbergh	Wednesday
Kirkby Lonsdale	Thursday
Ingleton	Friday
Bentham	Wednesday
Lancaster	Wednesday & Saturday

Museums

Lancaster	Castle	01524 46998	lancastercastle.com
	City Museum	" 64637	lancashire.gov.uk/education/ museums/lancaster/castle.asp

	Judges' Lodgings	" 32808	lancashire.gov.uk/education/ museums/lancaster/judges.asp
	Maritime Museum	" 382264	lancashire.gov.uk/education/ museums/lancaster/maritime.asp
	Ruskin Library	" 593587	lancs.ac.uk/users/ruskinlib/

Pubs (see also Hotels & Inns)

Tebay	Barnaby Rudge Tavern	015396 24328	
Sedbergh	Red Lion	" 20433	theredlionsedbergh.co.uk
Ingleton	Masons Arms	015242 41158	masonsarmsingleton.co.uk
Tunstall	Lunesdale Arms	" 74203	thelunesdale.co.uk
Bentham	The Byres	" 62846	
Wray	George & Dragon	" 21403	
Hornby	Royal Oak	" 21228	
Claughton	Fenwick Arms	" 21250	fenwickarms.co.uk
Brookhouse	Black Bull	01524 770329	
Halton	White Lion	" 812199	
Lancaster	Blue Anchor	" 66898	
	The Bobbin	" 32606	
	Boot & Shoe	" 63011	
	Duke of Lancaster	" 66909	
	George & Dragon	" 844739	
	Golden Ball	" 63317	
	Green Ayre	" 585240	
	John O'Gaunt	" 65356	
	Lord Ashton	" 841185	
	Royal Oak	" 65641	
	Sir Richard Owen	" 541500	
	Three Mariners	" 388957	
	Wagon & Horses	" 846094	wagonandhorsespub.co.uk
	Water Witch	" 63828	thewaterwitch.co.uk
	White Cross	" 33999	
	Yorkshire House	" 64679	yorkshirehouse.enta.net
Glasson	Dalton Arms	" 751213	
Winmarleigh	Patten Arms	" 791484	

Restaurants

Kirkby Lonsdale	Copper Kettle	015242 71714	
	Sorrel & Thyme	" 72772	
Ingleton	La Tavernetta	" 42465	
Bentham	Asian Spice	" 63400	
	Fish Inn	" 61317	
Lancaster	Bamboo Garden	01524 849948	
	Bella Italia	" 36340	bellapasta.co.uk
	Bombay Balti	" 844550	
	Casa Luca	" 843400	
	Gatehouse	" 849111	thegatehouserestaurant.co.uk
	Golden Dragon	" 33100	
	Golden Jade	" 847788	
	Il Bistro Morini	" 846252	
	Marco's Pizzeria	" 844445	
	Miyabi Japanese	" 848356	miyabi-restaurant.co.uk
	Moghuls	" 36253	
	Pizza Margherita	" 36333	pizza-margherita.co.uk
	Runcible Spoon	" 848049	
	Shabab Indian	" 388454	
	Quite Simply French	" 843199	quitesimplyfrench.co.uk
	Spaghetti House	" 846011	
	Sultan of Lancaster	" 61188	

Riding Centres

Aldcliffe	Low Wood Barn	01524 35343	
Overton	Lunebank Riding Centre	" 855397	lunebank-riding-centre.com

Tourist Attractions

Cautley	Cold Keld Walking Holidays	015396 23273	coldkeld.com
Garsdale	Sedgwick Geological Trail		
Sedbergh	Farfield Mill Arts & Heritage Centre	015396 21958	farfieldmill.org
	Holme Open Farm	" 20654	holmeopenfarm.co.uk
Dent	Craft Centre (Helmside)	" 25400	
	Village Heritage Centre	" 25800	dentvillageheritagecentre.co.uk
Mansergh	Mansergh Hall Farm Shop	015242 71397	manserghhall.co.uk
Ingleton	Ingleton Pottery	" 41363	ingletonpottery.co.uk
	Scenery Co. (Waterfalls Walk)	" 41930	ingletonwaterfallswalk.co.uk
	White Scar Cave	" 41244	whitescarcave.co.uk
Clapham	Ingleborough Show Cave	" 51242	ingleboroughcave.co.uk
	Reginald Farrer Trail		
Feizor	Yorkshire Dales Falconry Centre	01729 822832	falconryandwildlife.com
Arkholme	Docker Park Farm Visitor Centre	015242 21331	dockerparkfarm.co.uk
Bentham	Bentham Pottery	" 61567	benthampottery.com
Lancaster	Canal Waterbus	01524 389410	budgietransport.co.uk
	Castle	" 64998	lancastercastle.com
	Leisure Park	" 68444	
	Priory	" 65338	priory.lancs.ac.uk
	Williamson Park (Butterfly House)	" 33318	williamsonpark.com
Glasson	Smokehouse	" 751493	glassonsmokehouse.co.uk
general	Goldsworthy Sheepfolds		sheepfolds.org
	Settle-Carlisle Railway	08457 484950	settle-carlisle.com

Tourist Information Centres

Sedbergh	72 Main St.	015396 20125	
Kirkby Lonsdale	24 Main St.	015242 71437	kirkbylonsdale.co.uk/tic
Ingleton	Community Centre, Main St.	" 41049	visitingleton.co.uk
Bentham	26 Main St.	" 62549	
Lancaster	29 Castle Hill	01524 32878	visitlancaster.co.uk

Websites

Sedbergh	sedbergh.org.uk
Dent	dentdale.com
Kirkby Lonsdale	kirkbylonsdale.co.uk
Ingleton	ingleton.co.uk
Whittington	whittingtonvillage.fsnet.co.uk
Clapham	claphamyorkshire.co.uk
Bentham	benthamheritage.net
Wray	wrayvillage.org.uk
Hornby	hornbyvillage.org.uk
Caton	catonvillage.org.uk
general	forestofbowland.com
	outofoblivion.org.uk
	roughfellsheep.co.uk
	visitlunevalley.co.uk
	yorkshiredales.org

Index